PRAISE FOR *The President's Devotional*

"It is absolutely essential that all leaders receive daily direction, spiritual guidance, and soul-nourishing input from God's Word. Having served at the center of American government, Joshua DuBois understands better than many how draining leadership can be, and how we must refresh ourselves daily through time with God."

—Rick Warren, author of *The Purpose-Driven Life*

"The best leaders find moral courage, wisdom, and resolve by pursuing God. These words, drawn from ancient texts and trusted leaders, distill rare, urgent counsel during an age when we've never needed wisdom more."

—Stephan Bauman, president and CEO, World Relief

"Joshua has been the president's go-to bridge to spiritual leaders, to biblical wisdom, and to faith. Now he can be our bridge, too."

—Joel Hunter, senior pastor, Northland:
A Church Distributed

"Nothing uplifts American citizens more than knowing that our president is daily seeking the spiritual strength leadership demands, especially in times of great national and global challenges. We will all be blessed immeasurably as we journey through this amazing collection of presidential devotionals."

—Dr. Barbara Williams-Skinner, co-chair, National
African American Clergy Network and president,
Skinner Leadership Institute

"Whatever else history records of Barack Obama's years in the White House, it must include that this president was offered a type of spiritual nurture unique among America's chief executives—customized devotionals delivered daily by cell phone. Now, thanks to Joshua DuBois, we too can be instructed and inspired by words intended to sustain a president."

—Stephen Mansfield, *New York Times* bestselling author of
*The Faith of George W. Bush* and *The Faith of Barack Obama*

"No matter how busy and stressed you are; you're not busier or more stressed than the president of the United States, who read these devotionals every day in some of the highest-pressure days of his life. We can all learn from this book how to encourage and bless the leaders around us with wisdom and grace."

—Russell D. Moore, Ph.D., president, Ethics & Religious Liberty Commission, Southern Baptist Convention

"Joshua DuBois's devotions are life-changing, life-creating invitations to encounter God."

—Bishop Vashti Murphy McKenzie, presiding prelate, 10th Episcopal District, African Methodist Episcopal Church

"*The President's Devotional* is a surprisingly intimate journey. Joshua reveals a grace, courage, and humility that make this book an essential compass."

—Kevin Ryan, president and CEO, Covenant House International

"As we face mighty leadership challenges, we need a strong connection to our Almighty God. And now we have the privilege to learn from the same wisdom and insight that Joshua brought to the president during his amazing experience."

—Bobby Gruenewald, innovation leader, LifeChurch.tv and founder, YouVersion: The Bible App

"My friend Joshua DuBois, out of the context of one of the most intense environments in the world, imparts to us life-giving reflections that can help provide biblical guidance and insights to nourish our souls."

—Dr. Geoff Tunnicliffe, CEO and secretary general, World Evangelical Alliance

"This book will help all of us who are charging hard and intent on making a difference to stay grounded while accomplishing big things."

—Brad Lomenick, author of *The Catalyst Leader*

"Provides daily reflections, proven in the highest corridors of earthly power, that stand poised to inspire, inform, and impart the truth that God's mercies arrive new every morning. This devotional is a must-read for every leader in our land."

—Rev. Samuel Rodriguez, president, National Hispanic Christian Leadership Conference

"A concise daily educational exercise in Spiritual Formation."

—Rich Wilkerson, senior pastor, Trinity Church

"These devotions will prove valuable to each of us as we face the challenges of leadership."

—Michael A. Battle Sr., former president of the Interdenominational Theological Center

"I found a mix of courage and grace on almost every page. If you want to be challenged, encouraged, and inspired in your faith, look no further. *The President's Devotional* is a must-read book of spiritual reflections from one of America's most influential Christian leaders."

—Jonathan Merritt, senior columnist, *Religion News Service*, and author of *Jesus Is Better Than You Imagined*

"Inspire the leader within you with biblical and timely insights DuBois has learned from his personal relationship with the greatest Leader of all."

—Justin Mayo, executive director, RedEyeInc.org

"Filled with pastoral insights that can help guide us to make good choices."

—David Neff, former editor-in-chief, *Christianity Today*

"A uniquely valuable resource to help every person live a life that glorifies Christ and serves their neighbor."

—Mark Batterson, author of *The Circle Maker*

# THE PRESIDENT'S DEVOTIONAL

## THE DAILY READINGS THAT INSPIRED PRESIDENT OBAMA

## JOSHUA DUBOIS

HarperOne
*An Imprint of HarperCollinsPublishers*

HarperOne

THE PRESIDENT'S DEVOTIONAL: *The Daily Readings That Inspired President Obama*. Copyright © 2013 by Joshua DuBois. All rights reserved. Printed in the United States of America. No part of this book may be used or reproduced in any manner whatsoever without written permission except in the case of brief quotations embodied in critical articles and reviews. For information address HarperCollins Publishers, 195 Broadway, New York, NY 10007.

HarperCollins books may be purchased for educational, business, or sales promotional use. For information please e-mail the Special Markets Department at SPsales@harpercollins.com.

HarperCollins website: http://www.harpercollins.com

HarperCollins®, ▇®, and HarperOne™ are trademarks of HarperCollins Publishers.

FIRST HARPERCOLLINS PAPERBACK EDITION PUBLISHED IN 2014

Designed by Matthew Van Zomeren

Library of Congress Cataloging-in-Publication Data

DuBois, Joshua.
The president's devotional : the daily readings that inspired President Obama / Joshua DuBois. — FIRST EDITION.
pages cm
ISBN 978-0-06-226529-6
1. Obama, Barack—Religion.  2. Presidents—United States—Prayers and devotions. 3. Devotional calendars.  I. Title.
E908.3.D83     2013
973.932092—dc23      2013019524

14  15  16  17  18  RRD(H)  10  9  8  7  6  5  4  3  2  1

*To Michelle, David, Ralph, and Fannie Lou*

# PREFACE

~~~~

In the heat of the 2008 campaign season, I took a deep breath and sent the following e-mail to a young United States senator, who also happened to be running for president:

> Hi Senator,
>    I hope you're well. I've collected a few devotionals and scriptures that might provide encouragement in these last few weeks, including the one below. I'll send them in the morning from time to time, if it's helpful.
>
>    Best,
>    Joshua

Senator Obama—whom I'd been working for for several years by that time—replied saying that in fact, he would appreciate these morning messages very much. So every day, from that point on, I offered him a quote, prayer or interpretation of scripture to start his day.

Years later, after he had won the presidency and I became the White House faith-based office director, President Obama was having a conversation with reporters about an upcoming visit to the Pope. In an aside that took me off guard, the president started to reflect on the devotional messages that I had been quietly sending to him each day:

THE PRESIDENT: One last little note of sustenance, a little note is, is that Joshua does a wonderful service for me and he actually sends me a devotional on my BlackBerry every morning, which is actually something that he started doing I think when I was really having a tough time during the campaign.

MR. DUBOIS: It was a tough time.

THE PRESIDENT: And it was just such a wonderful practice that we've continued it ever since. So every morning I get something to reflect on, which I very much appreciate.

I still send President Obama these devotionals bright and early every morning. And now, with his permission, I'm glad to share a year's worth of them with you, along with twelve longer reflections to begin each month with lessons I've learned on faith, love, and leadership in the White House and in my own life.

The purpose of these readings has been to give the president a bit of nourishment to begin his day, a passage or prayer that inspires hope, illuminates life's key principles, or points him towards rest and replenishment. More generally, they've also been intended to assist him—and hopefully you, leaders in your own right across the country and around the world—in bridging the gap between the busyness of our temporal lives and the eternal calling of a changeless God.

The devotionals I send the president have always been Christian at their core, and their ultimate subject is Christ. They come from a range of sources—famous prayers and scriptures; songs and verse; and quotes from everyone from Abraham Lincoln to Fannie Lou Hamer, Helen Keller to Johnny Cash—but all are meant to trace back to the truth found in God's word. My hope has been that this truth, once found, would rest ever more securely in our souls.

I am deeply honored that you would include these devotionals and stories as a waypoint along your spiritual journey. I hope that they help you grow and bring you joy, as they have done for the president, and for me.

Joshua DuBois
Washington, D.C., May 2013

Transcript                                    February 7, 2013

## REMARKS BY THE PRESIDENT
## AT THE NATIONAL PRAYER BREAKFAST

Washington Hilton
Washington, D.C.
9:03 A.M. EST

THE PRESIDENT: Thank you very much. . . . Before I begin, I hope people don't mind me taking a moment of personal privilege. I want to say a quick word about a close friend of mine and yours, Joshua DuBois. Now, some of you may not know Joshua, but Joshua has been at my side—in work and in prayer—for years now. He is a young reverend, but wise in years. He's worked on my staff. He's done an outstanding job as the head of our Faith-Based office.

Every morning he sends me via e-mail a daily meditation—a snippet of scripture for me to reflect on. And it has meant the world to me.

# JANUARY

## GOD'S SURPRISES

I first heard the name Barack Obama in July of 2004 over a half-pound burger and fries on Capitol Hill. I was between two years of graduate school at Princeton, working in Washington for the summer for a feisty old member of Congress. The pay was meager—enough for gas for my beat-up Chevy Blazer and a tiny Craigslist apartment with two guys and a cat. But it was good to be in D.C. for a few months. And it was good to have some time to wrestle with what on earth I was going to do with my life.

But by the time my job was wrapping up in late July, I wasn't any closer to figuring things out. I knew I had a growing love affair with my faith—I had come to know Christ years earlier as a sophomore in college and became an associate pastor at a small church—and I wanted my vocation to be tied to my spiritual walk. I also knew I wanted to help folks who were struggling—my grandmother was active in the civil rights movement and my parents had made sure that working for greater justice and mercy in the world was in my bones. And finally, I knew that I had some serious student loans to pay back. What I didn't know was how to balance all three.

Late one day—July 27, 2004—I walked a couple blocks from the Rayburn House Office Building on Capitol Hill to my favorite neighborhood dive, a local spot named the Hawk 'n' Dove. There was always a happy hour burger special going on there, and the TVs played more Red Sox games than Yankees. As a Boston sports fan, this suited me fine.

I settled in to my food when the place became quiet—and the Hawk 'n' Dove was never quiet. There was some guy was on television, an Illinois state legislator named Barack Obama. And he was in the middle of delivering one heck of a speech.

I stopped and listened. The state senator touched on themes I had loved for a lifetime, of justice, of fighting for the vulnerable and sick, of patriotism and country. And then he said, almost out of nowhere, "We worship an awesome God in the blue states."

For some reason, that phrase hit me in my gut. It immediately blasted me back to childhood days of standing at bible camp in the Shenandoah Valley, arms raised, belting out whatever hurt and pain I was feeling with the mighty refrain of the worship song, "Our God . . . is an awesome God."

"Amen," I said to myself.

By the end of his speech, the purpose of my summer in Washington—and the trajectory of my life—got a little clearer. Progressive Democrats don't normally quote worship songs, I thought. And God doesn't generally reveal his purpose over a half-pound burger and fries at the Hawk 'n' Dove. But that evening I realized two things: first, this guy, Barack Obama, was pretty special, and I wanted to work for him. Second, and more important, Christ can show up anywhere. In anything. There is an opportunity to hear his voice in every mundane moment of our lives. Sure, it helps when we're looking for it. But even when we're not—he still surprises.

I went back to Princeton to complete my second year of graduate school and promptly sent a letter to Obama's campaign—and got a form-letter response. So I waited until after he was elected and drove down from New Jersey to the Senator's Washington transition office—and got turned away at the door ("too many applicants," they told me). A few months later I tried again, another three-hour drive each way. This time before rejecting me, they let me speak with a "senior official" in the senator's operation, who turned out to be the IT guy. Returning to school with my tail between my legs, I prayed hard and sent a last-ditch email to the senator's office, making a pleading case for why I was meant to work for Barack Obama. And, at long last, I got a response. After one phone interview and one in person, they were ready to hire me to write letters to Illinois constituents and eventually lead Obama's outreach to the faith community—at $29,000 a year, plus benefits.

Now, years later, that young state senator I watched on TV is the president of the United States, and in February 2013 I wrapped up my tenure as one of his longest-serving aides. I worked for President Obama in various capacities; most recently, he entrusted me with the responsibility of being the youngest-ever head of a White House office and leader of the administration's work with faith-based and not-for-profit organizations. But I've also come to know the president personally, praying with him and his family and walking with him through more peaks and valleys than I can count, including some stories that I'll share in the chapters ahead. And separate from my official duties, several years ago I began sending the leader of the free world a spiritual meditation to start his morning.

So that's how this story began—with something like a divine revelation over a burger and fries at the Hawk 'n' Dove, helped along by quite a speech. And all these years later, God still surprises.

# THIS HOUSE

Through wisdom a house is built,
and by understanding it is established.

—*Proverbs 24:3 (NKJV)*

What greatness has erupted in our house?

Emily Dickinson lived the majority of her life in a modest home at 280 Main Street in Amherst, Massachusetts, across the street from First Congregational Church. It was a nice, but by no means spectacular, dwelling, at the time painted the color of ochre and set among a small garden, where Emily tended her plants.

Dickinson rarely left this home. But inside, magic happened.

Nearly two thousand of some of the greatest poems the world has ever known were penned at 280 Main Street. From her upstairs bedroom, looking out through two large windows, she crafted lines that broke the mold of American verse. She defied convention and poured her soul into these elliptical appraisals of life, loss, and death. And the world was changed.

Look around. The space where we are standing, sitting, is an incubator for greatness. God can do wonderful things right here, in this place, if we take the risk. If we allow him to, and then if we move.

*Dear God, wherever I stand, you are with me, and therefore it is holy ground. Let my work and life reflect the sacred nature of this place you have gifted to me. Amen.*

# ON FRAILTY

Do not judge, or you too will be judged. For in the same way you judge others, you will be judged, and with the measure you use, it will be measured to you.

Why do you look at the speck of sawdust in your brother's eye and pay no attention to the plank in your own eye? How can you say to your brother, "Let me take the speck out of your eye," when all the time there is a plank in your own eye? You hypocrite, first take the plank out of your own eye, and then you will see clearly to remove the speck from your brother's eye.

*—Matthew 7:1–5 (NIV)*

In all people I see myself, none more and not one a barley-corn less,
     And the good or bad I say of myself I say of them.
               *—Walt Whitman,* Leaves of Grass

Let's think about our frailty. The greatest among us is nothing more than sin stitched together. The least among us is not much worse, and maybe a bit better. We're kept alive and thriving only by the grace of God.

These facts do not make us wretched beings. In fact, quite the opposite. When we realize that it is God's pure grace that binds the bodies and minds of our fellow man together, each person we encounter becomes more holy, special, worthy of care. Through this lens, it's harder to judge. And easier to love.

*Dear God, let me know my fellow man through your eyes, and through the lens of love. Remove the plank of judgment from my eyes that I might see. Amen.*

# SAFETY

In peace I will both lie down and sleep;
    for you alone, O LORD, make me dwell in safety.
                                          —*Psalm 4:8 (ESV)*

Don't play for safety. It's the most dangerous thing in the world.
                                   —*Hugh Walpole,* Fortitude

What does it mean to be *safe?*

There is physical safety—the protection of police and dogs and guns. But no matter the barriers placed between us and harm, there is always a greater harm that might break through. There is always a bigger gun.

There is economic safety—the security of our nest egg, our earnings and wealth. But we have seen deep crises wipe out even the most secure among us; even if wealth is retained, will it spare our bodies from sickness or harm?

So can we ever be safe? When every physical and economic precaution in the world is not enough, how can we ultimately be secure?

The Bible gives us a hint. "The beloved of the LORD dwells in safety. The High God surrounds him all day long" (Deuteronomy 33:12, ESV).

This does not mean that no harm will befall us. But come what may, we will always be closely quartered with an omnipotent God. We are his beloved, and secure in his arms. In that promise dwells eternal safety.

What a freeing notion! An encompassing love that neither death, nor life, nor physical nor economic nor emotional distress can take away. A love that must spur us to walk boldly and unafraid.

---

*Dear God, thank you for the safety that comes from your presence in my life. Let me feel that presence closely and be secure. Amen.*

# PEARLS

Who, by the power that enables him to bring everything under his control, will transform our lowly bodies so that they will be like his glorious body.

—*Philippians 3:21 (NIV)*

He who would search for pearls must dive below.
—*John Dryden,* The Poetical Works of John Dryden

We develop tough skin for our winters.

Like a diver plunging beneath chilly waters to snatch his reward, we'll need resilience to prosper, especially in lean times.

And that's what God is working in us now. The momentary challenges, the delays, the minor frustrations of this day will yield great benefit in the future, if only we learn to remain strong and peaceful through them. We are pearl divers, and we will never let a churning sea slow us on the way to the treasure Christ has in store.

*Lord, give me the spirit of a pearl diver today, the resilience to dive below. Amen.*

# HE SEES IN SECRET

God is not like a human being; it is not important for God to have visible evidence so that he can see if his cause has been victorious or not; he sees in secret just as well.

—*Søren Kierkegaard,* Works of Love

If I say, "Surely the darkness will hide me
    and the light become night around me,"
even the darkness will not be dark to you;
    the night will shine like the day,
    for darkness is as light to you.
For you created my inmost being;
    you knit me together in my mother's womb.

—*Psalm 139:11–13 (NIV)*

"He sees in secret just as well." *Into our past,* our furthest pasts, the moments that shaped our character and sentiments and belief. *Into our present,* our secret joys and hidden shames, the hopes that we cannot yet articulate, the worrisome pains we seek at all cost to avoid. *Into our future:* what is possible, what we're capable of, if only we stretch. Our future.

*Into his own nature.* God alone knows the expanse of love in his heart, the justice of his causes, the full measure of his power.

Left alone, we grope in the dark. But if we stretch out our arms and place them, even tentatively, on the shoulders of a waiting Savior, we can walk with confidence, even into darkness.

Because "he sees in secret just as well."

~∞∞∞~

*Dear Lord, when my vision is limited, help me learn to trust in you. I know that you see. Amen.*

# He Danced

Yes, to dance beneath the diamond sky with one hand waving free,
Silhouetted by the sea, circled by the circus sands,
With all memory and fate driven deep beneath the waves,
Let me forget about today until tomorrow.
　　　　　　　　　*—Bob Dylan, "Mr. Tambourine Man"*

Wearing a linen ephod, David was dancing before the LORD with
all his might.
　　　　　　　　　*—2 Samuel 6:14 (NIV)*

David, the king, the ruler of the nation of Israel, the man on whom the
mantle of God rested, and from whose lineage would emerge the Savior of
all humankind . . . David, in wild abandon, danced.

He danced because the Lord had been good. He danced because despite
unspeakable trials, he was still alive. He danced because it gave glory and
honor to the God who had formed him in his mother's womb. He danced
because the weight of sin had been lifted off of him. He danced, and
danced, and then danced some more, with all that he had, "with all his
might."

Let's pray for some of that joyful abandon today. Let's seek out the
moments when the seriousness of life melts away in the heat of God's glory,
and we are free to let loose, shout, and glorify God. And dance.

———⁙———

*Dear God, let me never be too serious to experience pure joy, to appreciate all
that you have done, and even, when the time is right, to dance. Amen.*

# RESISTANCE

I feared them so little, that the terrors, which until now oppressed me, quitted me altogether; and though I saw them occasionally, I was never again afraid of them—on the contrary, they seemed to be afraid of me. I found myself endowed with a certain authority over them, given me by the Lord of all, so that I cared no more for them than for flies. They seem to be such cowards; for their strength fails them at the sight of any one who despises them. These enemies have not the courage to assail any but those whom they see ready to give in to them, or when God permits them to do so, for the greater good of His servants, whom they may try and torment.

—*Teresa of Avila, "Divine Locutions"*

Resist the devil, and he will flee from you.

—*James 4:7 (NIV)*

Our tormentors are cowards; all they need is a little resistance. We don't have to muster much—just a mustard seed's worth will do—and God will amplify.

Look *temptation* in the face. Go eye to eye with *worry*. Stare directly at *anger*. Haters and despisers and enemies should get the fullness of our glare. And speak to them: "You will not have dominion. You will not have authority. For the Christ that is in me is bigger than the enemy within you."

And then, we will find ourselves "endowed with a certain authority over them, given [us] by the Lord of all, so that [we care] no more for them than for flies."

Victorious.

~~~~~

*Dear God, grant me victory today over all that assails. Help me square up to even the greatest challenges and claim authority over them, unafraid. Amen.*

# FEELING IMPORTANT

Do nothing from selfish ambition or conceit, but in humility count others more significant than yourselves. Let each of you look not only to his own interests, but also to the interests of others. Have this mind among yourselves, which is yours in Christ Jesus, who, though he was in the form of God, did not count equality with God a thing to be grasped, but emptied himself, by taking the form of a servant, being born in the likeness of men.

*—Philippians 2:3–7 (ESV)*

In 1946, shortly after the death of her husband, President Roosevelt, Eleanor Roosevelt was accosted by an admirer who went on and on about Mrs. Roosevelt's importance to the world. "I'm so glad I never *feel* important," Mrs. Roosevelt replied with smile. "It does complicate life."

*Lord, help us to not feel important. We know that we're but grains of sand, blown by the winds of this life. We do our work with humility today, acknowledging that we are just sinners, saved by grace. Amen.*

# STAY HOME AND KEEP THEM

Peace be within your walls
and security within your towers!

—*Psalm 122:7 (ESV)*

One day a man famed for his cutthroat approach to business said to the great author Mark Twain, "Before I die I mean to make a pilgrimage to the Holy Land. I will climb Mount Sinai and read the Ten Commandments aloud at the top."

"I have a better idea," Twain replied. "You could stay home in Boston and keep them."

As Twain implies, we would be wise to avoid grand gestures of piety and instead practice holiness right here at home. By serving God and giving generously. By loving our neighbors fully, in word and deed. We don't need to climb Mount Sinai to do that.

*Dear Lord, before I make a grand gesture, remind me to do the little things well. Amen.*

# WISDOM

> On that night God appeared to Solomon, and said to him, "Ask! What shall I give you?" . . . [Solomon replied], "Now give me wisdom and knowledge, that I may go out and come in before this people; for who can judge this great people of Yours?"
>
> —*2 Chronicles 1:7, 10 (NKJV)*

God appeared to King Solomon and told him to ask for whatever he wished, and he would have it.

Solomon could have requested anything in the world. But what did he ask for? Wisdom—and not just any wisdom. Wisdom to do the task that was in front of him.

And isn't that the most important thing? We can look down the road and seek greater blessings and provisions for what's to come. But there's work for us to do right here, right now, work for which we need God's help.

*Our prayer, oh Lord, is for wisdom to work this land in which we stand. We thank you in advance for your provision of wisdom, and for your grace. Amen.*

# AND THE HEAVENS OPEN

He mounted the cherubim and flew;
　　he soared on the wings of the wind.

　　　　　　　　　　　　　　　*—2 Samuel 22:11 (NIV)*

And something started in my soul,
fever or forgotten wings,
and I made my own way,
deciphering
that fire,
and I wrote the first faint line,
faint, without substance, pure
nonsense,
pure wisdom
of someone who knows nothing,
and I suddenly saw
the heavens
unfastened
and open.

　　　　　　　　　　*—Pablo Neruda, "Poesia"*

Isn't that what faith is? Walking right up to the edge of our present circumstance, closing our eyes, seeing the bright-red sparks of possibility dance beneath our lids, feeling the warm embrace of a God who wants ever greater and greater and greater things for us, whispering a silent prayer; then, we leap.

And the heavens open.

*Dear God, let me write the first line. Make the first move. Speak the first word. Love newly, radically. Let me leap, and let the heavens unfasten, and open. Amen.*

JANUARY 12

# No Lists

*If the world hates you, know that it has hated me before it hated you. If you were of the world, the world would love you as its own.*
*—John 15:18–19 (ESV)*

Humankind loves to be on lists.

We feel honored to be among the most accomplished, the brightest, the powerful. "She's the smartest person I know." "And the Oscar goes to . . ."

But we must remember that Jesus wasn't on any of those lists. He was counted among the outcasts, the rejects, the condemned. And Christ constantly reminds us: lists are overrated. If we want to be known as a friend of the world, then seek the world's accolades. But if we want to be a friend of the Most High, then we must seek to imitate him.

*Dear God, let me discount the value of place and position. Help me seek first your kingdom, your character, and your righteousness. Amen.*

# YOUR MYSTERIES

Great indeed, we confess, is the mystery of godliness:
>He was manifested in the flesh,
>>vindicated by the Spirit,
>>>seen by angels,
>proclaimed among the nations,
>>believed on in the world,
>>>taken up in glory.

—*1 Timothy 3:16 (ESV)*

The riddles of God are more satisfying than the solutions of man.
—*G. K. Chesterton,* The Book of Job: An Introduction

*We're satisfied with your mysteries today, dear God. We rejoice in knowing that there are things beyond our ability to comprehend.*

*We wonder and we wander, but we are never fully resolved outside of your grace. We delight in that fact, oh Lord. It makes us smile. Amen.*

# FIRE A BLESSING

You have heard that it was said, "Love your neighbor and hate your enemy." But I tell you, love your enemies and pray for those who persecute you, that you may be children of your Father in heaven. He causes his sun to rise on the evil and the good, and sends rain on the righteous and the unrighteous.

—*Matthew 5:43–45* (NIV)

Every time your enemy fires a curse, you must fire a blessing, and so you are to bombard back and forth with this kind of artillery. The mother grace of all the graces is Christian good-will.

—*Henry Ward Beecher,* Life Thoughts

Grace toward one another is our weapon. Time after time, battle after battle, we respond with it. The enemy will win some rounds, but when we respond with God's grace, we have already won the war.

*Dear Lord, every time my enemy fires a curse, help me to fire a blessing. Let me respond always in grace, and thereby overcome. Amen.*

# TOILING

When He had stopped speaking, He said to Simon, "Launch out into the deep and let down your nets for a catch."

But Simon answered and said to Him, "Master, we have toiled all night and caught nothing; nevertheless at Your word I will let down the net." And when they had done this, they caught a great number of fish, and their net was breaking."

—*Luke 5:4–6 (NKJV)*

My first pastor, Warren Collins from Calvary Praise and Worship Center in Cambridge, Massachusetts, is a mighty man of God. His sermons are gentle yet powerful, translating the words of Christ into practical ways that we can live out his purpose in the world. He preaches with few notes; the Holy Spirit within him is strong. I came to know Jesus under his ministry.

And yet, Pastor Collins has preached to a group of just thirty to fifty people every Sunday for over fourteen years. We don't know why the church doesn't grow; perhaps Cambridge is a tough place to plant a congregation. We know that it's not because of any lack of faithfulness on Pastor Collins's part, because he has been diligent every day. But it remains a very small congregation nonetheless, a fact that must bewilder him.

But here's the thing. Countless people—students at Harvard, MIT, or Boston University, visiting professors, businessmen—have spent brief periods of their lives in his pews. And, like me, for many it was a transformative experience. I know of disciples who brought Pastor Collins's teaching to NFL locker rooms, corporate boardrooms, and of course, even to the White House. His impact is much larger than even he imagines.

Like Peter in the fishing boat, and like Pastor Collins, many of us may have "toiled all night and caught nothing." But in reality God is doing something behind the scenes. And one day, if we continue to be faithful and follow his word, we'll throw down our nets and bring up a catch for the ages.

---

*Dear God, help me remember that evidence of my impact is not always apparent. I trust that you're moving behind the scenes. Amen.*

# RENEW OUR MINDS

I beseech you therefore, brethren, by the mercies of God, that you present your bodies a living sacrifice, holy, acceptable to God, which is your reasonable service. And do not be conformed to this world, but be transformed by the renewing of your mind, that you may prove what is that good and acceptable and perfect will of God.

—*Romans 12:1–2 (NKJV)*

Paul here speaks of the "renewing" of our minds, indicating that it's a process; we are not at once fully renewed.

Today, we ask God to move us along in that transformation process—toward ever-holier thoughts, ever-greater righteousness, ever-deeper love.

———∞∞∞———

*Lord, help us not be conformed to this world, but to be transformed by the renewing of our minds and to keep being transformed tomorrow. Move us along in this critical process. Amen.*

JANUARY 17

# THE COLOR OF
# OUR THOUGHTS

Finally, brothers, whatever is true, whatever is honorable, whatever is
just, whatever is pure, whatever is lovely, whatever is commendable,
if there is any excellence, if there is anything worthy of praise, think
about these things.

—*Philippians 4:8 (ESV)*

The soul is dyed the color of its thoughts. Think only on those things
that are in line with your principles and can bear the full light of day.
The content of your character is your choice. Day by day, what you
choose, what you think, and what you do is who you become. Your
integrity is your destiny . . . it is the light that guides your way.

—*Marcus Aurelius,* Meditations

We know that additional calories in the morning—say, a doughnut—will,
after a journey through enzymes and on to our bloodstream and liver,
eventually end up stored in our cells as fat. It's as plain as day. We know that
an additional dollar saved will grow at its rate of savings and yield a standard
return. There's no mystery there. Some created circumstances just naturally
lead to other circumstances. As Newton famously observed, "For every action
there is an equal and opposite reaction." The same is true with the Spirit.

Today, if we consume frantic media, gossipy conversation, indulgent
stimulation, or worrisome thoughts, then we will have frantic, gossipy,
indulgent, and worrisome lives. In the same manner, if we "think only
on those things that are in line with [our] principles and can bear the full
light of day," our character and our peace will grow stronger as a result. It
is just as certain as a banker's savings book, as sure as our digestive system
turning food into energy, protein, and fat.

*Dear God, help me purify my thoughts. When I am distracted, help me con-
stantly refocus on the things that matter most. Amen.*

# INTO SUBJECTION

Therefore I run thus: not with uncertainty. Thus I fight: not as one who beats the air. But I discipline my body and bring it into subjection, lest, when I have preached to others, I myself should become disqualified.

*—1 Corinthians 9:26–27 (NKJV)*

We don't run with uncertainty. We don't fight as one who beats the air. We press forward with a purpose, and our combat is sure.

And this old body of ours, which threatens to fail us when exhaustion and temptation rear their heads, this body, we beat it into submission. It listens to us, not the other way around.

We are ready. We are qualified. And we will finish this race.

*Amen.*

# CASTLES IN THE AIR

I learned this, at least, by my experiment; that if one advances confidently in the direction of his dreams, and endeavors to live the life which he has imagined, he will meet with a success unexpected in common hours. He will put some things behind, will pass an invisible boundary; new, universal, and more liberal laws will begin to establish themselves around and within him; or the old laws will be expanded, and interpreted in his favor in a more liberal sense, and he will live with the license of a higher order of beings. . . . If you have built castles in the air, your work need not be lost; that is where they should be. Now put the foundations under them.

—*Henry David Thoreau,* Walden

Do not lay up for yourselves treasures on earth, where moth and rust destroy and where thieves break in and steal; but lay up for yourselves treasures in heaven, where neither moth nor rust destroys and where thieves do not break in and steal. For where your treasure is, there your heart will be also.

—*Matthew 6:19–21 (NKJV)*

Being grounded is overstated. Yes, we should be humble. Yes, we should have a clear view of the world in front of us, the facts at hand.

But we are eternal beings. Our journey began when God foreknew us at the beginning of time itself, and it will continue until we greet him in paradise. Our efforts to create beauty in this world, to love our neighbors, to honor and worship God, these are infinite strivings—not bound by the mundaneness of any given hour.

"If you have built castles in the air," then that is just where they should be: stored-up treasures in heaven. And if anyone says our heads are in the clouds, the response should be, "Thanks!"

---

*Dear God, help me keep my eyes lifted up to you. Urge me on by a vision of eternal glory. Amen.*

# WHEN WE DON'T KNOW WHAT TO PRAY

> Likewise the Spirit helps us in our weakness. For we do not know what to pray for as we ought, but the Spirit himself intercedes for us with groanings too deep for words.
>
> —*Romans 8:26 (ESV)*

When we don't know what to pray.

When concern stacks upon concern, and tasks seem to merge together, and the demands on our psyche stretch us thin.

When we're needed, and we're goaded, and we're misunderstood; when the lump in our throat expands and blocks out words.

That's when the Spirit steps in, with "groanings too deep for words." The Spirit of God brings our message to the Father when we can't articulate it ourselves. When we're at wit's end. The Spirit prays for us when we don't know what to pray.

⚬⚬⚬⚬⚬

*. . . Amen.*

# SISTERS AND BROTHERS

You have heard that it was said, "Eye for eye, and tooth for tooth."
But I tell you, do not resist an evil person. If anyone slaps you on the
right cheek, turn to them the other cheek also. . . . You have heard
that it was said, "Love your neighbor and hate your enemy." But I tell
you, love your enemies and pray for those who persecute you, that
you may be children of your Father in heaven.
                                    —*Matthew 5:38–39, 43–45 (NIV)*

I can no longer condemn or hate a brother for whom I pray, no matter how much trouble he causes me. His face, that hitherto may have
been strange and intolerable to me, is transformed in intercession
into the countenance of a brother for whom Christ died.
                                    —*Dietrich Bonhoeffer,* Life Together

It is easy to love when we are loved. And, for believers, it is a bit more difficult but still a somewhat straightforward prospect, to love when we are
truly hated. There is something about pure hatred directed toward us that
intensifies a Christian's impulse to love.

The challenge often lies somewhere in the middle: not when we are
loved or hated, but when we are annoyed, when we are irritated, when our
family and our coworkers and our fellow sojourners exasperate us, at work,
on the roads, at home.

It is in these moments that we must live up to our spiritual discipline,
where we immediately say a word of prayer for the person on the other
end of the exasperation, the irritation. She or he is a sister or "brother for
whom Christ died." And these siblings are worthy of a measure of grace.

~∞∞~

*Dear God, remind me of my own fallibility, weaknesses, and flaws, so that I
might more easily show grace to others. Amen.*

# WE BUILT YOUR TEMPLE

The LORD has kept the promise he made. I have succeeded David my father and now I sit on the throne of Israel, just as the LORD promised, and I have built the temple for the Name of the LORD, the God of Israel.

—*2 Chronicles 6:10 (NIV)*

*Like Solomon, dear God, we want to look back and say: we built your temple. We carefully considered its dimensions, and brick by brick, we laid it down.*

*We loved fully. We worked diligently. We gave generously. We explored boldly. And we did our best to live your healing out in this broken world.*

*At the end of our lives, like Solomon, we desire to say, "I have built the temple for the Name of the LORD, the God of Israel." Today, Lord, we place another brick. Amen.*

# TO BE UNDERSTOOD

So shall my word be that goes out from my mouth;
  it shall not return to me empty,
but it shall accomplish that which I purpose,
  and shall succeed in the thing for which I sent it.

*—Isaiah 55:11 (ESV)*

The finest words in the world are only vain sounds if you cannot comprehend them.

*—Anatole France,* The Literary Life

‿◦◦◦⌒

*Oh God, we pray to be understood. Clarify our language. Crystallize our intent. Help us choose words that will best reach your people, and move them to action. Open the ears of our family, our loved ones, all in our circle of concern, and let them not just hear us, but comprehend. Amen.*

NOTE: This devotional was sent to President Obama around the time of his State of the Union address.

# FROM HIS HAND

O LORD our God, all this abundance that we have prepared to build You a house for Your holy name is from Your hand, and is all Your own.

—*1 Chronicles 29:16 (NKJV)*

The riches that mean anything are from God's hand. So we must hold them carefully and let them flow through us to worthy causes.

—◦◦◦◦—

*We pray the same prayer of David before the Israelites today: All this abundance you've given us, dear God, is from your hand. It is all your own. With our words, actions, and lives, we'll build your house today. Amen.*

JANUARY 25

# ECCLESIASTES PRAYER

What do workers gain from their toil? I have seen the burden God has laid on the human race. He has made everything beautiful in its time. He has also set eternity in the human heart; yet no one can fathom what God has done from beginning to end. I know that there is nothing better for people than to be happy and to do good while they live. That each of them may eat and drink, and find satisfaction in all their toil—this is the gift of God. I know that everything God does will endure forever; nothing can be added to it and nothing taken from it. God does it so that people will fear him.

Whatever is has already been,
and what will be has been before;
and God will call the past to account.

*—Ecclesiastes 3:9–15 (NIV)*

*Amen.*

# A HAPPY CHANGE OF NUISANCE

For to this you have been called, because Christ also suffered for you, leaving you an example, so that you might follow in his steps.
—*1 Peter 2:21 (ESV)*

British Prime Minister Lloyd George was going through a rough stretch. In succession, he had to confront World War I, a major economic crisis, the Sinn Féin Irish liberation movement, and many other challenges. When someone asked him how he kept such good spirits through it all, George replied, "I find that a change of nuisance is as good as a vacation."

Like Lloyd George, let's approach new challenges with joy.

We could have been consigned to a situation with no authority, no jurisdiction, or no responsibility over the trials in our lives. Yet God has seen fit to give us the opportunity to confront new problems today. We move from trial to trial embracing the opportunity each one presents to learn and grow.

*Dear God, help me embrace new trials. I'm grateful for the authority I have to shape, change, and resolve them. And while I'm doing so, I'll maintain my joy. Amen.*

# CONVERSATIONS WITH GOD

Teach us, O Lord, the disciplines of patience, for we find that to wait is often harder than to work.

When we wait upon Thee, we shall not be shamed, but shall renew our strength.

May we be willing to stop our feverish activities and listen to what Thou hast to say, that our prayers shall not be the sending of night letters, but conversations with God.

This we ask in Jesus' name. Amen.

*—Rev. Peter Marshall, D.D.,*
*prayer in congress, June 27, 1947*

Let's start a conversation with God. A give and a take.

*Lord, here's what I want. Here are my desires and dreams. I'm not sure of my motives; they're cloudy at times. But I know you can help clarify them. What do you want? What do you want, for me?*

And then, we listen. We keep watching, praying, and listening. As all around us, his answers unfold. *Amen.*

# THE WORLD WITHIN

I pray that out of his glorious riches he may strengthen you with power through his Spirit in your inner being.

—*Ephesians 3:16 (NIV)*

So hopeless is the world without,
The world within I doubly prize;
Thy world where guile and hate and doubt
And cold suspicion never rise;
Where thou and I and Liberty
Have undisputed sovereignty.

—*Emily Brontë, "To Imagination"*

---

*Lord, today, please cultivate my world within.*
   *The secret places where you and I commune.*
   *My motivations and desires, fears and deepest dreams.*
   *Out of your glorious riches, refine my inner self so that I can approach the outer world with confidence and calm.*
   *Amen.*

# POWER IN HIS BONES

Elisha died and was buried. Now Moabite raiders used to enter the country every spring. Once while some Israelites were burying a man, suddenly they saw a band of raiders; so they threw the man's body into Elisha's tomb. When the body touched Elisha's bones, the man came to life and stood up on his feet.

—*2 Kings 13:20–21 (NIV)*

The prophet Elisha was so infused with God's power that when the body of a dead man touched his dry bones, the body was raised to life. Elisha had power to spare.

*God, we ask for that power. To move into lifeless, loveless, hurting situations and be so infused with integrity, character, and your matchless love that the dead bodies around us are restored. We ask for the authority of Elisha, life-giving authority today. Amen.*

# MAKE THEM YOUR FRIENDS

Do not take revenge, my dear friends, but leave room for God's wrath, for it is written: "It is mine to avenge; I will repay," says the Lord. On the contrary:
If your enemy is hungry, feed him;
if he is thirsty, give him something to drink.
In doing this, you will heap burning coals on his head.
Do not be overcome by evil, but overcome evil with good.
—*Romans 12:19–21 (NIV)*

In the middle of the Civil War, President Lincoln attended a reception where he spoke about the Southerners. He referred to them as human beings who had committed grave errors, rather than as enemies to be completely destroyed.

One woman, fiercely committed to the Union cause, chastised President Lincoln for humanizing the foes to the south instead of seeking to destroy them. Lincoln responded to her calmly: "Why, madam, do I not destroy my enemies when I make them my friends?"

We can defeat our enemies by the sword and thereby create even more enemies. Or we can love them into submission.

President Lincoln had to do the former sometimes, but he much preferred the later. And the latter, of course, is the path of Christ.

---

*Dear Lord, help me love my enemies, not just out of charity, but because it is the most effective path toward bringing healing into this world. Let me love as you command. Amen.*

# OPEN HEARTS

And I will give you a new heart, and a new spirit I will put within you. And I will remove the heart of stone from your flesh and give you a heart of flesh.

*—Ezekiel 36:26 (ESV)*

There is a profound ground of unity that is more pertinent and authentic than all the unilateral dimension of our lives. This a man discovers when he is able to keep open the door of his heart. This is one's ultimate responsibility, and it is not dependent upon whether the heart of another is kept open for him.

*—Howard Thurman,* A Strange Freedom

*Open our hearts, God. To instruction, unheard. To possibility, unseen. To love, unfelt. To joy, unknown. If we have been closed off, we repent. And we ask you to open our hearts. Amen.*

# FEBRUARY

*⁓⁓⁓*

## THE VULNERABILITY TEST

My father died in the winter of 2005. He was in a federal prison in North Carolina, locked up on an arson charge. It was an insurance scam, the last desperate act of a troubled, brilliant, beautiful man. Paul DuBois's passing hit me pretty hard. I didn't think he knew Christ. And I was certain that I did not really know Paul.

My half siblings looked to me to make the arrangements. I drove seven hours to the prison to claim his ashes, put together a service to sprinkle them in his native upstate New York, and met with lawyers about his final affairs. I was twenty-two years old and had never done anything like that before.

Before hitting the road, I went into the office to grab a couple of file folders and some pens. While I was at my desk, I received a surprise call from the chief of staff: "The senator wants to speak with you. Can you come down for a few minutes?" I was a little shocked. I was not a high-flying member of his office. At the time, my title was legislative correspondent, which meant I wrote thousands of letters to the constituents of Illinois. And in the United States Senate, legislative correspondents didn't spend time with their senators, personal tragedy or not.

I walked downstairs and entered Senator Obama's office, frankly a bit dazed. He was sitting on his desk and rose to greet me, gave me a firm handshake, and walked me over to his couch. He sat across from me and asked me how I was doing. I mumbled something I don't recall.

"Joshua, I want you to know something," the senator said. He paused and looked me in the eye. And then he told me about his dad. His father's troubles. What it was like to learn from him as a teenager, about basketball, about jazz, in the two weeks they spent together. How it felt when he got the news that he had died. He concluded by giving me a hug. He said, "I'll be praying for you, and I want you to let me know if you need anything at all."

I have thought of that moment often, especially in my present role as a manager. We all have to be careful to guard our emotions and put the right boundaries around our lives. But sometimes, when prompted by God, we have to let our hearts break too. And share that heartbreak with others. It engenders loyalty and understanding like few other things can.

Christ knew this as well. In the Garden of Gethsemane, in a moment of startling vulnerability, Jesus took Peter, James, and John aside from the other disciples and confided in them. He said in a voice that must have been filled with hurt, with desperation, "My soul is overwhelmed with sorrow to the point of death. Stay here and keep watch with me."

Our Savior led with vulnerability. He led by sharing his heartbreak. It's a risky practice, but one with great reward.

# THE SONG ON OUR HEART

Praise the LORD! Praise God in his sanctuary; praise him in his mighty heavens! Praise him for his mighty deeds; praise him according to his excellent greatness! Praise him with trumpet sound; praise him with lute and harp! Praise him with tambourine and dance; praise him with strings and pipe! Praise him with sounding cymbals; praise him with loud clashing cymbals! Let everything that has breath praise the LORD! Praise the LORD!"

—*Psalm 150 (ESV)*

What is that song in your heart? The song that makes the corners of your mouth turn up into a wistful smile? What song can you hear pacing in the back of your mind in the quietest times? If sand is holding you gently on a beach, sun warming your feet and bright blue all around, what tune would complement the waves?

That song is the song in your heart. For Abraham Lincoln, it was an old Scottish love song, "Annie Laurie," which brought misty tears to his eyes. Coretta Scott King wrote in her journal that when Dr. King "needed a lift," he would turn to the African American spiritual "Balm in Gilead."

God wants us to find that song. He who made the sound of trumpets, the clang of cymbals, the tune of harps, knows that the happiness we feel from the songs in our hearts will be directed in praise toward him. Find that song this morning. And let it motivate great joy.

⁂

*Dear God, pace me today with the song in my heart. Let each footstep be to the rhythm of gladness, and let those steps be directed toward you. Amen.*

# FAST AND PRAY

Then Esther told them to reply to Mordecai: "Go, gather all the Jews who are present in Shushan, and fast for me; neither eat nor drink for three days, night or day. My maids and I will fast likewise. And so I will go to the king, which is against the law; and if I perish, I perish!"
—*Esther 4:15–16 (NKJV)*

Esther was about to make a very bold move—she was going to appeal to the king for the salvation of the Jews, against the king's closest adviser's wishes. And how did she prepare? She asked her people to fast with her, and pray.

Let's remember our brothers and sisters who are in tough situations today, overseas and here at home. Let's come around them in solidarity, sometimes with prayer and sometimes with fasting. We will seek God's will for them, and we will pray that they will do the same for us.

---

*Dear God, like Esther, when tough times come, we'll remember to fast and pray. Amen.*

# A HAMER SPIRIT

Blessed are you when others revile you and persecute you and utter all kinds of evil against you falsely on my account. Rejoice and be glad, for your reward is great in heaven, for so they persecuted the prophets who were before you.

*—Matthew 5:11–12 (ESV)*

One night I went to church. They had a mass meeting. And I went to church, and they talked about how it was our right, that we could register and vote. They were talking about [how] we could vote out people that we didn't want in office. . . . That sounded interesting enough to me that I wanted to try it. I had never heard, until 1962, that black people could register and vote. . . .

When they asked for those to raise their hands who'd go down to the courthouse the next day, I raised mine. Had it high up as I could get it. I guess if I'd had any sense I'd a-been a little scared, but what was the point of being scared. The only thing they could do to me was kill me and it seemed like they'd been trying to do that a little bit at a time ever since I could remember.

*—Fannie Lou Hamer, in* Modern America

⁓⧯⁓

*Dear God, give me a Fannie Lou Hamer spirit today. Help me take a bold step, and remind me that this earth is not my home. In Jesus's name, amen.*

FEBRUARY 4

# IMITATION

Imitate me, just as I also imitate Christ.

—*1 Corinthians 11:1 (NKJV)*

———⟡———

*Dear God, our prayer today is this: when we are not walking in your footsteps, we want no one to follow behind us. When we're not worthy of imitation, let the shadow of our presence be short indeed. But when we mimic you—when we work, and love, and pray like you—only then, send us imitators. So that others will follow not us, but Christ. Amen.*

# IN THE FINAL HOURS

Flee youthful passions and pursue righteousness, faith, love, and peace, along with those who call on the Lord from a pure heart.
—*2 Timothy 2:22 (ESV)*

A pleasure is full grown only when it is remembered. . . . What it will be when I remember it as I lie down to die, what it makes in me all my days till then—that is the real meeting. The other is only the beginning of it.
—*C. S. Lewis,* Out of the Silent Planet

Let's look beyond our momentary indulgences and consider the effects a generation from now. What ripples will our actions, our inactions, our conversations have in those distant, final hours?

If our deeds measure up to that standard, perfect; let's move forward with great joy. But if not, perhaps we should invest in more worthy pleasures and occupy ourselves with lasting things.

—∞∞∞—

*Dear God, let me not waste time with trifling indulgences. Rather, raise to my lips the cup of lasting joy. Amen.*

# THE PRAISE OF OTHERS

Paul gathered a pile of brushwood and, as he put it on the fire, a viper, driven out by the heat, fastened itself on his hand. When the islanders saw the snake hanging from his hand, they said to each other, "This man must be a murderer; for though he escaped from the sea, the goddess Justice has not allowed him to live." But Paul shook the snake off into the fire and suffered no ill effects. The people expected him to swell up or suddenly fall dead; but after waiting a long time and seeing nothing unusual happen to him, they changed their minds and said he was a god.

—*Acts 28:3–6 (NIV)*

Paul was shipwrecked on an island and then bitten by a viper. When the island's inhabitants saw this, they immediately thought that Paul must be a murderer to deserve such an awful fate. However, when Paul miraculously survived and thrived after the bite, they quickly changed their opinion; in their eyes, Paul was now a god.

Like Paul, when we overcome odds and experience success, we may become objects of worship by the same people who previously condemned us. But just as we did not let their condemnation stop us, neither should their worship inflate us. The God with us in our failures is also the God of our success, and to him we must return all praise.

---

*Dear God, help me avoid fealty to the praises of others. Accolades come and go; only faith in you and service to my neighbor is eternal. Amen.*

# COUGHLIN'S PRAYER

"After the earthquake came fire, but the Lord was not in the fire. And after the fire came a gentle whisper. When Elijah heard it, he pulled his cloak over his face and went out and stood at the mouth of the cave."

You, O Lord, are the subtle inspiration hidden in our deepest instincts to seek out goodness and love and content us with the whisper of truth and presence.

Lord, if we desire You to be a part of our busy lives we need to find some cave of Aloneness where we can heed Your voice and ponder Your Word with a clean heart.

Enable us and our children not to be afraid of silence.

Only from silence can come the depth of expression, the well-spring of beautiful and common language that will help us interpret all the sounds of our noisy world.

Lord, help us to keep silent so we may listen better. Help us to abide in the silence of prayer so prayer can live in us—now and forever. Amen.

*—Rev. Daniel P. Coughlin,*
*prayer at the opening session of Congress, April 23, 2009*

# ZOOM OUT

My thoughts are not your thoughts,
　Nor are your ways My ways.

*—Isaiah 55:8 (NKJV)*

If you look the right way, you can see that the whole world is a garden.

*—Frances Hodgson Burnett,* The Secret Garden

If we look around even now, we'll notice a certain ceiling to our vision. We cannot see beyond the wall in front of us or beneath the floor below. Even if we step out onto the balcony or into the backyard, a winding road or distant horizon will eventually bind the furthest reach of our glance. To be sure, there is beauty within our field of view. But we don't even know the half.

Each day we must ask God for the best and most expansive vision. And what is that vision? It is his. We will never know His full perspective, the widest reaches of his view of our lives. But perhaps if he gave us just a glimpse, we would know much more than we know right now.

*Help us "zoom out," oh God. Widen our perspective and extend our horizon, so that we can more fully know your purpose this day, and every day. Amen.*

# HOLDING OUR PEACE

> But the people held their peace and answered him not a word; for the
> king's commandment was, "Do not answer him."
>
> —*2 Kings 18:36 (NKJV)*

There's an old gospel song with a rising refrain: "If I hold my peace, and let the Lord fight my battles . . . victory shall be mine!"

King Hezekiah knew this to be true. In the face of accusations from Assyria's king, Hezekiah's command to the people of Israel was to be quiet. Do not respond. God will reveal his power in due time.

In the same manner, let's be careful not to answer every challenge. We could easily go from one retort to the next, but often our silence speaks louder than our response. God will enter that silence and show himself strong.

---

*Dear God, give me judiciousness in response today. Help me discern when to speak and when to hold my peace. In the end, I know that the victory will be yours, and mine. Amen.*

# RIGHTEOUS ANGER

> In your anger do not sin: Do not let the sun go down while you are still angry, and do not give the devil a foothold.
> —*Ephesians 4:26–27 (NIV)*

> Underneath his sweetness and gentleness was the heat of a volcano. He was a man of excitable and fiery nature; but through high self-discipline he had converted the fire into a central glow and motive power of life, instead of permitting it to waste itself in useless passion. "He that is slow to anger," saith the sage, "is greater than the mighty, and he that ruleth his own spirit than he that taketh a city." Faraday was *not* slow to anger, but he completely ruled his own spirit, and thus, though he took no cities, he captivated all hearts."
> —*John Tyndall,* Faraday as a Discoverer

There are few things as potent as passion, but portioning is key.

Too much, and the rising tide of our feelings spills over from day to night to day—uncontrolled, crashing down on those around us. Too little, and we become dry and listless, a parching force on those we love.

"Do not let the sun go down while you are still angry" implies that there is in fact a time for righteous anger—in controlled portions, while it is still day. Like the great scientist Michael Faraday, let us "through high self-discipline" convert the fire of our passion "into a central glow and motive power of life."

*Dear God, let my love for you, for justice, for righteousness burn bright; let righteous anger have its place in my life, but only the place you give it. Amen.*

# GLADNESS IN OUR HEARTS

You have put gladness in my heart,
> More than in the season that their grain and wine increased.
I will both lie down in peace, and sleep;
> For You alone, O LORD, make me dwell in safety.
>> —*Psalm 4:7–8 (NKJV)*

⸺⸎⸺

*We hold on to the promise of gladness in our hearts.*
*We hold on to the joy that lives within.*
*You have placed it there, God, and it cannot be moved.*
*We lie down in peace and rise in your safety.*
*And we hold on to the gladness in our hearts. Amen.*

# IN ONE MAN

Therefore, as through one man's offense judgment came to all men, resulting in condemnation, even so through one Man's righteous act the free gift came to all men, resulting in justification of life.
—*Romans 5:18 (NKJV)*

With one man, Adam, death came into the world; and with one man, Jesus, it was overcome.

As we thank God for the gift of his son, whose sacrifice was a perfect payment for our sin, we also marvel at the power that resides in a single human being.

We carry within us great authority to bring life and death into this world. Today, rather than falling into the temptations and traps of Adam, let's model ourselves on our Savior and use our power to bring healing and life.

*Dear God, I acknowledge the great power you've placed in my hands. And I will use it well. Amen.*

# FAIRNESS

Love your enemies and pray for those who persecute you, that you may be children of your Father in heaven. He causes his sun to rise on the evil and the good, and sends rain on the righteous and the unrighteous. If you love those who love you, what reward will you get? Are not even the tax collectors doing that? And if you greet only your own people, what are you doing more than others? Do not even pagans do that? Be perfect, therefore, as your heavenly Father is perfect.

*—Matthew 5:44–48 (NIV)*

Why should I love my enemy? He's my enemy! Why should the warm sun and cooling raining fall equally on me, the righteous, and on that guy, who is clearly unrighteous? Why should I greet in love those whose beliefs, whose core values, are so radically different from mine? And how on earth can I be perfect? Perfect, like God?

These are perhaps the most radically unfair verses in scripture, matching up perfectly with our radically unfair days. God is not a payroll clerk, providing grace and condemnation, sun and rain, in proportion to our good or evil works. It's a whole different calculation entirely.

Our days require us to strive to be like Jesus, nothing more, nothing less. When we accept that his love is sufficiently abundant for us and all the other undeserving beings who walk this earth, we will stop seeking fairness and instead simply accept His grace and desire it for others.

―∾∾∾―

*Dear God, help me shift from a worldly calculus to a godly one. I do not deserve the grace you extended to me. As I strive to live like you, let me extend grace to others who are also undeserving. Amen.*

# YOU LOVED US FIRST

This is how God showed his love among us: He sent his one and only Son into the world that we might live through him. This is love: not that we loved God, but that he loved us and sent his Son as an atoning sacrifice for our sins. Dear friends, since God so loved us, we also ought to love one another.

—*1 John 4:9–11 (NIV)*

Father in Heaven! You have loved us first, help us never to forget that You are love so that this sure conviction might triumph in our hearts over the seduction of the world, over the inquietude of the soul, over the anxiety for the future, over the fright of the past, over the distress of the moment. But grant also that this conviction might discipline our souls so that our hearts might remain faithful and sincere in the love which we bear to all those whom You have commanded us to love as we love ourselves.

—*Søren Kierkegaard,* The Prayers of Kierkegaard

*Father, you loved us first. Help us never forget it. And let us bear your love to all whom you have commanded. Amen.*

# HITTING THE HOLE

I want to be thoroughly used up when I die, for the harder I work, the more I live. I rejoice in life for its own sake. Life is no "brief candle" to me. It is a sort of splendid torch, which I have got hold of for the moment; and I want to make it burn as brightly as possible before handing it on to future generations.
　　　　　—*George Bernard Shaw, in* George Bernard Shaw,
　　　　　　　　　　　　　　　　　　His Life and Works

Since we have such a hope, we are very bold.
　　　　　—*2 Corinthians 3:12 (ESV)*

In football, there is a concept of a ball carrier "hitting the hole." This means that when offensive blockers move defenders aside and clear a path for a running back, that running back should attack the hole with as much speed, ferocity, and determination as possible. No matter how narrow it is, if you see daylight, you run toward it.

What if running backs decided to be cautious about the holes they "hit"? What if they chose to forgo the opportunities they saw, out of nervousness, fear, or some misplaced notion of prudence? We'd consider them crazy, and if they were on our favorite team, we'd pray for a trade.

And yet, every day, today, God opens up daylight. Opportunities—some wide, some narrow—emerge. He clears spaces for us to run through at full speed, with determination. When that happens, are we ready to "hit the hole"?

---

*God, give me a spirit of boldness. When you present an opportunity, I will take advantage of it. Amen.*

# AVOIDING OFFENSE

A brother offended is harder to win than a strong city,
　　And contentions are like the bars of a castle.
　　　　　　　　　　　　　　　　—*Proverbs 18:19 (NKJV)*

Let's be swift with apologies but avoid having to make them as much as we can. We pray that God would keep us from offense.

———∽∞∾———

*Lord, give us sensitivity to our brothers and sisters and help us avoid contention. When our neighbors are offended, we pledge to win them back, but help us not offend in the first place, as much as we can. Amen.*

# OUR CONTROL

There are only two kinds of people in the end: those who say to God, "Thy will be done," and those to whom God says, in the end, "*Thy will be done*." All that are in Hell, choose it. Without that self-choice there could be no Hell. No soul that seriously and constantly desires joy will ever miss it. Those who seek find. To those who knock it is opened.

—*C. S. Lewis,* The Great Divorce

Some things are out of our control—the pattern of our breathing, the actions of others, the sun or rain that beats down.

But those greater things—life or death, heaven or hell, joy or sorrow—those we, alone, determine. How freeing indeed!

Let's make wise choices. Chiefly among them, let's choose to work and pray for God's will to be done. As the captains of our souls, there is no worthier flag to raise.

~~~

*Dear God, thank you for free will. Thank you for the ability to determine the level of my joy and quantity of my peace. Help me at every decision point choose to do your will. Amen.*

# OUR FRIEND

What is man that You are mindful of him,
   And the son of man that You visit him?
For You have made him a little lower than the angels,
   And You have crowned him with glory and honor.

*—Psalm 8:4–5 (NKJV)*

—⁓⁓⁓—

*You call us friend.*

*The God of the universe calls us friend.*

*Who are we that you are mindful of us, oh God? Mere mortals, that you would spend time with us this day?*

*But you do; you're present; you're here. You've crowned us with the honor of your presence right now. We return that honor to you in the form of our obedience, and all our love.*

*Amen.*

# FOR THE FIRST TIME

We shall not cease from exploration
And the end of all our exploring
Will be to arrive where we started
And know the place for the first time.

—*T. S. Eliot,* Four Quartets

At that time Jesus said, "I praise you, Father, Lord of heaven and earth, because you have hidden these things from the wise and learned, and revealed them to little children. Yes, Father, for this is what you were pleased to do."

—*Matthew 11:25–26 (NIV)*

God must get a kick out of children. They've figured out the secret to laughter, erupting at even the silliest things—a funny face, a "knock-knock" joke, a gentle toss up into the air. They've figured out the secret to love—bursting into a classroom and embracing friends tall and short, black and white and brown, real and imaginary (teddy bears, of course)—before we've layered on top of them prejudice and difference. They've figured out the secret to boldness, donning costumes, capes, and wands, rushing into imaginary lands, slaying giants of all sorts—always conquering, never defeated.

Slowly, as time wears on, we forget these lessons. We grow judicious, cynical, and perhaps a bit afraid. But our prayer this day is to relearn the lessons we knew so long ago: how to laugh purely, act boldly, love innocently. Let's strive to mingle the wisdom we've been blessed with over the years with the lessons of childhood—to "arrive where we started and know the place for the first time."

*Dear God, as I appreciate the children around me, let me learn from them. Place within me their wonder and joy, and plant their laughter deep inside my soul. Amen.*

# REPAIR THE DOORS

> Hezekiah was twenty-five years old when he became king, and he
> reigned in Jerusalem twenty-nine years. His mother's name was Abi-
> jah daughter of Zechariah. He did what was right in the eyes of the
> LORD, just as his father David had done.
>
> In the first month of the first year of his reign, he opened the
> doors of the temple of the LORD and repaired them.
>
> —*2 Chronicles 29:1–3 (NIV)*

The first thing King Hezekiah did in the first year of his reign—in fact, in the very first month—was open "the doors of the temple of the Lord and [repair] them." He had his priorities straight.

Are we taking good care of the things of God? The things he's blessed us with, the items under our stewardship, the causes he's placed in our hearts, and his own house, the church?

---

*God, we pray that you would constantly order our priorities around what's most important. We pray that we would treat your things, what you've blessed us with, well. Amen.*

# YOU ARE THE FOUNDATION

His divine power has given us everything we need for a godly life
through our knowledge of him who called us by his own glory and
goodness.

*—2 Peter 1:3 (NIV)*

God is the foundation for everything
This God undertakes. God gives,
Such that nothing that is necessary for life is lacking.
Now humankind needs a body that at all times honors and
    praises God.
This body is supported in every way through the earth.
Thus the earth glorifies the power of God.

*—Hildegard of Bingen,*
*in* Meditations with Hildegard of Bingen

*Dear God, as the earth beneath my feet glorifies you, today, so do I. You are
the foundation, and nothing is lacking. In you, I am complete. Amen.*

# FORGIVING THE PAIN

If anyone says, "I love God," and hates his brother, he is a liar; for he who does not love his brother whom he has seen cannot love God whom he has not seen.

*—1 John 4:20 (ESV)*

I imagine one of the reasons people cling to their hates so stubbornly is because they sense, once hate is gone, they will be forced to deal with pain.

*—James Baldwin,* Notes of a Native Son

*Lord, if we have intense feeling—even hatred—for any of your creatures, we pray for its release. Search our emotions, and root out any ill will. We have reasons, good reasons, for certain antipathies—but today, we make an effort to forgive. And once we have forgiven, we ask you to help us deal with any underlying pain. Amen.*

# THE DIAMOND

> But we have this treasure in jars of clay to show that this all-surpassing power is from God and not from us. We are hard pressed on every side, but not crushed; perplexed, but not in despair; persecuted, but not abandoned; struck down, but not destroyed. We always carry around in our body the death of Jesus, so that the life of Jesus may also be revealed in our body.
>
> —*2 Corinthians 4:7–10 (NIV)*

Reflect for a moment on the sparkling treasure held in this frame of ours: A stranger walks beside us on the street, and after tapping us on the shoulder to get our attention, the stranger extends his hand. We hesitantly reach back, and in our palm this stranger places a perfectly formed diamond, larger than any museum piece, so bright it causes us to avert our gaze. We're unsure of its provenance, skeptical of its full worth. But when it is tested, it proves true. It turns out this is a priceless gift, given freely, into our feeble hands.

We walk around with such treasure, today and every day. Within these bodies, these fragile "jars of clay," is the Spirit of God, and life eternal, given freely to us through faith in Jesus Christ. We can never be too careful in cultivating that Spirit, listening for its voice and pointing our life toward its promptings. We have been given an extraordinary gift in these curiously ordinary frames.

---

*Dear Father, thank you for the gift of your salvation. I will never take it for granted; I will marvel at it all my days. Amen.*

# BEYOND OUR BORDERS

The world is shrinking together; it is finding itself neighbor to itself in strange, almost magic degree.
—*W. E. B. DuBois, in* The Wisdom of W. E. B. DuBois

But you will receive power when the Holy Spirit comes on you; and you will be my witnesses in Jerusalem, and in all Judea and Samaria, and to the ends of the earth.
—*Acts 1:8 (NIV)*

*Dear Lord, today, cast our thoughts beyond our borders. As we maintain and grow in love for our own country, remind us that your purpose for us knows no boundaries. Help us envision ways to bring your healing nature beyond this land of ours—"in all Judea and Samaria, and to the ends of the earth." Amen.*

# OLD PATTERNS

What shall we say then? Shall we continue in sin that grace may abound? Certainly not! How shall we who died to sin live any longer in it?

—*Romans 6:1–2 (NKJV)*

As believers, we must move beyond our old ways.

If we find ourselves stuck in the same patterns of sin even after accepting God's grace, let's pray that these patterns would be broken. "Shall we continue in sin that grace may abound. Certainly not!"

*Dear God, help me to break free from old patterns, old ways, old sins. I do not want to abuse your grace; it did not come cheaply. In you, I am set free. Amen.*

# FREE WILL

The heart of man plans his way,
    but the Lord establishes his steps.

—Proverbs 16:9 (ESV)

The glory of Him who moves everything penetrates through the universe, and is resplendent in one part more and in another less. . . . The greatest gift which God in His bounty bestowed in creating, and the most conformed to His own goodness, and that which He prizes the most, was the freedom of the will, with which the creatures that have intelligence, they all and they alone, were and are endowed.

—Dante, Paradiso

---

*Lord, you have given me free will, but I ask that you chain that will to your purposes. When I lift these feet to take a step, establish my steps in your path. Amen.*

# INTO BLESSINGS

> They hired against you Balaam the son of Beor from Pethor of Mesopotamia, to curse you. Nevertheless the LORD your God would not listen to Balaam, but the LORD your God turned the curse into a blessing for you, because the LORD your God loves you.
>
> —*Deuteronomy 23:4–5 (NKJV)*

Our God can turn curses into blessings.

The harmful habits we carried over from our mothers and fathers, the traits we've feared all our lives, can—in his hands—be molded for our good. The lies spoken against us, the attacks from our enemies, when shaped by him, can be our greatest weapons.

We should not fear the "curses" spoken over our lives. We serve a God more powerful than any chemist or alchemist indeed; he alone can turn curses into blessings.

~∞~

*Dear God, I hand over to you all the things spoken against me. I know that you know what to do. Amen.*

# BE STILL

Be still, and know that I am God.
—*Psalm 46:10 (NIV)*

*Amen.*

# MARCH

## THE POWER OF HUMILITY

In late April 2010, President Obama and First Lady Michelle Obama packed up their daughters and took them to a favorite vacation spot: the Grove Park Inn in Asheville, North Carolina. It was certainly time for a little rest.

From the campaign to the White House, it had been a rewarding but tough stretch. It certainly was for me: some of the more challenging issues we faced intersected with my work, from the president's former pastor to abortion and other related controversies. As the president's spiritual adviser and head of our government's faith-based initiatives, it was my job to handle these issues, and I was honored to do it. But I was also exhausted.

I can only imagine how President Obama felt. I thought he had done a phenomenal job responding to the economic crisis, making sure sick folks got health care, getting us out of Iraq, and leading the country in a difficult time. But after wrangling with Congress, managing the government, and trying to be a good dad and husband, the guy needed a breather.

When I heard the president would be heading to North Carolina, I mentioned that he may want to connect with Reverend Billy Graham, whose home in Montreat was about a half hour away, while he was in the area. It was an offhand suggestion: I figured he would probably just want to be with his family. But to my pleasant surprise, word came back from the road that President Obama would be delighted to visit with Reverend Graham, and he wanted me to join the meeting. I caught the next plane out of D.C. and met President Obama at his hotel. I went straight to the motorcade. To my relief, the president looked rested, revived. It had been a good vacation.

We hopped in "The Beast" (the president's weighty armored car) and began the short journey to Reverend Graham's house. The joy of seeing the world's most eminent pastor was tempered by real tragedy: just a few days earlier, an explosion at the Upper Big Branch Mine in West Virginia had claimed the lives of twenty-nine miners. After the meeting with Reverend Graham, the president was going straight from North Carolina to West Virginia to address the memorial service. On the way to Reverend Graham's house, we talked about what scripture the president would recite in the service. He settled on the 23rd Psalm.

It was quite a sight to see the full motorcade crawl slowly up the mountain, and neighbors filled the tree-lined path to catch a glimpse. We pulled into Reverend Graham's circular driveway and were greeted warmly by his assistant, who led us to the living room and Reverend Graham. There were four of us in the room: President Obama, myself, Graham's son Franklin, and Reverend Graham.

I had heard stories about this great man of God: how he had counseled presidents, saved millions of souls around the world, never missed an opportunity to share the Gospel of Jesus Christ. Even in his advanced age, he held a lofty position in my mind. I had no idea what to expect when we walked into that living room. And what I found quite simply floored me.

What I found in Rev. Billy Graham was an almost overwhelming, driving, powerful . . . humility. He was the most humble person I have ever met. His first words to President Obama were, "I am so proud of you!" It was a stunning sentiment from the greatest preacher who's ever lived. He went on to say that he had followed the president's career with great interest for years and had been praying for him every single day. He also related to the president a quick story about President Truman. (I won't go into the details here, largely because it was a cautionary tale about keeping presidential advice private.)

Reverend Graham drew the meeting to a close by earnestly thanking the president for making the trip up the mountain. We learned later that President Obama was the first sitting president to visit Billy Graham at his home, a fact surely not lost on Reverend Graham.

The last words, as one might expect, were in prayer. President Obama drew close to Reverend Graham in an antique wooden rocker and Reverend Graham sidled up to the president in his trusty padded sitting chair. Reverend Graham offered a beautiful prayer—one for the ages. And what happened next truly shocked me: President Obama began praying for Reverend Graham.

I don't know why he did it. Perhaps he was just grateful to God for the gift of Reverend Graham. Perhaps it was a show of humility to a man whose grace was so palpable in the room. Maybe he wanted to pray for the man who had prayed for so many. Whatever the reason, President Obama laid his hand on Reverend Graham's knee and thanked God for him. And I found myself quietly thanking God for both of them: for the pastor to so many presidents, and for a president who knew the power of prayer.

That day I thought, *If President Obama can find the boldness to pray for Billy Graham, surely I can pray for those whom I encounter as well, no matter who they are or where they're from.* Since that day, I have hardly gone twenty-four hours without asking someone, "How can I pray for you?" And, God's truth, it has never gotten a poor response.

# SLOWLY

The heart of the righteous studies how to answer,
But the mouth of the wicked pours forth evil.

*—Proverbs 15:28 (NKJV)*

Talk low, talk slow, and don't say too much.

*—John Wayne*

As a child, I always wondered why my grandfather, Homer Roberson, spoke so *slowly*. It seemed that by the time he answered my first question, I had five more ready. For a frequently impatient eight-year old, it was almost too much to bear.

So one day, I asked him, "Granddaddy Homer, why do you talk so *slow*?" It wasn't until I read Proverbs 15:28 years later that his answer made much sense. He said to me, "I speak slowly because I don't want my mouth to run laps around my brain. I'd rather my brain finish first."

A problem never went unsolved, or dispute unresolved, because of an answer delivered too slowly. Let us "study how to answer," before we speak, so that our replies will be godly and wise.

---

*Dear God, pace me. Let me not move in front of your wisdom, and let my language reflect study and care. Amen.*

# UPRIGHT

The LORD God is a sun and shield;
    the LORD will give grace and glory;
no good thing will He withhold
    from those who walk uprightly.

*—Psalm 84:11 (NKJV)*

What does it mean to "walk uprightly"? We know the metaphor—to live in a way that is honorable, just, and pure. But what if God literally meant "walk uprightly"?

Not bowed in shame because of hidden sin. Not darting from side to side, anxious about what is behind us and what is to come. Not slumped over with weariness, the pressures of the world resting upon our shoulders.

No—upright. Chin high. Resolved that we are children of God. Assured of His love for us. Ready to square our shoulders up to the blessings and wonder of this new day.

"No good thing will He withhold from them that walk uprightly."

*Dear God, let my physical presence in the world reflect what you are doing in my spirit. For you are surely doing a new thing. Amen.*

MARCH 3

# SELAH

The LORD of hosts is with us; the God of Jacob is our refuge. *Selah.*
*—Psalm 46:11 (KJV)*

A curious word is tucked at the end of various passages in the Psalms: *selah.*

Some bible scholars have said that *selah* is an instruction to the reader to pause and meditate on the passage's meaning. But according to other interpretations, it is so much more than that.

Historians point out that Selah was an actual, physical place: a walled city, "Selah Petra," in what is currently Jordan. And they say that instead of just calling us to meditation, when the Psalmist instructs us to *selah,* he is reminding us to *rest in the safety of God's arms.*

Knowing that we are protected. Knowing that the forces of this day, this world, this life cannot penetrate God's merciful fortress. In this security, we can experience true rest and release.

~~~

*Dear God, I follow your command to* selah *today. I reflect on your word and meditate, within the safety of your arms. Amen.*

# For Such a Time as This

> For if you remain completely silent at this time, relief and deliverance will arise for the Jews from another place, but you and your father's house will perish. Yet who knows whether you have come to the kingdom for such a time as this?
>
> —*Esther 4:14 (NKJV)*

These are the words of Mordecai to the great biblical heroine Esther, who saved the Jewish people from certain destruction by speaking boldly to her king. "Who knows whether you have come to the kingdom for such a time as this?"

Who knows?

Perhaps we are right here, right now, for a very particular reason. To declare a bold word. To write a brave phrase. To take a new step. To tell a hard truth.

If it is not our time, fine. As Mordecai said in his preface, God's will will still be done. But maybe, just maybe, this is our time. Such a time as this.

*Lord, if this is my time, my time to do a new thing, give me the courage to act boldly, unafraid. Amen.*

# VACANT PLACES, NEW BRICKS

Examine yourselves, to see whether you are in the faith. Test yourselves. Or do you not realize this about yourselves, that Jesus Christ is in you?—unless indeed you fail to meet the test!

—*2 Corinthians 13:5 (ESV)*

In the vacant places
We will build with new bricks.

—*T. S. Eliot,* The Rock

---

*Dear Lord, help us move into the vacant places today. Help us rediscover those parts of our cities, our world, even our own lives long since left behind. Remind us of these vacant places—and in them, help us build with new bricks. Amen.*

# OUR RAIN

The LORD is my shepherd; I shall not want. . . . Thou preparest a table before me in the presence of mine enemies: thou anointest my head with oil; my cup runneth over.

*—Psalm 23:1, 5 (KJV)*

Each morning, something nearly magical happens before we set foot out of the house. Hydrogen and oxygen atoms, connected by covalent bonds, spurred on by solar radiation, evaporate into the air. Rising air currents move these vapors into the cool atmosphere, where they condense into the beautiful figures above us, clouds. These masses of particles grow and collide with one another, and fall out of the atmosphere as precipitation. Precipitation then gathers together in deep underground aquifers, then on to a treatment facility, and then through a maze of pipes and tunnels into our homes. And at the conclusion of this process, above our heads, this converted rain, these strange particles, fall down upon us—as a shower. Heavenly, isn't it?

Each day, in some way, we are anointed. Each day, when we feel that water, we are reminded of the wonder of this world and the God who created it all. He "anoints our head" before we leave in the morning—his children, all. Let's revel in that notion today.

—∽∽∽∽—

*Dear God, thank you for the special care you have taken with your creation— the unique nature of my life, and my anointing. Let me return that care back to you in worship and in service. Amen.*

# SWEETNESS AND HEALTH

Kind words do not cost much. Yet they accomplish much.
—New York Evangelist

Pleasant words are like a honeycomb,
Sweetness to the soul and health to the bones.
—*Proverbs 16:24 (NKJV)*

*Dear Lord, make my words pleasant. Let them not just instruct or reprove, but bring sweetness and health to all I encounter. Amen.*

# GLOWING LIKE JO

About eight days after Jesus said this, he took Peter, John and James with him and went up onto a mountain to pray. As he was praying, the appearance of his face changed, and his clothes became as bright as a flash of lightning. Two men, Moses and Elijah, appeared in glorious splendor, talking with Jesus. . . . While he was speaking, a cloud appeared and covered them, and they were afraid as they entered the cloud. A voice came from the cloud, saying, "This is my Son, whom I have chosen; listen to him." When the voice had spoken, they found that Jesus was alone. The disciples kept this to themselves and did not tell anyone at that time what they had seen.

—*Luke 9:28–31, 34–36 (NIV)*

My wife has a friend named Jo. Jo is an African American woman, about fifty years old. We are fairly certain she's a real-life angel. Jo brightens every room she walks in. No matter what's happening on a given day, no matter the mood of those around her, Jo leaves a joyous imprint. With a brief word, or an offer of prayer, or a quiet look, Jo seems to quite literally . . . glow.

Jo has an aggressive form of cancer. In early 2012, doctors told her that her time may be drawing nigh. You couldn't tell by the expression on her face, though. She is still glowing.

I thought of Jo when I read about Jesus on the Mount of Transfiguration, when Moses and Elijah joined him across space and time, and the Spirit of God rested upon him, and "the appearance of his face changed, and his clothes became as bright as a flash of lightning."

When we are in Christ, living a life blessed by God, other folks should be able to tell that something's different about us. Our demeanor, our words, the spirit we emanate. Eventually the appearance of our face might even change. And like Jo and Jesus, we might seem to glow.

*Dear God, let me spread your light today. Not just by words and deeds, but by presence alone. Let those who are around me feel the Christ within me. Amen.*

# SURROUND US

"Am I only a God nearby,"
    declares the LORD,
"and not a God far away?
Who can hide in secret places
    so that I cannot see them?"
      declares the LORD.
    "Do not I fill heaven and earth?"
      declares the LORD.

*—Jeremiah 23:23–24 (NIV)*

God be in my head, and in my understanding;
God be in mine eyes, and in my looking;
God be in my mouth, and in my speaking;
God be in my heart, and in my thinking;
God be at mine end, and at my departing.

*—Sarum Primer*

*Surround us today, oh God. We don't want to take a step without your blessing. And when we finish, please be at our ending. Amen.*

# FULL-TIME PRAISE

And with them Heman and Jeduthun and the rest who were chosen,
who were designated by name, to give thanks to the LORD, because
His mercy endures forever.

*—1 Chronicles 16:41 (NKJV)*

King David found the cause of praise so important—the work of letting
God know how thankful he was for his many blessings—that he appointed
two full-time staff, Heman and Jeduthun, to help him give thanks to God!

While we may not have capacity for full-time praise staff, we should
spend a great deal of our own time in a spirit of thankfulness. There is
something enriching about praise: it reminds us of how far we've come, it
levels heady thoughts, and it brings joy to downcast hearts. Even a simple
"Thank you, Lord" is a good start.

———

*Dear God, I give all honor and praise to you. Your blessings have been so full
and rich, it's hard for me to describe. Thank you, Lord. Amen.*

# HE HAS PROTECTED US

Queen Jezebel was committed to killing the prophet Elijah.

> So Jezebel sent a messenger to Elijah to say, "May the gods deal with me, be it ever so severely, if by this time tomorrow I do not make your life like that of one of them."
>
> —*1 Kings 19:2 (NIV)*

But history records that forty days later, Elijah was still standing.

> So he got up and ate and drank. Strengthened by that food, he traveled forty days and forty nights until he reached Horeb, the mountain of God.
>
> —*1 Kings 19:8 (NIV)*

Let's take a moment to look back and see how many times the enemy's declarations over our lives have failed. Let's consider how the plots against us, the pessimism about us, have not come to pass. God has been a protector, and he has been faithful. So will he always be.

❧

*Dear Lord, thank you for your consistent protection. I have not had the easiest days, but I am still standing. And I know it's because of you. Amen.*

# BELIEVE THEM

The first time someone shows you who they are, believe them.
—*Maya Angelou, on* Oprah's Lifeclass

Then Mary took about a pint of pure nard, an expensive perfume; she poured it on Jesus' feet and wiped his feet with her hair. And the house was filled with the fragrance of the perfume.

But one of his disciples, Judas Iscariot, who was later to betray him, objected, "Why wasn't this perfume sold and the money given to the poor? It was worth a year's wages." He did not say this because he cared about the poor but because he was a thief; as keeper of the money bag, he used to help himself to what was put into it.

—*John 12:3–6 (NIV)*

Long before Judas Iscariot betrayed Jesus, he betrayed his own character to those who knew him.

Judas made a habit out of stealing from the "money bag" where people placed offerings for the poor. With Jesus and others around, Judas chided Mary for not selling a precious perfume and giving the proceeds to the poor—not out of a spirit of charity but because he intended to steal that same money. His later crime—handing Jesus over to the chief priest and the Romans to be crucified—was infinitely more severe, but this early betrayal of trust was telling.

When people reveal their character, we must listen—in forgiveness and love, but still listening. When the enemy is at work in people, they are susceptible to doing strange and destructive things, so we must be "wise as serpents, and as harmless as doves" (Matt. 10:16, ESV).

⁓⁓⁓

*Dear God, let my perception of the people around me be balanced with grace and wisdom. Let me be both innocent and wise. Amen.*

# A Prayer for Our Animals

A righteous man regards the life of his animal,
But the tender mercies of the wicked are cruel.

—*Proverbs 12:10 (NKJV)*

A prayer for our animals:

*And for these also, Dear Lord, the humble beasts, who with us bear the burden and heat of the day, and offer their guileless lives for the well-being of their country, we supplicate Thy great tenderness of heart, for Thou hast promised to save both man and beast. And great is Thy loving kindness, Oh Master, Savior of the world.* (Attributed to Saint Basil of Caesarea)

# WHAT YOU OUGHT TO SAY

Now when they bring you to the synagogues and magistrates and authorities, do not worry about how or what you should answer, or what you should say. For the Holy Spirit will teach you in that very hour what you ought to say.

—*Luke 12:11–12 (NKJV)*

How many times have the words just . . . come to us? And yet for some reason, we still doubt that they will.

God is not just a God of external blessings, of improved situations and needs that are met. He also blesses our language, particularly when we're under pressure, and we don't know what to say.

The next time we have to go in front of a crowd, let's seek the Holy Spirit's guidance. And he will "teach you in that very hour what you ought to say."

*Dear God, bless my language. Prepare me to say a word to your people today and each day in the future. And when I don't know what to say, I trust that you will step in. Amen.*

# A GOOD STORY

In the beginning, God created the heavens and the earth. The earth was without form and void, and darkness was over the face of the deep. And the Spirit of God was hovering over the face of the waters. And God said, "Let there be light," and there was light. And God saw that the light was good. And God separated the light from the darkness. God called the light Day, and the darkness he called Night. And there was evening and there was morning, the first day.

*—Genesis 1:1–5 (ESV)*

I believe that one of the principal ways in which we acquire, hold, and digest information, is via narrative. So I hope you will understand when the remarks I make begin with what I believe to be the first sentence of our childhood—that we all remember—the phrase "Once upon a time. . . ."

*—Toni Morrison, Nobel Prize lecture*

~∞∞∞~

*We want to tell a good story today, dear Lord. We want to write a new line in a chapter in this life of ours. A dramatic flair, a triumphant conclusion, a love song, a twist or turn.*

*You, God, continue to author the greatest story ever told—and you have placed within us a writer's heart. Today, help us tell and be a good story. Amen.*

# TAKE THIS BURDEN

Come to Me, all you who labor and are heavy laden, and I will give you rest. Take My yoke upon you and learn from Me, for I am gentle and lowly in heart, and you will find rest for your souls. For My yoke is easy and My burden is light.

—*Matthew 11:28–30 (NKJV)*

There is something wholly liberating about being honest with God. When our minds are cleared of hidden things, when we are transparent with ourselves and our God about the recesses of our thinking, he can remove the burdens of our souls.

It really is that simple: thoughts contained in a dark corner cannot be easily brought to light. But when we acknowledge that which belabors us—sin, worries, struggles, pain—then God can readily lighten the load. "For My yoke is easy and My burden is light."

<hr />

*Dear God, I bring to you all that burdens me. All of the ways I have fallen short, all my worries, all my concerns. Lord, take them from me and exchange them for your burden. Bring rest to my soul. Amen.*

# GUARDING OUR HEARTS

And the chief priests and the scribes that very hour sought to lay hands on Him, but they feared the people—for they knew He had spoken this parable against them.

So they watched Him, and sent spies who pretended to be righteous, that they might seize on His words, in order to deliver Him to the power and the authority of the governor.

—*Luke 20:19–20 (NKJV)*

Spies around Jesus clung to his words as friends and then used those words against him as enemies. In the same manner, we have to be shrewd about whom we trust with our thoughts, revelations, and dreams. Even smiling faces can mask ill intent.

My grandmother thought it wise to "never give anyone information they don't need to have—they won't know what to do with it, and they often do the wrong thing." There's wisdom there, but I might phrase it: never give anyone information that God does not want to reveal to them.

With that filter, we can share his revelations, but still guard our hearts.

---

*Dear God, place within me a spirit of holy circumspection. Let me be as wise as a serpent and as innocent as a dove. Amen.*

# PEOPLE OF REPENTANCE

There is no sin, and there can be no sin on all the earth, which the Lord will not forgive to the truly repentant! Man cannot commit a sin so great as to exhaust the infinite love of God. Can there be a sin which could exceed the love of God?

—*Fyodor Dostoevsky,* The Brothers Karamazov

But if we walk in the light, as he is in the light, we have fellowship with one another, and the blood of Jesus his Son cleanses us from all sin.

—*1 John 1:7 (ESV)*

Today, let's be people of repentance. Like buckets of water tossed in the ocean, we carry our faults to God. There is room enough, always room enough, for him to receive them and forgive. So we repent today of our sins, and we are made clean.

———∞∞∞———

*Father, forgive me of my sins, the ways I've fallen short of your purpose and plan. I repent and desire to sin no more. Amen.*

# THE COMING DAVIDS

Whatever mission Saul sent him on, David was so successful that Saul gave him a high rank in the army. This pleased all the troops, and Saul's officers as well.

When the men were returning home after David had killed the Philistine, the women came out from all the towns of Israel to meet King Saul with singing and dancing, with joyful songs and with timbrels and lyres. As they danced, they sang:

"Saul has slain his thousands,
    and David his tens of thousands."

Saul was very angry; this refrain displeased him greatly. "They have credited David with tens of thousands," he thought, "but me with only thousands. What more can he get but the kingdom?" And from that time on Saul kept a close eye on David.

—*1 Samuel 18:5–9 (NIV)*

This was the beginning of the end for Saul. King of Israel, personally selected by the prophet Samuel to lead God's people in their wars against the Philistines, Saul had everything he could possibly desire. But when a young man whom he had cultivated—David, the future king—showed success in battle, Saul couldn't handle it. He heard the voices of young women singing David's praises, and jealousy began to overwhelm him.

We must be careful to keep a gracious heart about those coming behind us. God has blessed us so that we might bless others; he creates "Sauls," in part, so that "Davids" will come along. When we encounter the Davids of our lives, let's rejoice for them, thank God for them, mentor them, and pray for their great success.

~~~~~~

*Dear God, thank you for the Davids who come behind me. Help me encourage them with humility, grace, and love. Let my focus not be on personal achievements but on building your kingdom, no matter who is doing the building. Amen.*

# OPTIMISTS

And we know that for those who love God all things work together for good, for those who are called according to his purpose.

—*Romans 8:28 (ESV)*

Every one of the great revolutionists, from Isaiah to Shelley, have been optimists. They have been indignant, not about the badness of existence, but about the slowness of men in realizing its goodness.

—*G. K. Chesterton,* The Defendant

*Dear Lord, today, help me be forcefully optimistic. Every negative thought, every downcast idea, let them shatter like a pane of glass. I know that all things work together for good, for those who love you and are called according to your purpose. And I stand on that promise. Amen.*

# CONSULTANTS

If any of you lacks wisdom, you should ask God, who gives generously to all without finding fault, and it will be given to you.

—*James 1:5 (NIV)*

It happened after this that David inquired of the LORD, saying,
"Shall I go up to any of the cities of Judah?"
And the LORD said to him, "Go up."
David said, "Where shall I go up?"
And He said, "To Hebron."

—*2 Samuel 2:1 (NKJV)*

We consult so many sources about that critical next step. Our attorneys, our financial advisers, experts on policy, leadership, history, and planning.

But have we stopped, in silence, to ask our Maker? A simple step, but one that takes a lot of faith. Just ask him. Like David, we ask, Lord, shall I go up? What shall I do?

Once asked, in a quiet place, let's be open to the response.

*Dear God, what would you have me do about ____? I sit in quiet and wait for your response. Amen.*

# WHERE HE WALKED

Let this mind be in you which was also in Christ Jesus, who, being in the form of God, did not consider it robbery to be equal with God, but made Himself of no reputation, taking the form of a bondservant, and coming in the likeness of men.

—*Philippians 2:5–7 (NKJV)*

Neil Armstrong, the great astronaut, once took a trip to the Old City of Jerusalem. He went to the Hulda Gate, which opens to the Temple Mount.

Armstrong asked a guide whether Jesus had in fact walked that same path, and when told that Christ had, he humbly replied: "I have to tell you, I am more excited stepping on these stones than I was stepping on the moon."

To walk the same earth, even the same path, that Jesus walked is an awesome thing. To place our footsteps near where he did, to bend down where he knelt before child and sinner and thief. Many will never get the opportunity to share in such a moment; for those of us who can, it's a time to be cherished.

---

*Dear God, thank you for the opportunities you've given me to walk in your footsteps. Let the echoes of your actions reverberate in my heart, from this day forward. Amen.*

NOTE: This devotional was sent to the president around the time of his trip to the Holy Land.

# I Choose You

*God, right now, I choose you.*

*I don't know where my mind will wander tomorrow. Where my flesh will try to take me.*

*I know I am tugged in a dozen different directions. By my past desires, my future strivings, my human weaknesses.*

*Perhaps not always in the future—certainly not always in the past—but right now, right now, Lord, I choose you. And I will keep choosing, consciously, each day that I walk this earth.*

*Amen.*

# DIFFERENCES

Welcome people who are weak in faith, but don't get into an argument over differences of opinion.

—*Romans 14:1 (GWT)*

My grandmother often said, "Never spend time arguing with a fool—because people from a distance can't tell who's who." Today, let's save our arguments for the things that matter most. In everything else, let's accept differences in opinion. There are few topics worth risking peace for.

———∽∾∾∾———

*Lord, help me minimize arguments and welcome those who disagree. Place love at the forefront of my mind in all my interactions. Amen.*

# DECLARED DISCIPLES

Nevertheless even among the rulers many believed in Him, but because of the Pharisees they did not confess Him, lest they should be put out of the synagogue; for they loved the praise of men more than the praise of God.

—*John 12:42–43 (NKJV)*

How many disciples might Jesus have had if men and women were bold enough to declare themselves as such?

The twelve disciples that have been forever recorded in the pages of history might have been joined by dozens, even hundreds more. Jesus's teachings touched this many, for sure, but there was one problem. Like the "rulers" described in John 12, many of those whom he touched were afraid to say it for fear of ridicule and shame. Perhaps they received some small private benefit from Jesus's words. But imagine what more God could have done through those rulers if they stepped out in faith and declared, "I am your disciple."

Whenever we have the opportunity, today or in the future, let us boldly declare our status as followers of Christ. And let history record that we were not ashamed.

~~~~~

*Dear God, let the private love I feel for you find ways to express itself publicly. Present me with an opportunity to let my brothers and sisters know how I feel about you. Amen.*

# SEPARATED

If your enemy is hungry, give him bread to eat,
and if he is thirsty, give him water to drink.
—*Proverbs 25:21 (ESV)*

Men hate each other because they fear each other; they fear each
other because they don't know each other; they don't know each other
because they cannot communicate with each other; they can't communicate with each other because they are separated from each other.
—*Dr. Martin Luther King Jr.,*
*in* The Papers of Dr. Martin Luther King, Jr.

⸎

*Lord, draw us closer to those on the "other side." Build bridges first of commu-
nication and then of love with our opponents. We accept this task today. Amen.*

# OUR SIN IS NOT JUST OUR OWN

So David said to Nathan, "I have sinned against the LORD."

And Nathan said to David, "The LORD also has put away your sin; you shall not die. However, because by this deed you have given great occasion to the enemies of the LORD to blaspheme, the child also who is born to you shall surely die." Then Nathan departed to his house.

*—2 Samuel 12:13–15 (NKJV)*

David committed a horrible sin: he slept with Bathsheba, the wife of one of his soldiers, and then sent Bathsheba's innocent husband to the battlefield to die.

God, in his infinite capacity for mercy, forgave David of that sin. But the ramifications of David's unfaithfulness remained. The prophet Nathan reminded David that his sin was not just between David and God. Others saw the sin as well; their faith was weakened as a result, and they used David's sin as a justification for blasphemy. In the minds of those who looked on, if David could so easily stray, then how powerful was his God?

We have to remember that our sin is not just our own. When leaders stumble, we cause waves of disobedience to ripple through those who look on. God forgives, but the impact on others lingers. It's a lesson for David, and for all of us.

⟿⟿⟿

*Dear God, nail me to your precepts, not just for my own benefit, but for the benefit of those who come behind me. Let me be grounded by the weight of leadership and lead me not into temptation on this path. Amen.*

# CLOSE

Our Saviour's great rule, that "we should love our neighbor as ourselves," is such a fundamental truth for the regulating human society, that, I think, by that alone one might without difficulty determine all the cases and doubts in social morality.

—*John Locke, "An Essay Concerning Human Understanding"*

I will remain in the world no longer, but they are still in the world, and I am coming to you. Holy Father, protect them by the power of your name, the name you gave me, so that they may be one as we are one.

—*John 17:11 (NIV)*

According to John, how close does Jesus want us to be with fellow believers? As close as he is to God. No separation. No distance. Enmeshed. One.

Let's remember that the next time the enemy desires to put trivial things in between us and our precious relationships. "That they may be one," Jesus said to God, "as we are one."

*Lord, help me remove any distance between me and those I love. Amen.*

# WE'RE SUBJECTS

Then He went down with them and came to Nazareth, and was subject to them, but His mother kept all these things in her heart. And Jesus increased in wisdom and stature, and in favor with God and men.

*—Luke 2:51–52 (NKJV)*

We're all subject to someone—even Christ. Jesus's public ministry—the disciples and crowds—did not begin until he was thirty years old. Until then, by all accounts he was a hardworking carpenter. The Gospel of Luke even says that Jesus was "subject to" his parents—meaning, he did his chores.

We will go in and out of seasons of authority. There are times when our words are given great merit and acted upon swiftly. But there are other seasons when those around us will have the authority, the power. Jesus teaches us to learn to be comfortable when we're not the one at the wheel; our season has come before and will come again.

---

*Dear God, help me to accept with peace and love the authority of others. When it's my time to be "subject to," let me remember that it is to you that I am always subject. Amen.*

# FANNIE LOU

> But He was wounded for our transgressions,
>   He was bruised for our iniquities;
> The chastisement for our peace was upon Him;
>   And by His stripes we are healed.
>
> *—Isaiah 53:5 (NKJV)*

On June 3, 1963, Fannie Lou Hamer arrived in Winona, Mississippi, by bus with a few fellow civil rights workers, intending to register African Americans to vote in that town. Policemen in the city had another idea, and they ordered Ms. Hamer and her friends off the bus and took them to the Montgomery County Jail. Fannie Lou Hamer continues the story:

> Then three white men came into my room. One was a state highway policeman, and . . . . they said they were going to make me wish I was dead. They made me lay down on my face and they ordered two Negro prisoners to beat me with a blackjack. . . . The first prisoner beat me until he was exhausted, then the second Negro began to beat me. I had polio when I was about six years old, and I have a limp. So I held my hands down and beneath me, trying to protect my weak side. . . . My dress pulled up, and I tried to smooth it down. One of the policemen walked over and raised my dress as high as he could. They beat me until my body was hard, 'til I couldn't bend my fingers or get up when they told me to.

But here's the thing: Ms. Hamer told this heartbreaking story a year later from the floor of the 1964 Democratic National Convention. Even after such a brutal experience, she was not just a survivor. She was a thriver.

We will endure trials today. However, we must remember the lashes that have come before. Suffering is persistent, varying in intensity from person to person, era to era, but our victory is everlasting. Let us rejoice in the fact that pain's shadow always, always portends triumph's light.

*God, I am thankful that I am an overcomer. When I forget that fact, remind me. And help me see the eternal even in this temporal day. Amen.*

# YOUR PLEASURES

The presence of God calms the soul, and gives it quiet and repose.
— *François Fénelon,* Spiritual Progress, Or,
Instructions in the Divine Life of the Soul

You will show me the path of life;
In Your presence is fullness of joy;
At Your right hand are pleasures forevermore.
—*Psalm 16:11 (NKJV)*

~⦅∞⦆~

*This is our prayer today, dear God. Show us the path of life. Bring us into your presence, where there is fullness of joy. Extend to us your right hand, and your pleasures, forevermore. Amen.*

# APRIL

## GOD'S WORD

As far as I can tell, our knowledge of the language of God—the extent to which His written words are implanted in our minds, our hearts, our marrow—is rarely tested when we are ready for the testing. Rather, the question of whether we know the Bible will be asked when we least expect it, when we're least prepared.

I was wrapping up from a pickup basketball game in the spring of 2006 when a number I didn't recognize flashed on my cell phone. It was a "773" area code—Chicago for sure—but not someone I had heard from before.

I let the first call go to voice mail; no message. Five minutes later, the phone rang again, and I answered, thinking maybe it was an emergency.

"Joshua," the caller said, in a familiar baritone. "This is Barack. How's it going?"

*Well,* I thought, *I'm a junior staffer in your office, you're a United States senator, you've never called me directly before, and I'm catching my breath after five straight games of three-on-three.* So of course, my answer was, "I'm great, Senator—how are you?"

"Doing great. Listen, I'm giving a speech about genocide at a 'Save Darfur' rally, and I'd like to begin with a word of scripture. I was thinking maybe something from the prophet Isaiah or a word from Jesus about the vulnerable. Any thoughts?"

Gulp.

A litany of unspoken excuses rushed through my brain—I've been so busy that I haven't been able to read my Bible as much; I'm really more of a reference guy, rather than a memorizer; it's Saturday afternoon, I'm leaving the gym, and I'm not exactly in the pews at church.

The pause in conversation stretched to the point of cringe-worthiness, and I was just about to tell him, "I'll e-mail you a few verses later," when something whispered to me—*"Proverbs 24, somewhere in the middle of the chapter—Rescue those being led away to death; hold back those staggering toward slaughter."* I repeated it to the senator, fumbling through the words.

"Perfect," Obama responded. "I like that—I think it works. I'll look at a few other verses and let you know where we end up."

Senator Obama did use Proverbs 24:11 at the "Save Darfur" rally, and I learned a critically important lesson that day. The words of God—his thoughts, his instructions, his creative promptings—are not luxuries to be toyed around with. They are necessities. People, from this future president to my own friends and family, were counting on me. God's word had to be planted so deeply within my bones that when asked for it, I couldn't afford to respond like a deer in headlights. I had to be ready to answer boldly.

This lesson was tested many times in the years to come. There was the phone call before Senator Obama's 2008 Democratic National Convention speech in Denver, when we landed on Hebrews 10:23 for a penultimate line. There was the e-mail as the president prepared to address a grieving nation after a massacre at a movie theater in Aurora, Colorado, when we decided that Revelation 21:4 would provide comfort in that sorrowful time. Learning to be ready with the word of God in these grand moments helped me prepare for more personal trials as well, on a smaller scale, but no less important. Like the time when a colleague was despairing nearly to the point of suicide and was in desperate need of comfort and prayer. Or when a close brother in Christ struggled with disillusionment in his marriage and was tempted to be unfaithful to his wife.

Our scriptural triggers must be primed, ready to unleash a healing message from God at a moment's notice. As 2 Corinthians 3:2 (NIV) declares, "You yourselves are our letter, written on our hearts, known and read by everyone." Our families, our friends, and this world need us—they need us to know the word of God.

# OUR RIGHT TO WORSHIP

There is neither Jew nor Greek, there is neither slave nor free, there is
no male and female, for you are all one in Christ Jesus.
—*Galatians 3:28 (ESV)*

On June 16, 1963, in the middle of an epic struggle for civil rights in
America, Rabbi Abraham Joshua Heschel sent a powerful telegram to
President John F. Kennedy:

> We forfeit the right to worship God as long as we continue to humili-
> ate Negroes. . . . The hour calls for moral grandeur and spiritual
> audacity.

When we demean, humiliate, debase God's beloved creation, the rabbi
said, we forfeit our very right to worship God.

※

*Dear God, help me remember to extend a full measure of dignity to all of your
creations, when it is easy and when it is not. And when the hour calls for it, let
me step up with moral grandeur and spiritual audacity. Amen.*

# ON THE LEFT AND RIGHT

"What do you want me to do for you?" he asked.

They replied, "Let one of us sit at your right and the other at your left in your glory."

"You don't know what you are asking," Jesus said. "Can you drink the cup I drink or be baptized with the baptism I am baptized with?"

"We can," they answered.

Jesus said to them, "You will drink the cup I drink and be baptized with the baptism I am baptized with, but to sit at my right or left is not for me to grant. These places belong to those for whom they have been prepared."

—*Mark 10:36–40 (NIV)*

What a wonderful thought: in heaven, there's a space each on Christ's left and right that are not even his to give. Rather, they're prepared for two special people. I wonder who will sit there.

Perhaps it's Moses's place, the forefather who led the people of Israel out of bondage and descended from a fiery mountain with God's great laws. Or maybe David, the beautifully flawed poet, close friend of God, whose spirit was such that the mere thought of God's goodness caused him to dance. Maybe Mary of Bethany, who trusted Jesus to raise her brother Lazarus from the grave; or the Apostle Paul, who brought the message of Christ to so many around the world. Or maybe they're rotating seats, and over time, Rosa Parks and Mother Teresa, Billy Graham and Fannie Lou Hamer, Dorothy Day and Saint Francis will take the places?

Of all the accomplishments in the world, all the fame and fortune, achievements and acclaim, maybe, just maybe, God will let us spend a short time, seated in the places that "have been prepared." What a wonderful aspiration!

---

*Dear God, thank you for preparing seats for the faithful. Help me keep my heart pure and my work steady so that I may spend eternal moments with you. Amen.*

# TO DIE FOR

And everyone who lives and believes in me shall never die. Do you believe this?

—*John 11:26 (ESV)*

What I really need is to get clear about what I must do, not what I must know, except insofar as knowledge must precede every act. What matters is to find a purpose, to see what it really is that God wills that I shall do; the crucial thing is to find a truth which is truth for me, to find the idea for which I am willing to live and die.

—*Søren Kierkegaard,* Søren Kierkegaard's
Journals and Papers, *vol. 5*

What are we willing to die for? For what would we put it all on the line?

Today, we pray that God crystallizes that thought. That he plants within us the idea for which we are willing to live and die. And that our work would flow from that notion, for his glory. *Amen.*

# THROW OUT THE PLAYBOOK

One Sabbath, when Jesus went to eat in the house of a prominent Pharisee, he was being carefully watched. There in front of him was a man suffering from abnormal swelling of his body. Jesus asked the Pharisees and experts in the law, "Is it lawful to heal on the Sabbath or not?" But they remained silent. So taking hold of the man, he healed him and sent him on his way.

Then he asked them, "If one of you has a child or an ox that falls into a well on the Sabbath day, will you not immediately pull it out?" And they had nothing to say.

*—Luke 14:1–6 (NIV)*

Despite rules forbidding work on the Sabbath, Jesus saw a man suffering and healed him. Doing so, he reminded us that we should never let legalism get in the way of the power of Christ.

When we are prompted to act, to love, to heal, to move, that's exactly what we have to do.

Throw out the playbook. Break through tradition. Like Christ healing a sick man on the Sabbath, rules should not disrupt God's calling on our lives.

⋙∘⋘

*Dear Lord, I come to you with abandon. I'm ready to do what you want me to do, regardless of rules or tradition. Reveal to me my calling today. Amen.*

# DRAW NEAR

> But Simon answered and said to Him, "Master, we have toiled all night and caught nothing; nevertheless at Your word I will let down the net." And when they had done this, they caught a great number of fish, and their net was breaking. So they signaled to their partners in the other boat to come and help them. And they came and filled both the boats, so that they began to sink. When Simon Peter saw it, he fell down at Jesus' knees, saying, "Depart from me, for I am a sinful man, O Lord!"
>
> For he and all who were with him were astonished at the catch of fish which they had taken; and so also were James and John, the sons of Zebedee, who were partners with Simon. And Jesus said to Simon, "Do not be afraid. From now on you will catch men."
>
> —*Luke 5:5–10 (NKJV)*

What's the best response to sin? The human response is often either ignorance or shame. Either we continue to press forward in our wrongdoing, blissfully ignoring its impact, or we hide our sin in the corner of our hearts and minds, ashamed of what we've done.

Peter felt this shame when he was approached by Jesus. When he felt God's power for the first time, Peter exclaimed to Christ, "Depart from me, for I am a sinful man, O Lord!"

But Jesus showed us the correct response. He beckoned Peter to draw close. He encouraged Peter not to be ashamed, to come near and follow him. "Do not be afraid," Jesus said. "From now on you will catch men."

The enemy would have us retreat away from God in guilt over the wrongs that we've done. But God wants the exact opposite. When we come to terms with our brokenness, he wants us to follow the One who can heal us. "Do not be afraid" of your sin. Just follow him.

*Dear God, I know I've done wrong in the past. I confess my sins to you, and I commit myself to not retreating in my wrongdoing. Instead, like Peter, I will draw closer to you. Amen.*

# WHEN WE'RE TRIUMPHANT

When the LORD your God brings you into the land you are entering to possess and drives out before you many nations . . . and when the LORD your God has delivered them over to you and you have defeated them . . . make no treaty with them, and show them no mercy. Do not intermarry with them. Do not give your daughters to their sons or take their daughters for your sons. . . . For you are a people holy to the LORD your God. The LORD your God has chosen you out of all the peoples on the face of the earth to be his people, his treasured possession.

*—Deuteronomy 7:1–3, 6 (NIV)*

We often derail our own progress, right at moments of success.

That was the case with the children of Israel. God gave them an important warning: when I deliver the land that I promise you, don't marry the people that you've conquered. It may seem a natural thing to do at first, but it will distract you, God said. Keep pressing forward to higher and higher heights. Don't wed yourselves to things of the past.

We must remember this lesson in our moments of triumph. Right when things are going well, and God is expanding our territory, we will be tempted to turn around, to remember our old ways, to look back.

We must keep moving forward. This is only an interim victory, a waypoint on the journey to a conquering greatness. Let's not let the intoxication of momentary triumph distract us from our broader purpose.

———❦———

*Dear God, thank you for the victories behind me, but I know there are many more ahead. Help me to not be distracted; keep my eyes on the prize. Amen.*

# PRACTICE WHAT YOU PREACH

> You, therefore, who teach another, do you not teach yourself? You who preach that a man should not steal, do you steal? You who say, "Do not commit adultery," do you commit adultery? You who abhor idols, do you rob temples? You who make your boast in the law, do you dishonor God through breaking the law?
>
> —*Romans 2:21–23 (NKJV)*

> Saint abroad, and a devil at home.
>
> —*John Bunyan,* The Pilgrim's Progress

We must practice what we preach.

Our exhortations cannot be hollow words. They'll ring as such on the ears of those around us if we don't back them up with our living. If we are consistent, we will lead others in a consistent path. If not, we'll lead them astray.

*Dear Father, I pray for internal consistency. Let me live honorably in private as well as in public. Amen.*

# STILL SPEAKING

I have much more to say to you, more than you can now bear. But when he, the Spirit of truth, comes, he will guide you into all the truth. He will not speak on his own; he will speak only what he hears, and he will tell you what is yet to come.

—*John 16:12–13 (NIV)*

God is still speaking.

Some call it a "still small voice." Others call it holy intuition. Jesus, before he left this earth, assured us that it is something else: the Holy Spirit.

Our Father and his Son are in heaven above, but they are also present on earth through their representative, who dwells among us. And the Spirit speaks on their behalf, if only we would listen.

---

*Let us extend an inch of faith in that direction: God, we believe that you've sent your Spirit as our guide. Help us listen as your wisdom unfolds. Amen.*

# TRUST

Some trust in chariots, and some in horses;
　　But we will remember the name of the LORD our God.
They have bowed down and fallen;
　　But we have risen and stand upright.
Save, LORD!
　　May the King answer us when we call.

*—Psalm 20:7–9 (NKJV)*

～∽◦∞◦∽～

A simple prayer for the day:
　　*Although some trust in chariots and others in horses, I remember the name of the Lord. When others bow and fall, I will stand upright.*
　　*Save us, Lord, and answer us when we call. Amen.*

# THE MASTER'S MASTERPIECE

> Through creation's rationality, God himself confronts us. Physics, biology, all the sciences generally, have offered us an account of the new and unheard of creation. Such great, new images help us to know the Creator's face. They remind us, yes, that in the beginning, and in the depth of every being, stands the Creator Spirit. The world has not issued forth from darkness and absurdity. It resonates intelligence, freedom, the beauty that is love. Seeing all this gives us the courage that makes living possible and makes us able to take up confidently on our shoulders the adventure of life.
>
> —*Joseph Ratzinger (Pope Benedict XVI),*
> *in* LCCC English Daily News Bulletin, *September 2, 2008*

We are the product of an extraordinary system, a weaving of the practical and divine never seen before and never to be experienced again. This body of ours, and the spirit that animates it, and the world in which it stands, are Bach's *Brandenburg Concertos* and Coltrane's "My Favorite Things," colored by Cézanne and bound by Picasso's angles, as sturdy and beautiful as any structure by Gehry or Gaudí, as lyrical as Maya Angelou or Tennyson at his best.

The same God who inspired these things created us. We are the Master's masterpiece. Today, let's take these diamond fingers of ours and etch out more beauty in his world.

~∞∞∞~

*Dear God, remind me of the beauty of your creation, as vested in me. Fill me with a sense of possibility this day, and let me do good work. Amen.*

# ETERNAL LIFE

And this is eternal life, that they may know You, the only true God, and Jesus Christ whom You have sent.

*—John 17:3 (NKJV)*

These words of Jesus before his arrest are telling.

What is eternal life? Eternal life is the knowledge of God and of his son, Jesus.

Eternal life is not found in medical breakthrough or mystical revelation. We cannot live forever through some vague notion of our "memory carrying on" after we are gone.

No, the path to eternal life is the knowledge of One who is eternal. When we grasp his hand in relationship, he pulls us through, behind the veil. And then we can feel the warmth of paradise.

———≈≈≈———

*Dear God, thank you for the blessing of life everlasting. Increase within me knowledge of you, that I may see you face-to-face in paradise. Amen.*

# IN SERVICE OF RELIGION

By religion I do not mean outward things, but inward states, I mean perfected manhood. I mean the quickening of the soul by the beatific influence of the divine Spirit in truth, and love, and sympathy, and confidence, and trust.

*—Henry Ward Beecher, "What is Religion?"*

And when He had said these things, one of the officers who stood by struck Jesus with the palm of his hand, saying, "Do You answer the high priest like that?"

*—John 18:22 (NKJV)*

In this scene, immediately before the crucifixion, a soldier raised his hand and slapped the face of Jesus, our Savior. Why? Because this officer felt that his duty to the high priests demanded as much.

We must be careful not to do violence to Jesus, or his commandments, in service of religion.

Those commandments are simple: the first is to love God, with all our hearts, and all our souls, and all our minds—and let all of our actions flow from that love. The second is to love our neighbor.

If we ever come to a crossroads where we must choose service to religion or service to Christ, the answer is clear. Never do violence to Jesus in service of religion.

*Dear God, order my priorities. Plant within me a deep love for you and for my fellow men and women. And let me give everything else, including religion, its proper place. Amen.*

# RECEIVE THE SPIRIT

Then, the same day at evening, being the first day of the week, when the doors were shut where the disciples were assembled, for fear of the Jews, Jesus came and stood in the midst, and said to them, "Peace be with you." When He had said this, He showed them His hands and His side. Then the disciples were glad when they saw the Lord.

So Jesus said to them again, "Peace to you! As the Father has sent Me, I also send you." And when He had said this, He breathed on them, and said to them, "Receive the Holy Spirit. If you forgive the sins of any, they are forgiven them; if you retain the sins of any, they are retained."

*—John 20:19–23 (NKJV)*

As Jesus breathed on the disciples, God has breathed on us this very morning; his Holy Spirit fills our frame. Our risen Christ is sending us out into the world in the same way that God sent his Son to earth. With that fullness of purpose, we greet this day. We are his chosen disciples. We're prepared for an awesome task. Let's allow that reality to ground us and then cause us to soar.

~∞~

*Lord, just as the disciples embraced your calling after the resurrection, so do I embrace the calling on my life. I'm ready, God. Let's go. Amen.*

# WAITING FOR WISDOM

Wisdom too often never comes, and so one ought not to reject it merely because it comes late.

*—Justice Felix Frankfurter,*
*in* The Great Justices, 1941–1954

For still the vision awaits its appointed time;
   it hastens to the end—it will not lie.
If it seems slow, wait for it;
   it will surely come; it will not delay.

*—Habakkuk 2:3 (ESV)*

And still we wait for wisdom. Like a conductor on the Underground Railroad, it may stop by infrequently, but when it does, oh the places we'll go—the freedom we'll see!

Patiently we'll bide our time. Diligently we'll work. And when the vision strikes, when God grants the wisdom, then we move. Then we shine.

*Dear God, I await your wisdom. And when you speak, I will listen. Amen.*

# JACKIE ROBINSON

Today we must balance the tears of sorrow with the tears of joy. Mix the bitter with the sweet in death and life. Jackie as a figure in history was a rock in the water, creating concentric circles and ripples of new possibility. He was medicine. He was immunized by God from catching the diseases that he fought. The Lord's arms of protection enabled him to go through dangers seen and unseen, and he had the capacity to wear glory with grace. Jackie's body was a temple of God. An instrument of peace. We would watch him disappear into nothingness and stand back as spectators, and watch the suffering from afar. The mercy of God intercepted this process Tuesday and permitted him to steal away home, where referees are out of place, and only the supreme judge of the universe speaks.

*—Jesse Jackson, eulogy for Jackie Robinson*

*Dear Lord, give us a Jackie Robinson spirit. Let us blaze new trails with dignity, determination, and grace. And God, like Jackie, immunize us from catching the very diseases we fight. In Jesus's name, amen.*

NOTE: This devotional was sent to the president on anniversary of Jackie Robinson's breaking into baseball's major league.

# THE BLISS POINT

He who loves pleasure will be a poor man;
He who loves wine and oil will not be rich.
*—Proverbs 21:17 (NKJV)*

The book *Salt Sugar Fat* by Michael Moss documents the decades-long efforts by the food industry to perfectly calibrate processed food to make us crave it more and more. One interesting fact *Salt Sugar Fat* uncovers is the notion of the "bliss point," a measurement developed by scientists in the food industry of the exact amount of sugar that consumers want in a given product. Any more and the buyer will be overwhelmed. Any less will not be enough.

Today, we pray that God would condition our "bliss points." Taking the words of Proverbs 21:17 seriously, we know that overconsumption and indulgence are not of God, and lead to destruction.

*God, shape our desires for the things of this world, bringing them into regulation and conformity with your will. We want our "bliss points" to be around things that truly make us happy rather than fleeting pleasures. Amen.*

# GOOD FRIDAY

The earthly form of Christ is the form that died on the cross. The image of God is the image of Christ crucified. It is to this image that the life of the disciples must be conformed; in other words, they must be conformed to his death.

The Christian life is a life of crucifixion. In baptism the form of Christ's death is impressed upon his own. They are dead to the flesh and to sin, they are dead to the world, and the world is dead to them. Anybody living in the strength of Christ's baptism lives in the strength of Christ's death.

—*Dietrich Bonhoeffer,* The Cost of Discipleship

Today, we mark Good Friday. A contradiction in terms, really. How can something so horrific be called "good"? Jesus was abused, berated, whipped, scorned. Executed in the worst way imaginable at the time. Left dead and hanging among common thieves.

And yet, as is often the case in moments of tragedy, there was more going on behind the scenes. God had sent his Son to the world as a perfect sacrifice. All the mess, the mire, the sin, and the sadness that we accumulate over a lifetime—in an act of divine grace, he took that upon himself. Our atonement.

Easter, the resurrection, is right around the corner. But today, we reflect on the sacrifice of Good Friday. We let our hearts well up with gratefulness for the fact that though we are weak, he has been strong.

~∞∞∞~

*Dear God, thank you for the sacrifice of Christ on Good Friday. Thank you for preventing my sins from following me to the grave. Thank you for your stripes, through which I am healed. Amen.*

NOTE: These next few devotionals were sent to the president around Easter.

# EASTER

Many indeed are the wondrous happenings of that time: God hanging from a cross, the sun made dark and again flaming out; for it was fitting that creation should mourn with its creator. The temple veil rent, blood and water flowing from his side: the one as from a man, the other as from what was above man; the earth shaken, the rocks shattered because of the rock; the dead risen to bear witness to the final and universal resurrection of the dead. The happenings at the sepulcher and after the sepulcher, who can fittingly recount them? Yet no one of them can be compared to the miracle of my salvation. A few drops of blood renew the whole world, and do for all men what the rennet does for the milk: joining us and binding us together.

—*Saint Gregory of Nazianzus,*
*in* Ancient Christian Commentary on Scripture

*Dear God, you took it on. My flaws, the deepest ones, my crimes. The sins that I remember and those that I've forgotten. My sorrows and those of whom I have made sorrowful. The wages of my sin was death—but you became my sacrifice. You took it on and gave me life. And I am grateful. Amen.*

# OVERWHELMED WITH GRACE

[Jesus said,] "There was a certain creditor who had two debtors. One owed five hundred denarii, and the other fifty. And when they had nothing with which to repay, he freely forgave them both. Tell Me, therefore, which of them will love him more?"

Simon answered and said, "I suppose the one whom he forgave more."

And He said to him, "You have rightly judged." Then He turned to the woman and said to Simon, "Do you see this woman? I entered your house; you gave Me no water for My feet, but she has washed My feet with her tears and wiped them with the hair of her head. You gave Me no kiss, but this woman has not ceased to kiss My feet since the time I came in. You did not anoint My head with oil, but this woman has anointed My feet with fragrant oil. Therefore I say to you, her sins, which are many, are forgiven, for she loved much. But to whom little is forgiven, the same loves little."

—*Luke 7:41–47 (NKJV)*

Blessed are the liars. Blessed are the thieves. Blessed are the bribers, the lusters, the doubters. Blessed are those who have been overcome by depression and addiction, anger and grief. Because, like the woman who wiped our Savior's feet in overwhelming gratitude, when God has made us right, we have more to rejoice for. We were deeply in debt, but he paid the price. And now we've been set free.

---

*Dear God, thank you for my past, for the ways that I've fallen short. You've brought me so far, and I will never forget. You've set me free. Amen.*

APRIL 20

# THE THORNS

While a large crowd was gathering and people were coming to Jesus from town after town, he told this parable: "A farmer went out to sow his seed. As he was scattering the seed, some fell along the path; it was trampled on, and the birds ate it up. Some fell on rocky ground, and when it came up, the plants withered because they had no moisture. Other seed fell among thorns, which grew up with it and choked the plants. Still other seed fell on good soil. It came up and yielded a crop, a hundred times more than was sown."

When he said this, he called out, "Whoever has ears to hear, let them hear."

—*Luke 8:4–8 (NIV)*

Sometimes the seeds of knowledge and character planted within us are just fine—it's the thorns that grow up around us.

We have to carefully watch our environment, our influences, our colleagues and friends. Jesus said as much in the parable of the sower. Even the strongest strain of seed can be choked if planted among thorns and never moved. To yield the harvest that God demands, we must be ready to cut them down.

———

*Dear God, help me discern the people and situations in my life that could be stopping my progress, choking my growth. And give me the boldness to take action, in love, and remove them. Amen.*

# CONFESSION

If we confess our sins, he is faithful and just to forgive us our sins and to cleanse us from all unrighteousness.

—*1 John 1:9 (ESV)*

"Confess" is in the present tense, which means that is to be the habitual practice of the believer.

—*Adrian Rogers,* The Power of His Presence

What is it that God wants us to confess?

What sin dwells in the furthest reaches, just beyond our regular grasp?

~∞∞∞~

*Search us, God, and bring dark things to light. We lay them at your altar and seek your forgiveness. We want to sin no more. Amen.*

# It Abides

Oh, these vast, calm, measureless mountain days, inciting at once to work and rest! Days in whose light everything seems equally divine, opening a thousand windows to show us God. Nevermore, however weary, should one faint by the way who gains the blessings of one mountain day; whatever his fate, long life, short life, stormy or calm, he is rich forever.

—*John Muir,* My First Summer in the Sierra

Your faithfulness endures to all generations;
    You established the earth, and it abides.

—*Psalm 119:90 (NKJV)*

These mountains have been here for thousands of years—even more, certainly not less. This ocean carried generations of creations long before it buoyed men. Underneath the asphalt and pavement is an old and earthen testament to God's creative impulses; the rocks beneath our feet, they run deep.

"You established the earth, and it abides."

And so too will we abide. Through seasons of change, through the blazing heat of summer and midnight cold of winter, we will abide. He established the earth, and he established us; his faithfulness endures to all generations.

*Dear God, help me rest within the bosom of your faithfulness; let me feel the security of your ageless embrace. Amen.*

# OUTWARD

A prayer for perspective:

*Dear God, let me lift my head off my own chest, and focus on the other. My family, my loved ones, my friends.*

*My neighbors, my "enemies," those loosely connected to me halfway across the world.*

*These eyes of mine are so frequently focused inward. Dear Lord, today, turn them out. And give me vision to see needs other than my own.*

*Amen.*

# MUTUAL EDIFICATION

Let us therefore make every effort to do what leads to peace and to mutual edification.

—*Romans 14:19 (NIV)*

There is a great man who makes every man feel small. But the real great man is the man who makes every man feel great.

—*G. K. Chesterton,* Charles Dickens

*Lord, today, let us raise others up. Help us delight in bringing a smile, a good feeling, a lifted head to our brothers and sisters. Let our words and actions be edifying to others, and let them be acts of worship to you. Amen.*

APRIL 25

# DEEP CALLS TO DEEP

Deep calls to deep
    in the roar of your waterfalls;
all your waves and breakers
    have swept over me.

*—Psalm 42:7 (NIV)*

*As the deepest parts within me cry out, our Lord, I hear you answer.*
    *When I can no longer stand, you rush in, and overwhelm.*
    *This voice of mine is just an echo; I speak and hear your pulsed and true reply.*

Deep calls to deep in the roar of your waterfalls; all your waves and breakers have swept over me.

*Amen.*

# GENEROSITY

Then the people rejoiced, for they had offered willingly, because with a loyal heart they had offered willingly to the Lord; and King David also rejoiced greatly.

—*1 Chronicles 29:9 (NKJV)*

I come in a world of iron . . . to make a world of gold.

—*Dale Wasserman,* Man of La Mancha

Let's rejoice in our giving; let generosity be our task.

We pray that the gifts of life, love, and resources that flow out of us will mean more to us than what we receive. We give willingly, without hesitation, and with open hearts.

———&e&e&———

*In this world of iron, dear God, through my giving, help me make a world of gold. Amen.*

# A BEAUTIFUL PICTURE

It is of the LORD's mercies that we are not consumed, because his compassions fail not. They are new every morning: great is thy faithfulness.

—*Lamentations 3:22–23 (KJV)*

Close your bodily eye, so that you may see your picture first with the spiritual eye. Then bring to the light of day that which you have seen in the darkness so that it may react upon others from the outside inwards. A picture must not be invented but felt. Observe the form exactly, both the smallest and the large and do not separate the small from the large, but rather the trivial from the important.

—*Caspar David Friedrich, in* The Romantic Imagination

*Lord, today, help me paint a beautiful picture. Remove the distractions, clarify my inner mind, and give me a vision. Lay out the canvas, oh God, and help me bring this picture to vivid life. Amen.*

# YOUR BEAUTY IS ENOUGH

He has made everything beautiful in its time. Also, he has put eternity into man's heart, yet so that he cannot find out what God has done from the beginning to the end.

—*Ecclesiastes 3:11* (ESV)

At some point in life the world's beauty becomes enough. You don't need to photograph, paint or even remember it. It is enough. No record of it needs to be kept and you don't need someone to share it with or tell it to. When that happens—that letting go—you let go because you can.

—*Toni Morrison,* Tar Baby

*I don't need to share it, take a picture of it, write it down. Lord, your beauty is enough. Today, God, I let go of the need to control, to hold on. I let your creation move freely around me, as I admire your good work. Dear Lord, your beauty in this world, it is enough. Amen.*

# JOHN PARKER

A wise man scales the city of the mighty,
  And brings down the trusted stronghold.
                              —*Proverbs 21:22 (NKJV)*

John Parker was destined to amount to nothing—if he lived at all. Born a slave in Virginia, as a child Parker was forced to walk, chained to another slave, all the way to Alabama. A feisty kid by nature, he ran away multiple times and was caught nearly as many. On more than one occasion—from riverboats on the Mississippi to backyards in Ohio—Parker stared down the barrel of an unfriendly gun. He really should have died.

But John Parker survived all this, purchased his freedom, and settled in the border town of Ripley, Ohio, across from slave-holding Kentucky. And there, he teamed up with the radical abolitionist minister Rev. John Rankin, and together they lit the institution of slavery on fire. Between the two of them, they conducted thousands of slaves along the Underground Railroad, sending them on their way to Canada. In the words of Proverbs, they scaled the "city of the mighty," and helped bring down "the trusted stronghold."

Parker and his compatriots have shown us that there are no institutions too strong, no giants too tall, no walls too high for us to scale. We're endowed with a particular spirit, a conquering one, and the enemy must yield in the face of a righteous cause.

———

*We pray for wisdom to pick our battles, and once picked, a ferocious courage to act and overcome. Amen.*

# PEACE TO THIS HOUSE

But whatever house you enter, first say, "Peace to this house."
—*Luke 10:5 (NKJV)*

A prayer to whisper when entering new buildings:
*Dear God, bless those in this house.*
*Let them feel your love. Let them know your wisdom. Let them encounter your peace, your grace.*
*Foster within them a true and lasting joy, unshakable by the world.*
*Bless the residents of this house. Amen.*

# MAY

## DONE IN SECRET

The White House is not supposed to be a place for brokenness. Sheer, shattered, brokenness. But that's what we experienced on the weekend of December 14, 2012.

I was sitting at my desk around midday on Friday the 14th when I saw the images flash on CNN: A school. A gunman. Children fleeing, crying.

It's sad that we've grown so accustomed to these types of scenes that my first thought was *I hope there are no deaths, just injuries.* I thought, *Maybe it's your run-of-the-mill scare.*

And then the news from Sandy Hook Elementary School, a small school in the tiny hamlet of Newtown, Connecticut, began pouring in. The public details were horrific enough: Twenty children murdered. Six staff. Parents searching a gymnasium for signs of their kids.

But the private facts we received in the White House from the FBI were even worse.

How the gunman treated the children like criminals, lining them up to shoot them down. How so many bullets penetrated them that many were left unrecognizable. How the killer went from one classroom to another and would have gone farther if his rifle would've let him.

That news began a weekend of prayer and numbness, which I awoke from on Saturday only to receive the word that the president would like me to accompany him to Newtown. He wanted to meet with the families of the victims and then offer words of comfort to the country at an interfaith memorial service.

I left early to help the advance team—the hardworking folks who handle logistics for every event—set things up, and I arrived at the local high school where the meetings and memorial service would take place. We prepared seven or eight classrooms for the families of the slain children and teachers, two or three families to a classroom, placing water and tissues and snacks in each one. Honestly, we didn't know how to prepare; it was the best we could think of.

The families came in and gathered together, room by room. Many struggled to offer a weak smile when we whispered, "The president will be here soon." A few were visibly angry—so understandable that it barely needs to be said—and were looking for someone, anyone, to blame. Mostly they sat in silence.

I went downstairs to greet President Obama when he arrived, and I provided an overview of the situation. "Two families per classroom . . . The first is . . . and their child was . . . The second is . . . and their child was . . . We'll tell you the rest as you go."

The president took a deep breath and steeled himself, and went into the first classroom. And what happened next I'll never forget.

Person after person received an engulfing hug from our commander in chief. He'd say, "Tell me about your son. . . . Tell me about your daughter," and then hold pictures of the lost beloved as their parents described favorite foods, television shows, and the sound of their laughter. For the younger siblings of those who had passed away—many of them two, three, or four years old, too young to understand it all—the president would grab them and toss them, laughing, up into the air, and then hand them a box of White House M&M's, which were always kept close at hand. In each room, I saw his eyes water, but he did not break.

And then the entire scene would repeat—for hours. Over and over and over again, through well over a hundred relatives of the fallen, each one equally broken, wrecked by the loss. After each classroom, we would go back into those fluorescent hallways and walk through the names of the coming families, and then the president would dive back in, like a soldier returning to a tour of duty in a worthy but wearing war. We spent what felt like a lifetime in those classrooms, and every single person received the same tender treatment. The same hugs. The same looks, directly in their eyes. The same sincere offer of support and prayer.

The staff did the preparation work, but the comfort and healing were all on President Obama. I remember worrying about the toll it was taking on him. And of course, even a president's comfort was woefully inadequate for these families in the face of this particularly unspeakable loss. But it became some small measure of love, on a weekend when evil reigned.

And the funny thing is—President Obama has never spoken about these meetings. Yes, he addressed the shooting in Newtown and gun violence in general in a subsequent speech, but he did not speak of those private gatherings. In fact, he was nearly silent on Air Force One as we rode back to Washington, and has said very little about his time with these families since. It must have been one of the defining moments of his presidency, quiet hours in solemn classrooms, extending as much healing as was in his power to extend. But he kept it to himself—never seeking to teach a lesson based on those mournful conversations, or opening them up to public view.

Jesus teaches us that some things—the holiest things, the most painful and important and cherished things—we are to do in secret. Not for public consumption and display, but as acts of service to others, and worship to God. For then, "your Father, who sees what is done in secret, will reward you," perhaps not now, but certainly in eternity. We learned many lessons in Newtown that day; this is one I've kept closely at heart.

# MIDWAY

"In righteousness you will be established:
Tyranny will be far from you;
   you will have nothing to fear.
Terror will be far removed;
   it will not come near you.
If anyone does attack you, it will not be my doing;
   whoever attacks you will surrender to you.

"See, it is I who created the blacksmith
   who fans the coals into flame
   and forges a weapon fit for its work.
And it is I who have created the destroyer to wreak havoc;
   no weapon forged against you will prevail,
   and you will refute every tongue that accuses you.
This is the heritage of the servants of the LORD,
   and this is their vindication from me,"
   declares the LORD.

*Isaiah 54:14–17 (NIV)*

The Battle of Midway was the most important battle of the Pacific Campaign in World War II. Strained by the attack on Pearl Harbor and losses at the Battle of Coral Sea, the American Navy was at great risk of defeat, and the Imperial Japanese Navy thought they had the U.S. fleets on the run. Instead, the Americans won decisively, inflicting irreparable damage on the Japanese armadas.

While the battle was fought from June 4 to June 7, 1942, the seeds of victory were in fact planted months earlier. Throughout the spring, Navy cryptoanalysts in Hawaii had been working to break Japan's vaunted "JN–25" code, allowing them to foil the coming Japanese ambush. Far from the seas of battle, these young code breakers—poring over an IBM punch card machine—paved the way for this epic American victory. And in many ways, these men helped win a war.

The same can be said of our Savior. Long before we entered into the battles we wage today, he has decoded the enemy's signal for us. He understands the approaches, the modes of attack, and he alone knows the outcome. Our job is to fight diligently and with honor in our present circumstance, and it is his role to prepare a way for us. And he always will, because "no weapon forged against you will prevail, and you will refute every tongue that accuses you. This is the heritage of the servants of the LORD, and this is their vindication from me."

—⦚⦚⦚—

*Dear God, I am thankful that the battle is not mine, but yours. Thank you that the victory is already won. I stand firmly on that promise, in Jesus's name. Amen.*

# LET'S LAUGH!

Laughter is the closest thing to the grace of God.
—*Karl Barth, in* The Harper Book of Quotations

Then our mouth was filled with laughter,
    and our tongue with shouts of joy;
then they said among the nations,
    "The Lord has done great things for them."
—*Psalm 126:2 (ESV)*

Six-year-olds laugh an average of three hundred times a day, while adults only laugh fifteen to one hundred times a day. Let's indulge our inner six-year-old and laugh a few extra times today!

—◦◦◦◦◦—

*Dear God, increase our laughter. Let the sides of our mouths curl up into a smile more than normal; let joy be on our hearts. Amen.*

# JUDE'S PRAYER

Now unto him that is able to keep you from falling, and to present you faultless before the presence of his glory with exceeding joy,

To the only wise God our Saviour, be glory and majesty, dominion and power, both now and ever. Amen.

*—Jude 1:24–25 (KJV)*

⊸∞∞⊷

*Amen.*

# NOT OF THIS WORLD

Jesus answered, "My kingdom is not of this world. If My kingdom were of this world, My servants would fight, so that I should not be delivered to the Jews; but now My kingdom is not from here."

*—John 18:36 (NKJV)*

"My kingdom is not of this world."

There's another place—where the streets are paved with unshakable stones, rocks bonded together by integrity. Where neighbors greet each other in love, for loving their neighbors is their morning thought. The sun does not always shine—there is rain—because without rain, nothing would grow. But in this place, people gleefully embrace the seasons; they know.

And God is glorified. He is glorified in the morning and when the noon sun is high. He's glorified at nighttime, when our worship fills the darkness. His glory is our chore, our gleeful task.

There is another kingdom—not this kingdom, but another one indeed. Let's never forget that awesome fact. "My kingdom is not of this world."

━━━∽∞∽━━━

*God, your kingdom come, your will be done, on earth, as it is in heaven. Amen.*

# FOOLISH FAITH

The LORD said to Moses, ". . . Speak to that rock before their eyes and it will pour out its water. You will bring water out of the rock for the community so they and their livestock can drink."

So Moses . . . said to them, "Listen, you rebels, must we bring you water out of this rock?" Then Moses raised his arm and struck the rock twice with his staff. Water gushed out, and the community and their livestock drank.

But the LORD said to Moses and Aaron, "Because you did not trust in me enough to honor me as holy in the sight of the Israelites, you will not bring this community into the land I give them."

—*Numbers 20:7–12 (NIV)*

God rewards foolish faith. In the book of Numbers, the children of Israel were complaining because they had no water. Parched, they demanded that Moses take action. Moses went to God, who gave a clear command: speak out loud to the rock in front of you and water will come forth.

Moses gathered the Israelites in front of the rock, but instead of speaking to it, he hit the rock with his rod. Water flowed, but Moses didn't do what God commanded; he didn't speak to the rock. Perhaps Moses wanted the water to seem like a natural phenomenon; perhaps he was embarrassed by the absurdity of crying out to a hunk of stone.

God was prepared to reward Moses's "foolish faith." If Moses had risked embarrassment, can you imagine the power and authority that he would have in front of the Israelites? Instead, God punished Moses for his disobedience. And Moses's leadership was limited in the days ahead.

Sometimes we have to step out on God's promises, even at the risk of appearing foolish. God rewards foolish faith, for those who are brave enough to practice it, even when others are watching.

*Dear God, is there something you want me to do that would appear foolish? If so, let me hear your voice and have the courage to take action. Amen.*

# IS IT RIGHT?

So whoever knows the right thing to do and fails to do it, for him it is sin.

—*James 4:17 (ESV)*

On some positions, cowardice asks the question, "is it safe?" Expediency asks the question, "is it politic?" Vanity asks the question, "is it popular?" But conscience asks the question, "is it right?" And there comes a time when a true follower of Jesus Christ must take a position that's neither safe nor politic nor popular but he must do it because it is right.

—*Dr. Martin Luther King Jr., "A Proper Sense of Priorities"*

～～～

*Dear Lord,*
*Let us not move out of a desire for safety.*
*Let us not move for good politics.*
*Let us not move to be popular.*
*No, Lord, today, we want to move when it's right.*
*Amen.*

# DIFFERENT MINISTRIES

> There are diversities of gifts, but the same Spirit. There are differences of ministries, but the same Lord.
>
> *—1 Corinthians 12:4–5 (NKJV)*

Today, let's remember the folks who keep this world from overflowing with disorder—the trash collectors who do their work out of view.

Let's pray for those who make our hallways sparkle and keep our workplace well supplied—the janitors who move with quiet discipline.

The drivers and officers. Cooks and groundskeepers. We are supported in a thousand different ways each day by professionals who work with dignity and excellence. As Paul's letter to the Corinthians tells us, their work comes from the same Spirit, and the same Lord. So we honor them.

---

*Dear God, remind me to respect all those who work quietly around me and to extend them honor however I can. Amen.*

# TEACH ME TO PRAY

One day Jesus was praying in a certain place. When he finished, one of his disciples said to him, "Lord, teach us to pray, just as John taught his disciples."

He said to them, "When you pray, say:
'Father,
hallowed be your name,
your kingdom come.
Give us each day our daily bread.
Forgive us our sins,
for we also forgive everyone who sins against us.
And lead us not into temptation.'"

*—Luke 11:1–4 (NIV)*

O Lord, make me an instrument of Thy Peace!
Where there is hatred, let me sow love;
Where there is injury, pardon;
Where there is discord, harmony;
Where there is doubt, faith;
Where there is despair, hope;
Where there is darkness, light, and
Where there is sorrow, joy.
Oh Divine Master, grant that I may not
so much seek to be consoled as to console;
to be understood as to understand;
to be loved,
as to love.
For it is in giving that we receive;
it is in pardoning that we are pardoned;
and it is in dying that we are born to Eternal Life.

*—The Prayer of Saint Francis*

Have we landed on a motto? What are the words written on our hearts? Saint Francis, the great and humble preacher from Assisi, who rejected wealth to commune with the poor, penned the prayer above as his regular meditation.

Our Savior, Jesus, suggested the Lord's Prayer as a go-to supplication.

Let God lead us to our own daily affirmation. If we don't choose one intentionally, one will be chosen for us; we'll meditate on traffic's honking horns, television's incessant buzz, or social media's never-ending stream.

We might borrow Saint Francis's or use the words of our Christ. Regardless, let's choose a go-to prayer to God to anchor our busy days.

—∞∞∞—

*Dear God, teach me to pray. Write words from heaven on my heart, and let me never forget them. Amen.*

# TRUSTWORTHY AND TRUE

Then I saw "a new heaven and a new earth," for the first heaven and the first earth had passed away, and there was no longer any sea. I saw the Holy City, the new Jerusalem, coming down out of heaven from God, prepared as a bride beautifully dressed for her husband. And I heard a loud voice from the throne saying, "Look! God's dwelling place is now among the people, and he will dwell with them. They will be his people, and God himself will be with them and be their God. 'He will wipe every tear from their eyes. There will be no more death' or mourning or crying or pain, for the old order of things has passed away."

He who was seated on the throne said, "I am making everything new!" Then he said, "Write this down, for these words are trustworthy and true."

—*Revelation 21:1–5 (NIV)*

"Write this down, for these words are trustworthy and true."

The coming reckoning and boundless rest. The closeness to our Lord and conquering of pain. Old things will pass away—and all things will become as new.

"Write this down, for these words are trustworthy and true." *Amen.*

# LET IT BE KNOWN THIS DAY

And it came to pass, at the time of the offering of the evening sacrifice, that Elijah the prophet came near and said, "LORD God of Abraham, Isaac, and Israel, let it be known this day that You are God in Israel and I am Your servant, and that I have done all these things at Your word. Hear me, O LORD, hear me, that this people may know that You are the LORD God, and that You have turned their hearts back to You again."

Then the fire of the LORD fell and consumed the burnt sacrifice, and the wood and the stones and the dust, and it licked up the water that was in the trench. Now when all the people saw it, they fell on their faces; and they said, "The LORD, He is God! The LORD, He is God!"

*—1 Kings 18:36–39 (NKJV)*

*Lord, show your power. Send your fire into my life. Let it be known this day that you are God. Amen.*

# THE LEAST

[Jesus said,] "For I was hungry and you gave me something to eat, I was thirsty and you gave me something to drink, I was a stranger and you invited me in, I needed clothes and you clothed me, I was sick and you looked after me, I was in prison and you came to visit me."

Then the righteous will answer him, "Lord, when did we see you hungry and feed you, or thirsty and give you something to drink? When did we see you a stranger and invite you in, or needing clothes and clothe you? When did we see you sick or in prison and go to visit you?"

The King will reply, "Truly I tell you, whatever you did for one of the least of these brothers and sisters of mine, you did for me."

*—Matthew 25:35–40 (NIV)*

Martin's soul grew glad. He crossed himself, put on his spectacles, and began reading the Gospel just where it had opened; and at the top of the page he read: "I was an hungered, and ye gave me meat; I was thirsty, and ye gave me drink: I was a stranger, and ye took me in." And at the bottom of the page he read: "Inasmuch as ye did it unto one of these my brethren, even these least, ye did it unto me" (Matt. xxv). And Martin understood that his dream had come true; and that the Saviour had really come to him that day, and he had welcomed him.

*—Leo Tolstoy, "Where Love Is, God Is"*

People are looking for a Savior to come to them. And Christ has given us instructions for how we can be his avatars in the world.

Nourishment to the hungry. Water to the thirsty. Shelter to the stranger. Covering to the naked. Healing for the sick. Comfort for the prisoner. Our King declares, "Whatever you did for one of the least of these brothers and sisters of mine, you did for me."

——◦◦◦◦——

*Dear Lord, today, that's what we'll do. Amen.*

# THROUGH THE MIDST

Then He said, "Assuredly, I say to you, no prophet is accepted in his own country." . . . So all those in the synagogue, when they heard these things, were filled with wrath, and rose up and thrust Him out of the city; and they led Him to the brow of the hill on which their city was built, that they might throw Him down over the cliff. Then passing through the midst of them, He went His way.
—*Luke 4:24, 28–30 (NKJV)*

Our life has been filled with unrecalled close calls. Somehow, someway, over and over again through the course of our lives, when we're on the brink of major disaster or really poor decisions, we have found our way to the other side. A few we'd like to consider our own doing, but there have been too many for that. If we consider each and every case—each accident that didn't happen, each bad call that turned out all right—we'll see the hand of providence, of God.

Just as Jesus, when backed up against a cliff, simply disappeared through the midst of the crowd, so does he help us press through the toughest of times in an almost miraculous fashion, with so much ease that we scarcely recall the crisis when the moment has passed. This should give us confidence in nightly challenges, because always, always, morning follows swiftly behind.

*Dear God, thank you for being a miracle worker. On so many occasions I've made it to the other side, too many for me to remember or recount. I rest in the knowledge that you will do it again and again, for your greater glory. Amen.*

# THE WAVE

No temptation has overtaken you except such as is common to man; but God is faithful, who will not allow you to be tempted beyond what you are able, but with the temptation will also make the way of escape, that you may be able to bear it.

—*1 Corinthians 10:13 (NKJV)*

But Satan now is wiser than of yore,
  And tempts by making rich, not making poor.

—*Alexander Pope,* Moral Essays

The wave is coming. Its crest high, thundering, overwhelming. We see it from far off and tremble at what it portends. The great wave of temptation.

It would have us believe that no one has survived it, that all have succumbed to its crashing terror. But it is a liar. Because "no temptation has overtaken" us, "except such as is common to man." People have weathered this storm before. They've come out whole. And so will we.

*Dear God, I know temptation is coming. Give me the mettle to withstand. Amen.*

# BREAKING FREE

So the LORD's anger was aroused against Israel, and He made them wander in the wilderness forty years, until all the generation that had done evil in the sight of the LORD was gone. And look! You have risen in your fathers' place, a brood of sinful men, to increase still more the fierce anger of the LORD against Israel.

—*Numbers 32:13–14 (NKJV)*

It is incumbent on all believers to learn lessons from the previous generation—both the good and the bad. The children of Israel saw the same patterns occur over and over again: first they were tried, then God told them how to avoid the trials, then they were disobedient, then God delivered them anyway, and finally they were punished for continued unbelief. Yet, these patterns persisted, to Moses's dismay. "And look! You have risen in your fathers' place."

What are the patterns of our ancestors, our parents, and our loved ones, from which we must break free? Meditating on these things is not a show of disrespect to the previous generation; rather it is an act of service to the next. For when God roots out these harmful patterns, those who will come behind us will face fewer burdens as a result.

*Dear God, what do you want me to learn from those who came before? Search me and find patterns that I must address, and liberate me from prior sins. Amen.*

# WHEN TO SPEAK

My dear brothers and sisters, take note of this: Everyone should be quick to listen, slow to speak and slow to become angry.

*—James 1:19 (NIV)*

There's a story told about a young Albert Einstein. His parents were concerned that although Albert was growing in years, he had not spoken yet. One evening at dinner, the boy finally opened his mouth to speak, declaring, "The soup is too hot!"

His parents rejoiced and asked Albert why it had taken him so long to talk. Albert replied, "Because up to now everything was in order."

Like Einstein, we should be careful to be judicious with our words. Our tongues have great power and are best used when they're truly needed. Until then, let's cultivate a listening spirit.

⌐∞∞∞⌐

*Dear God, help me use words sparingly, and help me be quick to listen. Amen.*

# A DOER

But be doers of the word, and not hearers only, deceiving yourselves.
*—James 1:22 (ESV)*

Lose this day loitering, 'twill be the same story
Tomorrow—and the next more dilatory;
Thus, Indecision brings its own delays
And days are lost lamenting over days.
Are you earnest? Seize this very moment;
What you can do, or dream you can, begin it.
Courage has genius, power, and magic in it;
Only engage, and the mind grows heated.
Begin it, and the work will be completed.
*—Johann Wolfgang Von Goethe,* Faust

Begin it, and the work will be completed!

Just go. Do. Jump. Speak. Write. Emerge.

Yesterday is behind, and tomorrow is not promised. It's time for us to do, to go.

*God, today I'll be a doer, not just a hearer of your word. I'm ready to go. Amen.*

# GOOD FRUIT

> John said to the crowds coming out to be baptized by him, "You
> brood of vipers! Who warned you to flee from the coming wrath?
> Produce fruit in keeping with repentance. And do not begin to say
> to yourselves, 'We have Abraham as our father.' For I tell you that
> out of these stones God can raise up children for Abraham. The ax is
> already at the root of the trees, and every tree that does not produce
> good fruit will be cut down and thrown into the fire."
> "What should we do then?" the crowd asked.
> John answered, "Anyone who has two shirts should share with
> the one who has none, and anyone who has food should do the same."
> —*Luke 3:7–11 (NIV)*

We can't earn our salvation; it's given to us freely by belief in Christ alone.
But we can bear good fruit in the world, and there's one sure way to do it.

When John the Baptist addressed the multitude of people seeking
baptism, he reminded us of our wretched state: "Brood of vipers!" he
exclaimed. John then implored the crowd to be trees that "produce good
fruit," and when asked what "good fruit" means, John simply said: give a
significant portion of what you have to the poor.

It's not complicated. This great prophet tells us that service to the
poor and vulnerable will yield a harvest of fruit worthy of our Lord. Let's
recommit ourselves to that task, following the pattern of John, and of
Christ.

*Dear God, help me remember those who have less. Place within my heart the
same love that you have for the poor, and let it motivate my daily walk. Amen.*

# CROWDED KINDNESS

I have said these things to you, that in me you may have peace. In the world you will have tribulation. But take heart; I have overcome the world.

—*John 16:33 (ESV)*

Do not let the empty cup be your first teacher of the blessings you had when it was full. Do not let a hard place here and there in the bed destroy your rest. Seek, as a plain duty, to cultivate a buoyant, joyous sense of the crowded kindnesses of God in your daily life.

—*Alexander Maclaren, in* Dictionary of Burning Words of Brilliant Writers

---

*Lord, who lends me life, lend me a heart replete with thankfulness, no matter the circumstance. Give me a joyous sense of your crowded kindness this day. Amen.*

# WHAT DEFILES

Again Jesus called the crowd to him and said, "Listen to me, every-one, and understand this. Nothing outside a person can defile them by going into them. Rather, it is what comes out of a person that defiles them."

—*Mark 7:14–15 (NIV)*

Food can make us fat. A poor diet can cause high cholesterol, heart disease, and early demise. These preventable problems are critically important to address.

Jesus tells us, though, that an equal priority for believers must be what comes out of us, in addition to what goes in: the words that we speak, the thoughts toward others that we think, our outwardly focused desires. It's these egressing things that can truly "defile" a person and make us unclean.

The United States Department of Agriculture found in a recent study that Americans spend about sixty-seven minutes every day eating and drinking. With every bite, perhaps we can be reminded to take equal care of what comes out as of what goes in.

---

*Dear God, thank you for the gift of sustenance and nourishment. Please use my meals to remind me to be mindful of my thoughts, words, and desires so that my "inner self" can be just as strong as my outer. Amen.*

# The Courage of Life

For God has not given us a spirit of fear, but of power and of love and of a sound mind.

—*2 Timothy 1:7 (NKJV)*

Without belittling the courage with which men have died, we should not forget those acts of courage with which men . . . have lived. The courage of life is often a less dramatic spectacle than the courage of a final moment; but it is no less a magnificent mixture of triumph and tragedy. A man does what he must—in spite of personal consequences, in spite of obstacles and dangers and pressures—and that is the basis of all human morality. . . . In whatever arena of life one may meet the challenge of courage, whatever may be the sacrifices he faces if he follows his conscience—the loss of his friends, his fortune, his contentment, even the esteem of his fellow men—each man must decide for himself the course he will follow. The stories of past courage can define that ingredient—they can teach, they can offer hope, they can provide inspiration. But they cannot supply courage itself. For this each man must look into his own soul.

—*John F. Kennedy,* Profiles in Courage

*Dear Father, give me the courage of life. Create in me an urge to press past all obstacles, to go beyond imposed limits, to break this day's mold. This I pray in Jesus's name. Amen.*

# RAIN IN ITS SEASON

*If you walk in My statutes and keep My commandments, and perform them, then I will give you rain in its season, the land shall yield its produce, and the trees of the field shall yield their fruit.*
—*Leviticus 26:3–4 (NKJV)*

Sometimes we want more than our portion. More money, more power, more success, more satiated desires. Like the cries of a parched man in the desert, we want God to fill our lives with rain.

In the book of Leviticus, God does promise rain to those who follow his commandments. But our Lord says that this rain will only come "in its season." Why would God limit his abundance? Simple, really: any more would result in a flood.

Too much money at the wrong time corrupts and eventually makes one poor. Too much power before we're ready leads our human nature toward abuse. Simply stated, there is in fact such a thing as too much rain.

Let's be delighted with what we have. Our territories will be enlarged at the appropriate time, but for now, let's enjoy whatever rain God provides.

———

*Dear God, help me enjoy the abundance in my life, the rain that you have given me. I don't want more, and I am glad I don't have less; thank you for providing rain in its season. Amen.*

# THE LITTLE MOMENT

Exhaust the little moment, soon it dies
And be it gash or gold, it will never come
Again in this identical guise
                    —*Gwendolyn Brooks, "Annie Allen"*

Enter his gates with thanksgiving
    and his courts with praise.

                    —*Psalm 100:4 (NIV)*

Every day is precious. This one is no exception.

How can we honor this day? What unique enthusiasm, distinctive approach can we bring to it?

It is the some-odd-thousandth anniversary of our birth—a present gift wrapped by God, begging to be opened. Let's fully "exhaust the little moment," right here, right now.

---

*Dear God, let me honor this day with gladness in my heart. Increase the joy within me, and the gratitude I feel for this life. Amen.*

# KEEPING CLOSE TO JESUS

> When you see the ark of the covenant of the LORD your God, and the Levitical priests carrying it, you are to move out from your positions and follow it. Then you will know which way to go, since you have never been this way before. But keep a distance of about two thousand cubits between you and the ark; do not go near it.
>
> —*Joshua 3:3–4 (NIV)*

Here's the wondrous aspect of a relationship with Jesus: in times past, the holiest objects were kept at a distance. Everyone except the priests and the Levites had to stay two thousand cubits (about three thousand feet) from the ark of the covenant of the Lord, where God's spirit dwelled. God spoke directly to Moses but no others.

But then Christ came to earth. He broke all the rules of distance between God and humanity. By taking human form, Jesus showed us that we too can touch, feel, and abide with God. We just need to draw close to him. And he will draw near to us.

---

*Dear God, thank you for shrinking the distance between me and the ark of your covenant. The only distance is that which I impose. I want to draw close to you now and commune with your spirit. I humbly ask for your presence. Amen.*

# CLEANSE ME

O Lord, the house of my soul is narrow;
enlarge it, that you may enter in.
It is ruinous, O repair it!
It displeases your sight; I confess it, I know.
But who shall cleanse it, or to whom shall I cry but unto you?
Cleanse me from my secret faults, Lord,
and spare your servant from strange sins.
>                    —*Augustine of Hippo, in* Living and Praying in Jesus' Name

*Cleanse me from my secret faults, O Lord.*
*And spare your servant from strange sins.*
*Amen.*

# BEING RIGHT

I've learned that people will forget what you said, people will forget what you did, but people will never forget how you made them feel.
—*Maya Angelou*

Be careful, however, that the exercise of your rights does not become a stumbling block to the weak.
—*1 Corinthians 8:9 (NIV)*

We can do anything today—and we'd probably be right.

Our statements are likely backed by unassailable facts and solid figures. Our postures toward those who have wronged us are probably justified. The judgment we cast on others is likely warranted, given their misdeeds.

But is being right . . . worth it? Once we've summited the mountain of our own correctness, what great prize will we receive?

Paul, echoed by the poet Maya Angelou, reminds us of what is most important. Not our correctness nor the exercise of our multitude of rights. Rather, what is most important is the impression we leave behind on our brothers and sisters, the edification that is left in our wake, and the echoes of our love.

*Dear God, let me put first things first—not my own "rightness" but my love for you and for others. Amen.*

# THE LAND'S REST

I will scatter you among the nations and draw out a sword after you;
your land shall be desolate and your cities waste.
Then the land shall enjoy its sabbaths as long as it lies desolate and
 you are in your enemies' land;
then the land shall rest and enjoy its sabbaths.
As long as it lies desolate it shall rest—
for the time it did not rest on your sabbaths when you dwelt in it.
—*Leviticus 26:33–35 (NKJV)*

We are called to be stewards of this earth. To use its resources wisely, to be gentle caretakers, and every now and then, to give it rest.

God gave the ancient Israelites the same task, and they ignored him. They abused the land and rejected his commandments.

After years of disobedience, the Lord said: Enough. My land must have some rest. He let the children of Israel be scattered among the nations, and fall victim to conquering swords.

God's message is clear. Either we take good care of his creation, or be forced to reckon with the results. One way or another, the land will have its Sabbath. Let's be a part of the solution and find ways to give a bit of rest to this beautiful gift of earth.

*Dear God, thank you for the ground on which I walk, the water I drink, the air I breathe. Let me return to your creation the same care with which you formed it. Help me give rest to this land. Amen.*

# RECKLESS LEAPS, OUTSTRETCHED HANDS

In the same way, I tell you, there is rejoicing in the presence of the angels of God over one sinner who repents.

—*Luke 15:10 (NIV)*

For blows on the fort of evil
That never shows a breach,
For terrible life-long races
To a goal no foot can reach,
For reckless leaps into darkness
With hands outstretched to a star,
There is jubilation in Heaven
Where the great dead poets are.

—*Joyce Kilmer, "Apology"*

What do they celebrate in heaven? What makes the hosts rejoice?

Do they look kindly on our wealth, our authority and power? Or do they cheer for other things?

For lost souls led to the comfort of God's love. For the vulnerable being protected. For evil being confronted. "For reckless leaps into darkness with hands outstretched to a star."

For these things, heaven rejoices.

———

*Dear God, let me hear heaven's applause in the recesses of my mind as I go about your work today. I'm not afraid to make a reckless leap with outstretched hands. Amen.*

# FIRST THINGS

Religion that God our Father accepts as pure and faultless is this: to look after orphans and widows in their distress and to keep oneself from being polluted by the world.

—*James 1:27 (NIV)*

Our being Christian today will be limited to two things: prayer and righteous action among humanity.

—*Dietrich Bonhoeffer,* A Year with Dietrich Bonhoeffer

We have a lot of rules and regulations to follow today.

Red, yellow, and green stoplights. The taxes we pay. Basic decorum to colleagues, relational standards with family and friends.

But when it comes to being a Christian, the journey boils down to two things: are we living a life of purity, and are we giving of ourselves to the poor?

Simple enough to remember—important enough to never forget.

❧

*Dear God, in the midst of modern rules, let me keep your most important precepts in mind. Let me be a Christian in my personal righteousness and public work. Amen.*

# REFINING FIRE

These have come so that the proven genuineness of your faith—of greater worth than gold, which perishes even though refined by fire—may result in praise, glory and honor when Jesus Christ is revealed.

*—1 Peter 1:7 (NIV)*

In a multitude of testings I [God] would perfect your understanding. I am not unaware of the pressures thus inflicted upon you, but as the trials come and go, I not only turn them into a means of blessing, but I never fail to make available My comfort and My sustaining strength.

*—Frances Roberts,* Progress of Another Pilgrim

Our trials are making us stronger, day by day. Each weighty task, each lesson learned, each tribulation persevered strengthens our souls. A refined faith is precious, and we are goldsmiths at the forge.

⎯⎯∾≫∾⎯⎯

*Dear God, thank you for your refining fire. I rejoice in any hindrance, knowing that I will emerge stronger from it. In Jesus's name, amen.*

# REMEMBER FORGETTING

Then Peter came to Jesus and asked, "Lord, how many times shall I forgive my brother or sister who sins against me? Up to seven times?"

Jesus answered, "I tell you, not seven times, but seventy-seven times."

—*Matthew 18:21–22 (NIV)*

There is a story told about Clara Barton, the great founder of the Red Cross, who was said to never hold a grudge. One day she encountered someone who had done her wrong in years past. Another friend said to her of the slight, "Clara, don't you remember?"

"No," Ms. Barton replied without hesitation. "I distinctly remember forgetting that."

As believers, we must be intentional about forgiveness. A grudge left to fester, slightly addressed or not at all, will come back to haunt. It will weigh down our souls like an anchor, preventing movement from darker waters into light.

*Dear God, who do I need to forgive today? What old wrongs must I forget? Help me bring them into the light and throw them into the sea of forgetfulness, as you have done for me. Amen.*

# YOUR FACE I SEEK

Come now, little man,
turn aside for a while
from your daily employment,
escape for a moment
from the tumult of your thoughts.
Put aside your weighty cares,
let your burdensome distractions wait,
free yourself awhile for God
and rest awhile in him.
Enter the inner chamber of your soul,
shut out everything except God
and that which can help you in seeking him,
and when you have shut the door, seek him.
Now, my whole heart, say to God,
"I seek your face, Lord,
it is your face I seek."
—*Anselm of Canterbury, in* Theology for a Troubled Heart

*Come now, escape for a moment.*
*Enter the inner chamber of your soul.*
*And say to God,*
*"It is your face I seek."*
*Amen.*

# JUNE

~~~

## OUR SENIORS

It was an odd way for the president of the United States to spend a
Wednesday afternoon.

Around 1 P.M. on June 13, 2012, President Obama found himself sitting around a picnic table at Kenny's BBQ in northeast Washington, D.C.,
hunched over white Styrofoam containers of ribs, chicken, and turnip
greens with two elderly barbers. The president was crackling with laughter
as he listened to the two men, both north of seventy years old—Nurney
Mason and Otis "Big O" Gamble—talk about their families, their time in
the armed services, and lessons they learned growing up in the South and
moving to Washington, D.C.

Ostensibly, we were at Kenny's to mark Father's Day: that year the
White House kicked off a new program where we'd partner with barbers
around the country to help disconnected dads reconnect with their families. But really, President Obama just wanted to have a good laugh, eat a
slab of ribs, and soak in some wisdom from Nurney and Big O, two men
who had been around for a while and seen a few things.

For whatever reason, in my time in the White House, it seemed like we
were often surrounded by our elders.

There was the Martin Luther King Jr. Day when the president eschewed
the normal glitzy reception and instead invited African American senior
citizens from around the country to join him in the Oval Office, a place
most had never been. Dr. Dorothy Height, the pioneering civil rights
leader and advocate for families, was rolled in her wheelchair into the Oval

Office at that time, and she whispered a few truths to President Obama, shortly before she passed away.

There were the long hours that President Obama spent with Rev. Joseph Lowery, the "dean of the civil rights movement" and close friend of Dr. Martin Luther King Jr. The two of them became so close that whenever Reverend Lowery fell ill with the flu or something worse, the president and his senior staff would call to check on the reverend's health.

From Billy Graham to Joseph Lowery, Ted Kennedy to Dorothy Height, when I reflect on the meetings and occasions that seemed to mean the most to the president—and to me—there was often a senior citizen at the center. Perhaps that's because of the president's own background, having been raised by his grandparents, their wisdom shaping his early life. Or maybe it was the fact that as a relatively young president, sworn in at the age of forty-seven, he recognized that there was still much to learn.

I remember when President Obama and First Lady Michelle attended Dr. Dorothy Height's funeral in April 2010. It was one of the few times that I saw our president choke up, as he recalled what that great woman meant for the African American community and all families around the nation. I have to believe that he thought back to that quiet moment in the Oval Office, away from the cameras and the glitz, when he had the chance to seek Dr. Height's wisdom in her final days. I'm sure he smiled, thinking that moments spent with our seniors are a great use of a busy man's time.

I've tried to keep that pattern in the days since, drawing close to grandparents, older mentors, and elderly friends. God's commandment in the book of Leviticus grows truer and sweeter with each day: "You shall stand up before the gray head and honor the face of an old man, and you shall fear your God."

And I've found that the cordoned perspective of youth seems to me to stretch wider on each encounter with someone who has lived more life than I.

# GOOD BEHAVIOR

Jesus entered the temple courts and drove out all who were buying and selling there. He overturned the tables of the money changers and the benches of those selling doves. "It is written," he said to them, "'My house will be called a house of prayer,' but you are making it 'a den of robbers.'"

—*Matthew 21:12–13 (NIV)*

In 1900, the Daughters of the American Revolution (DAR) gave a rare honorary membership to Jane Addams, the great social reformer of the early twentieth century and fighter for racial equality and women's rights. However, years later when Addams, a committed pacifist, opposed World War I and supported jury trials even for subversive criminals, the DAR rescinded her membership. Addams is said to have remarked that while she thought the DAR honor was for life, "apparently it was for good behavior."

Christ shows us that we are not on this earth for "good behavior." When Jesus confronted money changers using the temple of God as a "den of robbers," he did something decidedly impolite: he turned over the tables and wrecked the shops.

When Jane Addams had to decide between being polite or following her notion of justice, she chose the latter, regardless of how it would be perceived.

We can't be afraid to mix things up, to be unpopular, to rock the boat. The greatest change agents often do just that.

*Dear God, give me wisdom on the use of righteous indignation, and when it wells up within me, let me make sure it's truly righteous. Amen.*

# TRUE WEALTH

When you enter the land the LORD your God is giving you and have taken possession of it and settled in it, and you say, "Let us set a king over us like all the nations around us," be sure to appoint over you a king the LORD your God chooses. He must be from among your fellow Israelites. Do not place a foreigner over you, one who is not an Israelite. The king, moreover, must not acquire great numbers of horses for himself or make the people return to Egypt to get more of them, for the LORD has told you, "You are not to go back that way again." He must not take many wives, or his heart will be led astray. He must not accumulate large amounts of silver and gold.

*—Deuteronomy 17:14–17 (NIV)*

God instructed Moses in the book of Deuteronomy that when Israel finds a king, that person "must not acquire great numbers of horses" or "accumulate large amounts of silver and gold." At first the instruction seems counterintuitive; so much of what we know about kings and queens is defined by their opulence.

But we often see in the Bible that the pursuit of riches draws men and women away from God and toward certain destruction.

As we grow in worldly stature, we must remember not to internalize the world's definition of success. Following God's standard for wealth is the best way to leave a lasting foundation.

⁓∽∘∽⁓

*Dear God, let me learn from the counsel of your word and prioritize spiritual wealth over material accumulation. Let me be wary of idolizing "large amounts of silver and gold." Amen.*

# JOY IN THE GOING

This is the day which the LORD hath made; we will rejoice and be glad in it.

—*Psalm 118:24 (KJV)*

Ours is the pain of constantly pitching our tent and folding it up again, of befriending strangers and bidding them goodbye, of loving the world but never truly being satisfied with it, of pouring our heart and soul into a project others have begun and still others will finish. If we would not be torn in two by the tensions of this truth, we must learn to live provisionally—to measure the road well. We need to make the most of the occasions when we gather by the roadside to break bread together and compare directions. Joy must be discovered in the going as we never really arrive, not even in a lifetime.

—*Kristine Malins, in* Medical Missionary Magazine

*Dear God, give me joy "in the going." I've never walked this way before, and I'd like to enjoy it. Today, reveal pearls of your wisdom and reflections of your glory, and help me take them in. Amen.*

# FOR OURSELVES

When he takes the throne of his kingdom, he is to write for himself on a scroll a copy of this law, taken from that of the Levitical priests. It is to be with him, and he is to read it all the days of his life so that he may learn to revere the LORD his God and follow carefully all the words of this law and these decrees.

—*Deuteronomy 17:18–19 (NIV)*

There's something beautiful about this passage. In these verses, God, through Moses, provides instructions for all the future kings of Israel. And the first thing God commands a king to do when he sits on the throne is to "write for himself . . . a copy of this law."

These kings should not use scribes. They should not assign the task to underlings. In a private and holy ritual, these rulers are to take out their writing instruments and copy down God's laws for themselves. And they should then return to that copy over and over again, reading it "all the days" of their lives.

We must know God's word, for ourselves. We must read it, for ourselves. We must keep it close to us, in a private place, perhaps even copied from our own hands. This writes God's words upon our hearts, where no circumstance can remove it. And it brings us into alignment with his kings.

~~~~~

*Dear God, help me learn your word for myself. Give me rituals and patterns that write your words on my heart. In doing so, let me draw nearer to you. Amen.*

# IS IT TRUE?

Let every one of us cultivate, in every word that issues from our mouth, absolute truth. I say cultivate, because to very few people—as may be noticed of most young children—does truth, this rigid, literal veracity, come by nature. To many, even who love it and prize it dearly in others, it comes only after the self-control, watchfulness, and bitter experience of years.

—*Dinah Craik,* A Woman's Thoughts About Women

And you will know the truth, and the truth will set you free.

—*John 8:32 (ESV)*

Truth: the sieve through which our every action must flow. Yes, it's allowable; yes, it's beneficial; yes, it's profitable; but is it true? Only we know the answer—and to this standard we must keep. "Let every one of us cultivate, in every word that issues from our mouth, absolute truth."

---

*Dear God, grow within me the desire for truth in all things so that I might be set free from the bondage of falsehood. Let veracity be my nature. Amen.*

# NEVER RECORDED

And there are also many other things that Jesus did, which if they were written one by one, I suppose that even the world itself could not contain the books that would be written. Amen.
—*John 21:25 (NKJV)*

This concluding verse in the book of John is fascinating to me. We often want our good deeds to be noticed, recorded, written down. But even Christ himself did not think it was important to ensure that every good and holy act of His be recorded in history. John reveals that there were many more powerful works of Jesus, works we'll never know. And that's okay.

Like Christ, let's live out goodness in the world irrespective of our legacy. History will take care of itself, and our unspoken, unrecorded works will have the impact intended for them.

*Dear God, let me tend to the tasks at hand, and let history take care of itself. Amen.*

# DOUBLE VISION

The power and attraction Jesus Christ exercises over men never comes from him alone, but from him as Son of the Father. It comes from him in his Sonship in a double way, as man living to God and God living with men. Belief in him and loyalty to his cause involve men in the double movement from world to God and from God to world. Even when theologies fail to do justice to this fact, Christians living with Christ in their cultures are aware of it. For they are forever being challenged to abandon all things for the sake of God; and forever being sent back to the world to teach and practice all the things that have been commanded them.

—*H. Richard Niebuhr,* Christ and Culture

For I gave them the words you gave me and they accepted them. They knew with certainty that I came from you, and they believed that you sent me.

—*John 17:8 (NIV)*

*Dear Lord, give me double vision today. I want to see you in your glory, worship you, and sit before your feet. I also want to live fully in this world, serving your people, living out your love. Place me in the world, but make me not of it. This I pray in your name. Amen.*

# SMALL CHANGES

Search me, God, and know my heart;
   test me and know my anxious thoughts."

*—Psalm 139:23 (NIV)*

The great author, journalist, and explorer Ernest Hemingway was sitting down one day when his son Patrick came to him and asked him to edit a short story the young man had written.

The elder Hemingway pored over the manuscript like it was one of his own and returned it to Patrick in due time. Patrick was shocked when he reviewed his father's edits: "But, Papa," he cried, "you've only changed one word!"

Hemingway said in response: "If it's the right word, that's a lot."

Hemingway shows us: small adjustments can make a world of difference.

~~~~~

*Lord, we pray that you would help us identify the minor changes in our lives that can dramatically increase our productivity, our compassion, our service to you. When we identify that change, give us the courage to make it. Amen.*

# GREAT GRACE

Now the multitude of those who believed were of one heart and one soul; neither did anyone say that any of the things he possessed was his own, but they had all things in common. And with great power the apostles gave witness to the resurrection of the Lord Jesus. And great grace was upon them all.

—*Acts 4:32–33 (NKJV)*

———

*Dear God,*

*Like the early church, we pray for "great grace." We pray that your grace follows us wherever we go. To our work, and in our home. In community, and in our quiet moments.*

*Like the earliest believers, let us come together and know your heart. And let "great grace" be upon us today, upon us all.*

*Amen.*

# TRY THE SPIRITS

You may say to yourselves, "How can we know when a message has not been spoken by the LORD?" If what a prophet proclaims in the name of the LORD does not take place or come true, that is a message the LORD has not spoken. That prophet has spoken presumptuously, so do not be alarmed.

*—Deuteronomy 18:21–22 (NIV)*

It is perfectly appropriate to "try the spirits." God's word and the things he has revealed directly to us: those things we know are true.

But other spiritual instructions must meet a test of discernment. The Old Testament tells us to reject a prophet whose words do not "come to pass"; and the New Testament admonishes us to "try the spirits," discerning whether instructions are from God or from human sources only.

We should draw closely to God, close enough to hear the promptings from his Spirit. And then operate in discernment.

~∞∞∞~

*Dear God, teach me to "try the spirits" in love, and determine which lessons are from you and which are not. Amen.*

# FOR ORDER

That there be no breaking in or going out;
  That there be no outcry in our streets.
Happy are the people who are in such a state;
  Happy are the people whose God is the LORD!
                              —*Psalm 144:14–15 (NKJV)*

Today, like David, we pray for order.

We pray that the law is followed and justice reigns.

That the vulnerable are protected and the protectors remain safe.

That our homes and workplaces, cities and towns, know peace, unshaken by criminality or strife.

"That there be no breaking in or going out; That there be no outcry in our streets." *Amen.*

# SINCERITY

For we are not, like so many, peddlers of God's word, but as men of sincerity, as commissioned by God, in the sight of God we speak in Christ.

—*2 Corinthians 2:17 (ESV)*

A bizarre sensation pervades a relationship of pretense. No truth seems true. A simple morning's greeting and response appear loaded with innuendo and fraught with implications. . . . Each nicety becomes more sterile and each withdrawal more permanent.

—*Maya Angelou,* Singin' and Swingin'
and Gettin' Merry Like Christmas

Let's focus on sincerity today. From our motives to our words to the impressions we leave behind, let's avoid pretense and be pure. As Christ's words left timeless impressions with simple truth, so may ours.

———✸———

*Dear God, leaven me with sincerity. Remove any pretense and help me approach this day with truth. Amen.*

# CHRIST WITHIN

Neither shall they say, Lo here! or, lo there! for, behold, the kingdom of God is within you.

*—Luke 17:21 (KJV)*

Christ be with me, Christ within me,
Christ behind me, Christ before me,
Christ beside me, Christ to win me,
Christ to comfort and restore me.
Christ beneath me, Christ above me,
Christ in quiet, Christ in danger,
Christ in hearts of all that love me,
Christ in mouth of friend and stranger.

*—Saint Patrick's Breastplate Prayer*

*Lord, we affirm that you are God within us. We navigate these hours with the full knowledge of your presence in our lives, this day and every day. Amen.*

# IN SILENCE

Now it came to pass, about eight days after these sayings, that He took Peter, John, and James and went up on the mountain to pray. As He prayed, the appearance of His face was altered, and His robe became white and glistening. And behold, two men talked with Him, who were Moses and Elijah, who appeared in glory and spoke of His decease which He was about to accomplish at Jerusalem. But Peter and those with him were heavy with sleep; and when they were fully awake, they saw His glory and the two men who stood with Him. Then it happened, as they were parting from Him, that Peter said to Jesus, "Master, it is good for us to be here; and let us make three tabernacles: one for You, one for Moses, and one for Elijah"— not knowing what he said.

—*Luke 9:28–33 (NKJV)*

Peter shows us that sometimes in the presence of holiness, it behooves us to be quiet.

When God roars in the wind or shines in the morning sun. When his spirit is evident to us in our solitary times or he draws near on a walk alone.

Like Peter, we may be tempted to interrupt this move of God with words or actions. But in these moments, there's really nothing to say.

Let's just experience his presence around us. Be awed by his work in the world. And be silent.

※

*God, in your presence, I sit in silence.*

# LET IT GO

Whatever you do, work at it with all your heart, as working for the
Lord, not for human masters.

*—Colossians 3:23 (NIV)*

When you feel restless, sad, sorrowful and embittered, look for the
cause, and if it is not worth being sorry about (and nothing that does
not offend God is worth being sorry about), get rid of your anxiety;
if you do not see the causes but feel restless and dissatisfied all the
same, put up with it, arm yourself with patience, let the storm pass,
and your inner peace will return.

This union, my sister, demands a heart at peace, calm, unalter-
able, like some place in heaven, and we can and must acquire it fighting hard whatever threatens if from outside ourselves.

*—Francisco Palau, "Letter to Juana Gratia"*

We should not be harder on ourselves than God is.

Yesterday, there were things we could not get to, people we could not
accommodate, places we simply were unable to be. If this "falling short"
did not offend God or violate his commandments, then we must learn to
let it go, like a single exhalation in a long lifetime of deep breaths.

*Dear God, help me let go of the obligations, worries, and demands that are not
important. Clear my mind so that I can better follow you. Amen.*

JUNE 16

# THE THOUGHTS OF OUR HEARTS

Then a dispute arose among them as to which of them would be greatest. And Jesus, perceiving the thought of their heart . . .
—*Luke 9:46–47 (NKJV)*

In these verses, Jesus's disciples were in a power struggle. They were wondering which of them was the greatest. But here's the thing: nothing in the Bible says that the disciples revealed this dispute to Jesus out loud, or even to each other. Instead, it only says that Christ perceived "the thought of their heart."

We have to be careful not just with what we say, but also with the thoughts of our hearts. These unspoken meditations can lead us astray as easily as a misplaced word. Let's ask God to purify our thoughts, and create in us a clean heart.

—◦◦◦—

*Dear God, you know the silent pulses of my heart. Rid me of jealousies, petty envies, selfish desires. Let there be no arguments within me, spoken or unspoken. Amen.*

# YESTERDAY'S EBENEZERS

To look backward for a while is to refresh the eye, to restore it, and
to render it the more fit for its prime function of looking forward.
> —*Margaret Fairless Barber,* The Roadmender

Here I raise my Ebenezer;
Here by Thy great help I've come;
And I hope, by Thy good pleasure,
Safely to arrive at home.
> —*Robert Robinson, "Come Thou Fount of Every Blessing"*

*Dear God, we raise "Ebenezers" in our yesterdays. We place markers of remembrance in the past, recalling the goodness you've showed us, the mercy that sustained us, the love that surrounded us, your hand that protected us. We begin this day with the full knowledge that as you've guided us in the past, you will also move us forward, and bring us home. Amen.*

# WEEPING OVER THE CITY

> As he approached Jerusalem and saw the city, he wept over it and said, "If you, even you, had only known on this day what would bring you peace—but now it is hidden from your eyes."
>
> —*Luke 19:41–42 (NIV)*

Jesus wept over the city.

He wept because humankind just didn't get it—they just didn't know what would make them whole, even though the answer was right in front of them. He wept for the brokenness around him, the needless suffering and lack of peace.

He wept because we were blind and deaf to our own circumstance.

And after he wept, he acted.

When's the last time we wept for our city? Has the world around us broken our hearts? Let's picture Christ on a hilltop, looking over rooftops and people milling about—and weeping. Let our hearts break as well. And then, let's act.

*Dear God, I am thankful that your heart was broken for the city. Allow mine to break too—and then motivate me to healing action. Amen.*

# THE OBJECTS OF OUR WORSHIP

A person will worship something, have no doubt about that. We may think our tribute is paid in secret in the dark recesses of our hearts, but it will out. That which dominates our imaginations and our thoughts will determine our lives, and our character. Therefore, it behooves us to be careful what we worship, for what we are worshipping we are becoming.

*—attributed to Ralph Waldo Emerson*

Jesus answered, "It is written: 'Worship the Lord your God and serve him only.'"

*—Luke 4:8 (NIV)*

What are the things that capture our hearts when no one's looking? Where do we retreat when there's no obligation? If we could have any indulgence, with what would we indulge? These are the objects of our worship.

If it is God and his Kingdom, his beautiful creation in the world, then our minds are captured by the right things. If not, perhaps we have some praying to do. We must ask God to right the objects of our worship.

---

*Dear God, clarify to me the things that I worship. If I have not placed holy priorities first, send your Spirit to help me reorient. I trust that you can do it. Amen.*

# CONTROL

Now John answered and said, "Master, we saw someone casting out demons in Your name, and we forbade him because he does not follow with us."

But Jesus said to him, "Do not forbid him, for he who is not against us is on our side."

*—Luke 9:49–50 (NKJV)*

The world is full of co-laborers. Let's pray that their work will flourish.

We don't always need control. We don't always need oversight. We don't even need to know everything that's going on. If people are about God's business, if they are bringing his truth to the world or helping their people, let's be careful to "not forbid" them. "For he who is not against us is on our side."

⎯⎯∾⎯⎯

*Dear God, remove from me any unhealthy desire to control. Let your work in the world be unlimited, through many workers. Amen.*

# HOW HE LOVES US

For God so loved the world that he gave his one and only Son, that whoever believes in him shall not perish but have eternal life.

*—John 3:16 (NIV)*

When He died in the Wounded World He died not for men, but for each man. If each man had been the only man made, He would have done no less. Each thing, from the single grain of Dust to the strongest eldil, is the end and the final cause of all creation and the mirror in which the beam of His brightness comes to rest and so returns to Him. Blessed be He!

*—C. S. Lewis,* Perelandra

It's you, it's me, that he loves.

When we stir in the morning and our eyes open to a new day, our Father in heaven looks down at his creation and smiles.

He is jealous for us—desiring our time, our focus, our requited love. And when other lesser passions have subsided and we return to his embrace, God is still here, waiting.

Oh, how he loves us. How he loves us. How he loves.

---

*God, I can never love you like you love me, but today, I want to do my best, in the way I honor you through my decisions, in the way I care for others. Thank you for how you love me. Amen.*

# SOMETHING OUT OF NOTHING

Give thanks in all circumstances; for this is the will of God in Christ Jesus for you.

—*1 Thessalonians 5:18 (ESV)*

My parents had a way of making something out of nothing. When I was five, my mother was raising me by herself and didn't have much money. She had hoped to take me to Chuck-E-Cheese's to celebrate my birthday, but when the day rolled around there was nothing in the bank.

My mom told me we couldn't have the party, and I was disappointed to the point of tears and saw her eyes water as well. But then she drove me to a self-service car wash. She asked me to get out of the car, handed me a hose, and proceeded to spray me. Astonished, I laughed and sprayed her back. We spent an hour spraying each other, laughing and playing, until she ran out of quarters. We were thoroughly soaked and every single tear was washed away. It was the best birthday I've ever had.

When my stepfather—father, really—Antoni Sinkfield, married my mom, they both worked jobs that paid minimum wage; we had to stretch to pay the bills. But I never felt poor. One day he took us to the local department store. The way he described this vacuum cleaner—its bells and whistles, features and colors—made it sound like we had bought a brand-new car. I left the store with my chest poked out and a new sense of pride: my dad could really take care of us.

Sometimes we grow in wealth and stature and lose our sense of perspective. But a central quality of leadership—in our families, our workplaces, and our communities—is the ability to inspire gratitude with what we have right now, without always seeking more. Let's make much of what we have today, and find satisfaction in the task.

———

*Dear God, thank you for my present circumstance. In it I will find great joy. Amen.*

# OPPOSING IMPULSES

The strong man holds in a living blend strongly marked opposites. . . . The idealists are usually not realistic, and the realists are not usually idealistic. The militant are not generally known to be passive, nor the passive to be militant. Seldom are the humble self-assertive, or the self-assertive humble. But life at its best is a creative synthesis of opposites in fruitful harmony. The philosopher Hegel said that truth is found neither in the thesis nor the antithesis, but in the emergent synthesis which reconciles the two.

—*Dr. Martin Luther King Jr. in "Strength to Love"*

*Dear God, balance my opposing impulses. When I am angry, mix calm into my soul. When I lack vision, give me the perspective of a wide horizon. When I am tempted to lose discipline, put a workman's spirit within me. Give me equal measures of strength and love. Amen.*

# OUR REFLEX

Now it came to pass, when the time had come for Him to be received up, that He steadfastly set His face to go to Jerusalem, and sent messengers before His face. And as they went, they entered a village of the Samaritans, to prepare for Him. But they did not receive Him, because His face was set for the journey to Jerusalem. And when His disciples James and John saw this, they said, "Lord, do You want us to command fire to come down from heaven and consume them, just as Elijah did?"

But He turned and rebuked them, and said, "You do not know what manner of spirit you are of. For the Son of Man did not come to destroy men's lives but to save them." And they went to another village.

—*Luke 9:51–56 (NKJV)*

Look at how Jesus dealt with embarrassment and rejection. He was walking along the way to Jerusalem and wanted to stop in a Samaritan village. But before he could settle in, the villagers rejected him and sent him on his way.

The disciples welled up with righteous indignation and threats of holy fire. But Jesus simply said, I'm not here to condemn them. Quite the opposite; I want them to be saved.

How do we respond when someone embarrasses us, fails to give us our due respect? Do we rebuke them angrily? Or do we pray God's best for them and for their salvation? Only one way is the path of Christ.

---

*Dear God, condition my embarrassment reflexes. When I am rejected, help me respond with love and care, as you did. Amen.*

# TRULY

Even in literature and art, no man who bothers about originality will ever be original: whereas if you simply try to tell the truth (without caring twopence how often it has been told before) you will, nine times out of ten, become original without ever having noticed it.

—*C. S. Lewis,* Mere Christianity

Rather, let our lives lovingly express truth [in all things, speaking truly, dealing truly, living truly]. Enfolded in love, let us grow up in every way and in all things into Him Who is the Head, [even] Christ (the Messiah, the Anointed One).

—*Ephesians 4:15* (AMP)

"Speaking truly, dealing truly, living truly"—that pretty much sums it up, doesn't it? In all things, in all circumstances, when joyful, when pained, when hurt, when cornered, when afraid: the truth. Across the millennia, it has never steered a soul wrong. Nor will it for us.

———

*Dear God, bind me to the truth. When the enemy prompts me otherwise, let my impulse be in the direction of honesty, integrity, and truth. Amen.*

# DON'T LOOK BACK

And another also said, "Lord, I will follow You, but let me first go and bid them farewell who are at my house."

But Jesus said to him, "No one, having put his hand to the plow, and looking back, is fit for the kingdom of God."

—*Luke 9:61–62 (NKJV)*

Whatever we do, we must not look back.

The past is the past. It's over, done. God's grace is sufficient for whatever was in our rearview mirror; he wants us to focus on the road ahead. The work God has in store for us is too tough and too rewarding to waste one ounce of energy on backward thinking. "No one, having put his hand to the plow, and looking back, is fit for the kingdom of God."

Don't look back.

—∼∾∽—

*Dear God, focus my mind on the road ahead instead of on what's behind me. While I'm doing your work, remind me to never look back. Amen.*

# FAMOUS

For by the grace given me I say to every one of you: Do not think of yourself more highly than you ought, but rather think of yourself with sober judgment, in accordance with the faith God has distributed to each of you.

—*Romans 12:3 (NIV)*

All of us failed to match our dreams of perfection. So I rate us on the basis of our splendid failure to do the impossible. . . . If I had not existed, someone else would have written me, Hemingway, Dostoyevsky, all of us. Proof of that is that there are about three candidates for the authorship of Shakespeare's plays. But what is important is *Hamlet* and *A Midsummer Night's Dream,* not who wrote them, but that somebody did. The artist is of no importance. Only what he creates is important, since there is nothing new to be said. Shakespeare, Balzac, Homer have all written about the same things, and if they had lived one thousand or two thousand years longer, the publishers wouldn't have needed anyone since.

—*William Faulkner, interview in* The Paris Review

*God, I don't want to be famous; I want you to be famous. Remind me that it's not about me. Place within me the creative fire to make beautiful, constructive, healing things that point this world back to you. In Jesus's name, amen.*

# TAKE THE LOWEST PLACE

When you are invited, take the lowest place, so that when your host comes, he will say to you, "Friend, move up to a better place." Then you will be honored in the presence of all the other guests. For all those who exalt themselves will be humbled, and those who humble themselves will be exalted.

*—Luke 14:10–11 (NIV)*

Go and sit down in the lowest place.
   Don't rush to the front.
   Don't edge out the eager.
   Don't look for recognition by taking the prime seat in the house.
   Jesus commands, "Take the lowest place."
   And let him who sees our humble heart call us up higher. *Amen.*

JUNE 29

# A BARBER'S JOY

Rejoice always, pray continually, give thanks in all circumstances; for
this is God's will for you in Christ Jesus.
—*1 Thessalonians 5:16–18 (NIV)*

A leaf fluttered in through the window this morning, as if supported
by the rays of the sun, a bird settled on the fire escape, joy in the taste
of coffee, joy accompanied me as I walked.
—*Anaïs Nin,* Diary of Anaïs Nin

Nurney Mason is well beyond eighty years old and was a barber in the U.S.
House of Representatives for over fifty of those years. Mr. Mason cut hair
out of a tiny booth in the basement of the Rayburn House Office Building; his stall has seen nearly as much history as the floor of the Capitol
itself. And every day, even now in his retirement, he wears a smile.

"Hello, Congressman!" he'd say to approaching customers, with a solid
handshake and a knowing grin. I used to wonder how Mr. Mason stayed
upbeat, day after day, cut after cut, the vibrations from his clippers surely
jarring his wrists over the half century. One day while getting a haircut,
I asked Mr. Mason how he stays so happy all the time. He replied, "I just
make it right here. I create joy where I stand."

*Dear God, help me create joy where I stand. In the daily tasks, the things that
might otherwise drive me crazy, let me make my own happiness. And let the
light that flows from you to me be passed on to those around me. Amen.*

# A Prayer for Action

I think one's feelings waste themselves in words, they ought all to be distilled into actions and into actions which bring results.
—*Florence Nightingale, "Letter to a Friend"*

Dear children, let us not love with words or speech but with actions and in truth.
—*1 John 3:18 (NIV)*

~~~~~~

A prayer for action:

*Dear God, you did not just say that you would bring the children of Israel out of Egypt; you brought them.*

*You did not just promise to deliver Daniel from the lion; you delivered him.*

*You did not just assure Mary that she would bear a child; you came into the world.*

*You did not just offer yourself as a sacrifice for our sin; you were and are our sacrifice.*

*In the same manner, let me live out my words into the world today. Let this day be one of action.*

*Amen.*

# JULY
## ON DISAGREEMENT

So what do you do when you disagree with your boss, and your boss's boss, and maybe even the president of the United States?

That's where I found myself in the fall and winter of 2011, on one of the most important challenges of our day: religious liberty and a historic conflict with the Catholic Church.

The issue was fairly clear. President Obama's Affordable Care Act—popularly known as Obamacare—made preventative services, including contraception, free for millions of American women, paid for by their employers (I thought that was a very good thing). But the unresolved question before President Obama in late 2011 and early 2012 was whether employers that objected to contraception on religious grounds—say, for instance, the Catholic Church—would have to pay for it as well. Faith-based organizations like the U.S. Conference of Catholic Bishops were on one side of this debate, and women's rights groups like NARAL and Planned Parenthood were on the other.

And in the White House, opinions fell roughly around the same fault lines.

On one side, I stood with two very senior officials who were closely connected to the Church and had grown up sitting in pews. In our opinion, it was blindingly obvious that government just can't force religious organizations to pay for things they don't believe in. I also believed that President Obama's decision on this issue would send a broader signal about religious liberty in our country and permanently shape his relationship with faith-based groups. In my view, there had to be another way to make sure women had access to contraception without infringing on the rights of the Church.

On the other side of the issue were several White House and agency officials—also much more senior than I—most of whom had deep histories with the women's advocacy community. In their view . . . well, for months I didn't understand their view at all! I knew their opinions had to do with women's access to contraception regardless of where they worked, but to me, it didn't add up. Their inability to make this relatively small concession to religious organizations seemed to me unreasonable at best, and at worst, destructive.

For months the two sides battled it out, in large staff meetings, small group discussions, and private e-mails. The Catholic Bishops, women's groups, and U.S. congressmen and senators were feverishly lobbying the president as well, which didn't help a bit. On several occasions—particularly the large group meetings we would have in the Roosevelt Room, that imposing wood-lined conference room in the White House's West Wing—I felt like I was the only voice advocating for religious liberty, while other staff, years my senior and far more persuasive, were lined up on the other side. Every time I had to address the issue, I had the sensation of a very small man about to jump off a very high cliff.

And then, the big day came—the day President Obama would announce his decision. I was up all night the night before with a knot in my stomach, in fervent prayer. The next morning—a sunny one, unseasonably warm for a January day—I walked into my office on Jackson Place, a row of townhouses directly across from the White House, and made a few calls to West Wing staff to see if there was an update on the president's decision. Strangely, I couldn't get through to anyone. I waited a few hours and then called again—no answers. I decided to go for a walk around the West Wing and the Eisenhower Building, where many of the president's staffs' offices are, to see if I could find someone; no one was available to see me.

I returned to my desk and saw the voice mail indicator flashing on my phone—finally, some news. I checked the message, and it was a polite voice mail from one of our senior staff asking me to give her a call back.

However, at the end of the voice mail, she thought she had hung up the phone, but the line was still active. I could hear her say to her assistant: "I just called Joshua back, but I don't really want to talk with him; at this point, there's really nothing to say. If he calls back, take a message."

My heart dropped, and I slumped into my chair. That was it; I had my answer. I didn't need to hear it formally. The president had clearly decided to not exempt religious groups from the requirement to buy contraception. This was, in my opinion, a historic breach of relationship with the Church, much bigger than this particular issue. And it also meant that I had failed.

I felt a wave of shame and regret. Perhaps if I had fought harder or taken a different approach, the religious community would have been better protected and the president better served. But mostly, I was angry, very angry. *They manipulated him!* I thought, believing that staffers on the other side of this issue had unfairly used outside voices to lobby the president. *How could they not understand how important this is? They never wanted the right result; they just wanted to win.*

I was sick to my stomach the rest of the afternoon and evening, and into the next day. The public reaction was as I anticipated; the religious community was livid, and all I could do was watch. As the calls poured in from friends and allies, my anger burned hotter, and eventually I'd had enough. I marched into the office of one of the most senior staffers in the White House, a neutral party on this issue, and I let it rip.

"How could they? . . ." "Their arguments were so specious, dishonest . . ." "Don't they know what this will do to the president, to the country?" I didn't hold anything back. Then I settled back into the chair and stared at him, daggers in my eyes.

The recipient of my wrath—a Washington veteran with many more battles under his belt than I—took it in calmly, even empathetically. But his reply still rings in my ears to this day. He said: "Joshua, I understand why you're upset; it's a huge issue. But I need you to know that as passionately as you feel right now, as angry as you are, as hurt as you feel on behalf of the people you serve—there are people on the other side who feel just as passionately, would have been just as angry and just as hurt.

"For you," he continued, "faith is a big part of your context; it's the space in which you work and live. But other people have other contexts.

I know some people in this building—people I've known for twenty years—for whom the protection of women's rights is as deep in their marrow as religious liberty is in yours. For them, it is unthinkable—really unthinkable—that even one woman would have unequal access to medical care.

"You can question policy decisions. You can disagree with people, even vehemently. But you should be very, very careful before you question others' motives. Not only is it not fair, but in this case, I truly believe your attacks on them are wrong. They do care about the president. And they care about the country. They just ended up in a different place. How would you feel if someone said behind your back that you really didn't care for the president or the religious community, and just wanted to win? Would that be accurate? Would it be right?"

I sat there, temperature still high and hands still shaking, but fighting a new reality that was beginning to settle in. A reality where I felt just as passionately about religious liberty and was just as confident in my view, but where my opponents weren't evil or dishonest—just in sincere, passionate disagreement with me. And I started to realize that in this country, that's a place they are allowed to be.

The issue did not go away, and in fact the president made some significant adjustments to the contraception policy. Eventually, I believe we moved toward a place where both religious liberty and the rights of women were protected. But for me, there was an even larger point.

The book of Proverbs, chapter 21, verse 2 (ESV), tells us, "Every way of a man is right in his own eyes, but the LORD weighs the heart." The Lord weighs the heart—not me, not anyone else, but God. And until the time when I can ask him face-to-face about someone else's motives, I have no business questioning them myself. My job was to fight as hard as I can and as fair as I can, and in the meantime to love every person I come into contact with. And let God work out the rest.

# AIRPLANE HOLY

Once you have tasted flight, you will forever walk the earth with your eyes turned skyward, for there you have been, and there you will always long to return.

*—attributed to Leonardo da Vinci*

But just as he who called you is holy, so be holy in all you do; for it is written: "Be holy, because I am holy."

*—1 Peter 1:15–16 (NIV)*

In the unexamined abstract, airplanes don't make much sense at all. Think about it. A hunk of metal, over 450 tons, can fly, unsupported, through the air?

And then physics unfolds. Newton's Third Law bears itself out as the thrust from massive engines counters the drag of wind, creating a force of lift greater than the weight of the airplane, which then rises. Startlingly simple; yet it took millennia to discover.

Holiness is something like that. In the abstract it makes little sense and seems unattainable. How are we, with all of our mess, supposed to be holy, like God?

And then God's word unfolds. Love him fully, totally, now. Love our neighbor in precisely equal measure to how much we love ourselves—in all of our interactions. Read his word and strive daily to follow its instructions. Love God, and love our neighbor. Startlingly simple, imminently attainable; yet we still have not fully discovered it. Today, perhaps we can.

*God, I cannot be holy on my own. Yet you can make me holy. Do it today; this is my earnest plea. Amen.*

# COME IN

Therefore if any man be in Christ, he is a new creation: old things are passed away; behold, all things are become new.

*—2 Corinthians 5:17 (KJV)*

Imagine yourself as a living house. God comes in to rebuild that house. At first, perhaps, you can understand what He is doing. He is getting the drains right and stopping the leaks in the roof and so on: you knew that those jobs needed doing and so you are not surprised. But presently He starts knocking the house about in a way that hurts abominably and does not seem to make sense. What on earth is He up to? The explanation is that He is building quite a different house from the one you thought of—throwing out a new wing here, putting on an extra floor there, running up towers, making courtyards. You thought you were going to be made into a decent little cottage: but He is building a palace. He intends to come and live in it Himself.

*—C. S. Lewis,* Mere Christianity

⚬⚬⚬

*Lord, my doors are open to you. Wherever you want to move, move. Whatever you want to change, change. Create in me a clean heart, and renew and right my spirit. Make me yours. Amen.*

# LESSER "GODS"

> If there arises among you a prophet or a dreamer of dreams, and he gives you a sign or a wonder, and the sign or the wonder comes to pass, of which he spoke to you, saying, "Let us go after other gods"— which you have not known—"and let us serve them," you shall not listen to the words of that prophet or that dreamer of dreams, for the LORD your God is testing you to know whether you love the LORD your God with all your heart and with all your soul.
>
> —*Deuteronomy 13:1–3 (NKJV)*

As God instructs in Deuteronomy, we cannot serve other gods—even if the work of these gods appears to come to pass. God is testing us, and watching.

Sometimes the work of this world, those other gods, yields results. Dishonest dealings can still bring profit. Manipulation in relationships can cause others to respond to us. Vengeful actions can overtake our enemies. In the words of Deuteronomy, false prophets and dreamers of dreams can still cause signs or wonders to come to pass.

But these wins from lesser gods are fleeting, their yield short-lived. In the long run, we've betrayed our God and our purpose and will suffer the consequences.

*Dear God, let me look past lesser "gods" and short-term wins, and look only to you. Amen.*

# FOR OUR COUNTRY

I shall need, too, the favor of that Being in whose hands we are, who led our fathers, as Israel of old, from their native land and planted them in a country flowing with all the necessaries and comforts of life; who has covered our infancy with His providence and our riper years with His wisdom and power, and to whose goodness I ask you to join in supplications with me that He will so enlighten the minds of your servants, guide their councils, and prosper their measures that whatsoever they do shall result in your good, and shall secure to you the peace, friendship, and approbation of all nations.
—*Thomas Jefferson, inaugural address, March 4, 1805*

Let's pray for our country today. Let's join in prayers across the ages—from Thomas Jefferson to citizens praying at this moment, now, today—and lift her up.

———❦———

*Lord, we pray that the ropes that bind our nation together, though frayed, will never break; that the greatest of our natural resources—the love of our people—will abound, flowing even beyond our shores; that our flinty determination will cause sparks of innovation to fly but never set wildfires of anger that we are not big enough to extinguish. And most of all, that you will be with us, as you have always been. Amen.*

# GOD'S SURPRISES

See, the former things have taken place,
   and new things I declare;
before they spring into being
   I announce them to you.

*—Isaiah 42:9 (NIV)*

My whole life has largely been one of surprises. I believe that any man's life will be filled with constant, unexpected encouragements of this kind if he makes up his mind to do his level best each day of his life—that is, tries to make each day reach as nearly as possible the high-water mark of pure, unselfish, useful living.

*—Booker T. Washington,* Up from Slavery

Are we ready for God to surprise us? When he does a new thing, are we primed to respond? Let's not be so expectant of the ordinary that we fail to seek the remarkable. Let's live a life like Booker T. Washington's—"one of surprises." Today, perhaps God has a few in store.

*Dear God, thank you for the unexpected. My eyes are open, anxious to see bright lights in new spaces. Amen.*

# FOR BOLDNESS

And when they had prayed, the place where they were assembled together was shaken; and they were all filled with the Holy Spirit, and they spoke the word of God with boldness.

—*Acts 4:31 (NKJV)*

There was something about the prayers of Peter and John and other early Christians. When they prayed in the assembly, the walls shook—and God's Spirit fell down.

What were the words of that prayer? What invocation was so powerful that it provoked the Holy Spirit to fall fresh and shake the very foundation of the building in which they gathered?

The preceding verses offer some clue. In order for signs and wonders to be done, and for the walls to shake, Peter and John prayed for "boldness," and they invoked Christ's holy name.

~~~

*Father, I pray for boldness. I pray for the audacity to move wherever you prompt, to fight through worldly trials toward eternal glory. And I pray this in the name of your son Jesus Christ, the son of the living God. Amen.*

# A SIMPLE PRAYER

I do not have the courage to force myself to search out *beautiful* prayers in books. There are so many of them it really gives me a headache! And each prayer is more *beautiful* than the others. I cannot recite them all and not knowing which to choose, I do like children who do not know how to read, I say very simply to God what I wish to say, without composing beautiful sentences, and He always understands me. For me, *prayer* is an aspiration of the heart, it is a simple glance directed to heaven, it is a cry of gratitude and love in the midst of trial as well as joy; finally, it is something great, supernatural, which expands my soul and unites me to Jesus.

—*Thérèse of Lisieux,* Comfort in Hardship

And when you pray, do not keep on babbling like pagans, for they think they will be heard because of their many words.

—*Matthew 6:7 (NIV)*

⁓᥆᥆᥆⁓

*Lord, I come to you with a simple prayer. I worship you for your presence in the world, and for this life of mine. I repent of my sins, the ways I've fallen short, and I desire a new path. I ask for your provision for my family and friends, and those near and far. I open myself to your service, however you desire to use me, in the building of your kingdom. Amen.*

# DEFENSIVE PRAISE

Now when they began to sing and to praise, the Lord set ambushes against the people of Ammon, Moab, and Mount Seir, who had come against Judah; and they were defeated.

—*2 Chronicles 20:22 (NKJV)*

Like the people of Israel facing down a warring enemy, praise is our best defense. Against depression. Against anxiety. Against a defeatist attitude, or despair.

As we open our mouths in praise—thanking God for who he is and what he's done in our lives—the strongholds of these enemies will begin to fall. And like "the people of Ammon, Moab, and Mount Seir, who had come against Judah," they will be defeated.

*Dear Lord, I shout down every attack against me with the music of praise. There's no darkness that can muffle the sound of my thankful voice. I praise you now, oh God, even in the midst of challenges. And I hear victory marching in the distance. Amen.*

# THE BLESSING BUSINESS

Since God is unchangeable, He will continue to be mindful of us in the future as He has been in the past; and His mindfulness is tantamount to blessing us. But we have here not only the conclusion of reason but the declaration of inspiration; we have it on the Holy Ghost's authority—"He will bless us." This means great things and unsearchable. The very indistinctness of the promise indicates its infinite reach. He will bless us after His own divine manner, and that forever and ever. Therefore, let us each say, "Bless the Lord, O my soul!"

—*Charles H. Spurgeon,* Faith's Checkbook

Every good gift and every perfect gift is from above, coming down from the Father of lights with whom there is no variation or shadow due to change.

—*James 1:17 (ESV)*

My grandmother Kathryn Russell likes to say: "God is in the blessing business." One of the grand benefits of a relationship with our Savior is his unbreakable promises to us. And one of those promises, from the book of Ephesians, is that God will do "immeasurably more than all we ask or imagine, according to his power that is at work within us" (3:20, *NIV*).

We must expect these blessings. We must gleefully receive them. Because as sure as we are living, God will bless.

*Dear God, with eager expectation, I trust in your power to bless me. And I will receive these blessings with humility and gratitude today. Amen.*

# OUR PRAYER OF THANKS

God,
For the gladness here where the sun is shining at evening on the
        weeds at the river,
    Our prayer of thanks.

God,
For the laughter of children who tumble barefooted and bare-
        headed in the summer grass,
    Our prayer of thanks.

God,
For the sunset and the stars, the women and their white arms that
        hold us,
    Our prayer of thanks.

God,
If you are deaf and blind, if this is all lost to you,
God, if the dead in their coffins amid the silver handles on the
        edge of town, or the reckless dead of war days thrown
        unknown in pits, if these dead are forever deaf and blind
        and lost,
    Our prayer of thanks.

God,
The game is all your way, the secrets and the signals and the sys-
        tem; and so for the break of the game and the first play and
        the last,
    Our prayer of thanks.

—*Carl Sandburg, "Our Prayer of Thanks"*

# WHY WE REJOICE

And He said to them, "I saw Satan fall like lightning from heaven. Behold, I give you the authority to trample on serpents and scorpions, and over all the power of the enemy, and nothing shall by any means hurt you. Nevertheless do not rejoice in this, that the spirits are subject to you, but rather rejoice because your names are written in heaven."

—*Luke 10:18–20 (NKJV)*

Let's never love our own power. If our Lord can send Satan tumbling from heaven to earth, if he can give his disciples authority over every attack of the enemy and still maintain a spirit of humility, then so can we.

Let's rejoice in the fact that God loves us. Let's rejoice in his grace, in the knowledge what we are forgiven. Let's shout aloud because "your names are written in heaven." But let's never exult in our own power; there should be no rejoicing there.

※

*Dear God, let me never grow so hungry for power that it becomes the thing I praise. Let power come and power go, while my mind is ever fixed on you. Amen.*

# TO EXPLORE

That what is true of business and politics is gloriously true of the professions, the arts and crafts, the sciences, the sports. That the best picture has not yet been painted; the greatest poem is still unsung; the mightiest novel remains to be written; the divinest music has not been conceived even by Bach. In science, probably ninety-nine percent of the knowable has to be discovered. We know only a few streaks about astronomy. We are only beginning to imagine the force and composition of the atom. Physics has not yet found any indivisible matter, or psychology a sensible soul.

*—Lincoln Steffens, "This World Depression*
*of Ours Is Chock-full of Good News"*

He stretches out the north over the void
    and hangs the earth on nothing.

*—Job 26:7 (ESV)*

God's greatest is all around us, but so much of it is undiscovered. What will we find today?

Will we articulate a word of his voice through our writing? Will we show courage through our leadership? Will we mimic some element of God's creativity through the beauty we create in the world?

So much yet to explore. So much to discover. So much beauty to unveil. It makes for an exciting day.

※

*Dear God, open my eyes to the wonder of your world. Place within me an explorer's spirit, and help me go out boldly. Amen.*

# GO AND DO THE SAME

Jesus answered by telling a story. "There was once a man traveling from Jerusalem to Jericho. On the way he was attacked by robbers. They took his clothes, beat him up, and went off leaving him half-dead. Luckily, a priest was on his way down the same road, but when he saw him he angled across to the other side. Then a Levite religious man showed up; he also avoided the injured man.

"A Samaritan traveling the road came on him. When he saw the man's condition, his heart went out to him. He gave him first aid, disinfecting and bandaging his wounds. Then he lifted him onto his donkey, led him to an inn, and made him comfortable. In the morning he took out two silver coins and gave them to the innkeeper, saying, 'Take good care of him. If it costs any more, put it on my bill—I'll pay you on my way back.'

"What do you think? Which of the three became a neighbor to the man attacked by robbers?"

"The one who treated him kindly," the religion scholar responded.

Jesus said, "Go and do the same."

*—Luke 10:30–37 (MSG)*

Let's go and do the same. *Amen.*

# BETWEEN US

And when you pray, do not be like the hypocrites, for they love to pray standing in the synagogues and on the street corners to be seen by others. Truly I tell you, they have received their reward in full. But when you pray, go into your room, close the door and pray to your Father, who is unseen. Then your Father, who sees what is done in secret, will reward you. . . .

When you fast, do not look somber as the hypocrites do, for they disfigure their faces to show others they are fasting. Truly I tell you, they have received their reward in full. But when you fast, put oil on your head and wash your face, so that it will not be obvious to others that you are fasting, but only to your Father, who is unseen; and your Father, who sees what is done in secret, will reward you.

—*Matthew 6:5–6, 16–18 (NIV)*

There are things to confess that enrich the world, and things that need not be said.

—*Joni Mitchell*

We are a world of sharers. In media, on social networks, even with our family and friends—we lay bare our thoughts and ideas so frequently. In many ways this is a good thing—conversation clarifies.

And yet, Christ commands us to keep some things—holy things—separate, unshared, apart. Because even the most careful and delicate human hands are still just that—human. And holy things might be corrupted if we entrust them to earthly hands.

Let us cherish the whispers that are just between us and God. A sly smile will edge upward on lips when we savor those secrets. It's just for him, and for us.

*Dear God, thank you for the disciplines, practices, and revelations that are just between you and me. Let me think on these things and honor that privilege. Amen.*

# FICKLE PRAISE

You can't let praise or criticism get to you. It's a weakness to get caught up in either one.

*—Coach John Wooden, in* Coach Wooden:
The 7 Principles That Shaped His Life and Will Change Yours

A very large crowd spread their cloaks on the road, while others cut branches from the trees and spread them on the road. The crowds that went ahead of him and those that followed shouted,

"Hosanna to the Son of David!"

"Blessed is he who comes in the name of the Lord!"

"Hosanna in the highest heaven!"

When Jesus entered Jerusalem, the whole city was stirred and asked, "Who is this?"

The crowds answered, "This is Jesus, the prophet from Nazareth in Galilee."

*—Matthew 21:8–11 (NIV)*

Both crowds and the wind blow hot and cold, and change directions just as fast.

On his triumphant ride into Jerusalem, in a spontaneous burst of worship, the Jewish people welled up in celebration and cried, "Hosanna! Hosanna to the highest!" They caught a glimpse of Jesus's true worth, and their gratitude overwhelmed. A week later, that same crowd cried: "Crucify him!" And they did.

Our value must not be built from the brittle mortar of man's acclaim. That foundation crumbles in an instant. Instead, we must know our worth as a child of the Most High God, sent here to do a great work in him. His applause for our service is worth all the praise in the world.

*Dear God, let me neither dismiss nor indulge in man's praise. Let me love and work with steady diligence, regardless of the public response. Amen.*

# WHEN BLESSINGS OVERTAKE

Now it shall come to pass, if you diligently obey the voice of the LORD your God, to observe carefully all His commandments which I command you today, that the LORD your God will set you high above all nations of the earth. And all these blessings shall come upon you and overtake you, because you obey the voice of the LORD your God.

—*Deuteronomy 28:1–2 (NKJV)*

When we walk in obedience, God's blessings won't just surprise us. They will *overtake* us. Out of nowhere. Overwhelming. Unexpected. In undeserved measure.

Let's do our part. Let's walk as closely to him as we can. Let's love God and love our neighbor. Let's reduce our fleshly desires and pray that the Spirit of God will increase within us.

And wait for his blessings to overtake us.

⸻⸺⸻

*Dear God, I know you have some surprises up your sleeve. I'll walk this road of obedience, and let you do your work. Amen.*

# READY

The king's command was so urgent and the furnace so hot that the flames of the fire killed the soldiers who took up Shadrach, Meshach and Abednego, and these three men, firmly tied, fell into the blazing furnace.

Then King Nebuchadnezzar leaped to his feet in amazement and asked his advisers, "Weren't there three men that we tied up and threw into the fire?"

They replied, "Certainly, Your Majesty."

He said, "Look! I see four men walking around in the fire, unbound and unharmed, and the fourth looks like a son of the gods."

—*Daniel 3:22–25 (NIV)*

It is stern work, it is perilous work, to thrust your hand in the sun
And pull out a spark of immortal flame to warm the hearts of men:
But Prometheus, torn by the claws and beaks whose task is never done,
Would be tortured another eternity to go stealing fire again.

—*Joyce Kilmer, "The Proud Poet"*

Like Daniel in the den, we are prepared to confront lions.

Like Shadrach, Meshach, and Abednego, thrown in the fiery furnace, we do not flinch before the flame.

Let's rush in, swords bared, ready to fight for what God has promised us. And when the battle is over, we'll be ready to do it all over again.

*Dear God, I'm ready for a fight, a righteous one. Prepare me for battle; steel me for the task. Amen.*

# CONTEND WITH HIM

And of Levi he said:
"Let Your Thummim and Your Urim be with Your holy one,
Whom You tested at Massah,
And with whom You contended at the waters of Meribah."
—*Deuteronomy 33:8 (NKJV)*

God can withstand our testing.

When we doubt him, let him hear it.

When we're angry with him, cry out.

When we are unsure even of his existence, when we beg to feel his presence, let those requests be known.

The ancients tested God. They wrestled with him at Massah and contended with him at the waters of Meribah.

He's strong enough to withstand. And he honors those who, with a good heart, bring him these tests.

*Dear God, instead of running from you when I feel holy tension, remind me to bring it to you. I know you value the honesty; I know you can withstand the test. Amen.*

# HONESTY

Then you will know the truth, and the truth will set you free.
—*John 8:32 (NIV)*

It is the glistening and softly spoken lie; the amiable fallacy; the patriotic lie of the historian, the provident lie of the politician, the zealous lie of the partizan, the merciful lie of the friend, and the careless lie of each man to himself, that cast that black mystery over humanity, through which any man who pierces, we thank as we would thank one who dug a well in a desert.
—*John Ruskin, "The Seven Lamps of Architecture"*

*Dear Lord, in all things, make me honest. With myself. With my loved ones. With my colleagues. With you. Pull me toward the truth like a moth to a flame. And let me never waiver in my honesty. Amen.*

# IN OUR FOOTSTEPS

And they buried him within the border of his inheritance at Tim-nath Serah, which is in the mountains of Ephraim, on the north side of Mount Gaash.

Israel served the Lord all the days of Joshua, and all the days of the elders who outlived Joshua, who had known all the works of the Lord which He had done for Israel.

—*Joshua 24:30–31 (NKJV)*

Joshua served God so fully, so well, that even among the often-recalcitrant Israelites, his message and character continued on in Israel after he passed away. Simply put, Joshua's lessons stuck.

Let us pray for the same. That when we've left our institutions, and even when we leave behind our family, our footsteps will have left impressions clear enough for others to follow. We want not just our actions to live on in the hearts of those we love—but our character to linger as well.

*Dear God, help me walk carefully now so that others can walk confidently in my footsteps later. Amen.*

# WE WAKE UP

What use is it to slumber here,
Though the heart be sad and weary?
What use is it to slumber here,
Though the day rise dark and dreary?

For that mist may break when the sun is high,
And this soul forget its sorrow;
And the rosy ray of the closing day
May promise a brighter morrow.
—*Emily Brontë, "What Use Is It to Slumber Here?"*

Let the morning bring me word of your unfailing love,
    for I have put my trust in you.
Show me the way I should go,
    for to you I entrust my life.

        —*Psalm 143:8 (NIV)*

We wake up. We shake off yesterday's tiredness and ignore tomorrow's fear, and wake up.

There's a new morning before us. The dawn has beat us to it, and the day stretches out like a runway, awaiting our flight. We've no more use for slumber; we wake up. And we start this day with joy!

—◦◦◦◦◦—

*God, thank you for the new morning and the promise it brings. Invigorate me today, so I can know its blessings. Amen.*

# AS HE WHO SERVES

Now there was also a dispute among them, as to which of them should be considered the greatest. And He said to them, "The kings of the Gentiles exercise lordship over them, and those who exercise authority over them are called 'benefactors.' But not so among you; on the contrary, he who is greatest among you, let him be as the younger, and he who governs as he who serves."

—*Luke 22:24–26 (NKJV)*

Even in the time of Christ, there was a campaign finance system. Jesus revealed how the structure worked: "The kings of the Gentiles exercise lordship over them, and those who exercise authority over [the kings] are called 'benefactors.'"

But he continued: "But not so among you; on the contrary, he who is greatest among you, let him be as the younger, and he who governs as he who serves."

Jesus reminds us that although we have to do what we have to do in the spheres of politics and power, we must always keep in mind the true hierarchy of things. The ones who govern must act "as he who serves."

<hr>

*Dear God, constantly renew within me a servant's heart. Let me be last and least, before I yearn to be first. Amen.*

# WHO EXISTS?

The first man was of the dust of the earth; the second man is of heaven.

—*1 Corinthians 15:47 (NIV)*

The worst sin toward our fellow creatures is not to hate them, but to be indifferent to them: that's the essence of inhumanity.

—*George Bernard Shaw,* The Devil's Disciple

Who exists to us? Not who do we see; at some point our glance falls on everyone within our field of vision. But who really *exists*?

Do the faces in the crowd exist? Do we care about their well-being, their families, their lives? Do passing acquaintances exist? Are we hopeful for their future?

Certainly, we should guard our hearts, and be careful whom we let in. But in this callous world, too often people fail to really exist to us. They become shadows and avatars, cardboard cutouts where humans might have been. Let's make sure we extend the presumption of human dignity, of real existence, to all those whom we meet. Because in this world, there are no lesser beings.

*Dear God, help me to see my brothers and sisters as you do. Help me acknowledge their existence and extend to them dignity and worth. Amen.*

# MAKE ME A MOUNTAIN

Those who trust in the LORD are like Mount Zion,
  which cannot be moved, but abides forever.

—*Psalm 125:1 (ESV)*

*Lord, make me a mountain.*

*Let my base run wide and deep, sturdy and immovable.*

*Let my peak break through the clouds: let me see for miles all around.*

*Though I crumble from time to time, let me never break.*

*And let my posture always, always, be pointed upward, toward worship, toward you.*

*Lord, make me a mountain, like Mount Zion. "Which cannot be moved, but abides forever." Amen.*

# STADIUM MUSIC

Be strong and courageous. Do not be afraid or terrified because of them, for the LORD your God goes with you; he will never leave you nor forsake you.

—*Deuteronomy 31:6 (NIV)*

I love the sound of stadium music—the raucous bands that play when my favorite players are announced. For Michael Jordan's Bulls, it was "Sirius," by the Alan Parsons Project. No one knew the name of the song, but everyone knew the feeling when Jordan took the floor.

These words spoken by Moses over Joshua and the people of Israel are our stadium music. We can hear them thumping, driving in the background as we tackle this day:

"Be strong and courageous," when the morning unfolds.

"Be strong and courageous," when tough times hit.

"Be strong and courageous," when we're standing alone.

"Be strong and courageous," when it's all on the line.

For the Lord our God is with us, always. Wherever we go. *Amen.*

# THINGS ABOVE

In the long run men hit only what they aim at. Therefore, though they should fail immediately, they had better aim at something high.
—*Henry David Thoreau,* Walden

Set your minds on things above, not on earthly things.
—*Colossians 3:2 (NIV)*

Let's set our minds on things above today. Let's aim as high as we can.

Aim for Christ's love. For truly selfless service. For the boldest possible adventures and the deepest possible calm.

We may not hit the mark exactly, but God willing, we'll come close. When our minds are set on things above, not on earthly things.

---

*Dear God, renew my mind today. Make it purer than yesterday, and tomorrow make it purer still. Amen.*

# SUSTAINING FOOD

> On the evening of the fourteenth day of the month, while camped
> at Gilgal on the plains of Jericho, the Israelites celebrated the Pass-
> over. The day after the Passover, that very day, they ate some of
> the produce of the land: unleavened bread and roasted grain. The
> manna stopped the day after they ate this food from the land; there
> was no longer any manna for the Israelites, but that year they ate the
> produce of Canaan.
>
> —*Joshua 5:10–12 (NIV)*

For a time, under Joshua's leadership, God provided the children of Israel
with "manna," or food from heaven. The Israelites were starving, wan-
dering in the desert, and in desperate need of provision. But eventually,
God weaned them off manna. The Israelites learned to work the land of
Canaan, and the manna stopped. This was a good thing: God had moved
them from temporary miraculous provision to sustainable food.

It's the same with us. When we are babes in the spirit, we can be satiated by God's miraculous provision. But eventually, God shows us how
to grow in faith, toward a more mature dependence on him that involves
our own disciplined work. We should not be satisfied with being fed like
spiritual infants; instead, we should seek the role of adult farmers in the
kingdom—responsible for working his land.

---

*Dear God, help me move from spiritual childhood to adulthood. Connect me
with the people and resources to grow in my faith, so that I move from manna
to sustainable food. Amen.*

# OBEDIENCE MORE THAN SACRIFICE

But Samuel replied:

> "Does the LORD delight in burnt offerings and sacrifices
>> as much as in obeying the LORD?
> To obey is better than sacrifice,
>> and to heed is better than the fat of rams."
>
> —*1 Samuel 15:22 (NIV)*

Use, do not abuse; the wise man arranges things so. I flee Epictetus and Petronius alike. Neither abstinence nor excess ever renders man happy.

> —*Voltaire,* Sept Discours en Vers sur l'Homme

Sometimes we vacillate between indulgence and grand sacrifice when all God really wants is obedience.

The slow and steady work of right living. One foot in front of the other, pointed toward him.

Reading the Bible. Communicating daily with God. Loving our neighbor. Fulfilling our obligations. With seeds he has planted and the diligent watering of obedience, our harvest will surprise.

*Dear God, let me not swing to the extremes of indulgence or sacrifice but instead remain steady on the path of obedience to your word. Amen.*

# THE OTHER GODS

> Now therefore, fear the LORD, serve Him in sincerity and in truth, and put away the gods which your fathers served on the other side of the River and in Egypt. Serve the LORD! And if it seems evil to you to serve the LORD, choose for yourselves this day whom you will serve, whether the gods which your fathers served that were on the other side of the River, or the gods of the Amorites, in whose land you dwell. But as for me and my house, we will serve the LORD.
> —*Joshua 24:14–15 (NKJV)*

Put away the gods on the other side of the river. The gods that got you nowhere—that wasted days, months, and years.

The gods that flashed a smile only to disappear as quickly as they came.

The gods of worry, of desire, of pride, of wrath, that never left us feeling edified, whole.

Our God has proven his worth. Those other gods have shown their weakness. As Joshua commanded Israel, let's put aside the gods on the other side of the river—and serve the Lord.

---

*Lord, I know how far you've brought me, and I remember what it was like to be outside of your presence, on the other side of the river. I don't want to go back, and I'm committed to going forward. Amen.*

# EARNING OUR SALARY

I have told you these things, so that in me you may have peace. In this world you will have trouble. But take heart! I have overcome the world.

—*John 16:33 (NIV)*

October 1962 was, of course, a tense time for our country. When the Russians made a decision to install ballistic missiles in Cuba, President Kennedy was adamant that the missiles had to be removed, bringing the two superpowers to the brink of nuclear war. Finally, as the clock counted down, Soviet Premier Nikita Khrushchev ordered the missiles withdrawn. At the height of the standoff, President Kennedy is said to have remarked: "I guess this is the week I earn my salary."

Like President Kennedy, there will be those weeks when we earn our salaries. As Jesus said, "In this world you will have trouble." But the next part is critical: "Take heart! I have overcome the world."

The conclusion is just around the corner. The resolution is near. In the meantime, we press forward, holding on to God's promises with each step.

~~~

*Dear Lord, thank you for moments of trials—times when we "earn our salaries." We know these moments are building strong muscles within us and they're precursors to a coming reward. Amen.*

# MERCY AND TRUTH MET

Mercy and truth have met together;
    Righteousness and peace have kissed.
Truth shall spring out of the earth,
    And righteousness shall look down from heaven.
Yes, the LORD will give what is good;
    And our land will yield its increase.
Righteousness will go before Him,
    And shall make His footsteps our pathway.

*—Psalm 85:10–13 (NKJV)*

<hr>

*"Mercy and truth have met together; Righteousness and peace have kissed."*
    *We are the union of God's beautiful purposes. When we follow his word and stay in his presence, the earth around us springs forth with goodness; the land bears an increase.*
    *"Yes, the LORD will give what is good;*
*And our land will yield its increase.*
*Righteousness will go before Him,*
*And shall make His footsteps our pathway."*
*Amen.*

# AUGUST
## A GLIMPSE OF CHRIST

I was introduced to Jesus on a street corner in Boston. I should've met him much earlier than that.

I had grown up in the church. My stepfather was a pastor and I spent formative years in bible camps, youth choirs, and crawling between and underneath pews. With so much stained glass around me and religion in the air, as a teenager I figured that I must automatically be a Christian. I knew the words to all the right songs and how to nod my head at appropriate times.

But by the time I got to Boston University in 1999, I had about as much church as I could handle. So I stopped going. I guess I figured that all of my past experience with religion would be enough. I never said it this way, but I think that I believed my parents' faith would cover for the fact that I didn't truly have a faith of my own. As soon as I left home, seeking God was the last thing on my mind.

So it caught me off-guard one evening when a man named Eugene Schneeberg invited me to his church. I was standing on a street corner on Commonwealth Avenue, participating in a political protest, and not at all looking for a place to worship. It didn't help that Eugene looked nothing like the Christians I had previously known: his pants were baggier than those of some of my favorite rappers, and his fitted baseball cap reminded me more of a DJ than an evangelist.

"There's no way," I thought to myself, "that this guy knows more about God than me."

I brushed Eugene off, but not before grudgingly giving him my phone number and e-mail address. And empowered with my contact info, Eugene kept on me. Week after week he'd invite me to worship with him, and each time I'd decline. But one Saturday night, after a particularly intense night of partying, I felt an ache in my chest that I couldn't shake. I looked in the mirror at my face, swollen by drinking, and down at fingernails encrusted with ashes of various sorts. "Who am I?" I wondered. I didn't recognize myself, and couldn't answer that basic question.

So I called Eugene and asked him to pick me up for church the next morning. When he arrived in his black SUV, I thought that our next stop would be a gleaming white building with a steeple on top. Instead, he pulled over in front of a middle school where Calvary Praise and Worship Center was at the time renting space for its service. "Where on earth is this guy taking me?" I must have muttered.

We enter a small auditorium and I saw a smattering of people greeting each other. A few embraced me warmly, and I thought that maybe these kind folks were part of the choir, preparing for service. But then the pastor, Warren Collins, kicked things off, and I realized that this wasn't just the choir—it was the entire congregation.

No more than twenty people. No organ, no piano. Belting out worship songs to words displayed on a dim slide projector. A scripture reading, and then right into the message. This was a bare-bones service if I had ever seen one, and I looked down my holy nose at it.

And then Pastor Collins started preaching. Just a few written notes, no "three-part structure" that I had grown used to in my years in church, no sing-songy voice. He just talked, in a deeply personal way, about Jesus.

Jesus of Nazareth. Who he was. How he was raised. Why God sent him to earth. How precisely he loved the people around him. Why he died, and what that death and resurrection meant for me, personally: Joshua DuBois, from Nashville, Tennessee, a kid with some brokenness and in need of redemption.

There was no pulpit, no grandeur, no church-fan to wave or even a choir to echo his words. But stripped bare of all of these sanctified accessories, I was finally able to catch a glimpse of Christ. And I liked—loved—what I saw.

It took a few more trips with Eugene but one Sunday morning, I just knew. I finally summoned the courage to admit that even with my supposedly righteous past, with all of that church under my belt, I was not a Christian. My pastor welcomed me into his arms, and walked me through a simple prayer, a confession of faith in Jesus, an admittance of my own frailty, and an acceptance of his love.

I have reflected on that day many times since. There have been occasions in my life—from the campaign to the White House and other moments as well—where I became distracted by the "trappings" of religion: the relationships with famous leaders, the splendor of large churches, the politics of social issues, the beauty of ceremonies and events. But I am then quickly reminded that when it comes to real, sustaining faith—the way to tackle each day with joy and purpose—none of that other stuff matters. What matters is knowing Christ personally, spending time in conversation with my God, reading his word, and serving those whom he loves.

I didn't learn that in a cathedral or through an elaborate message filled with the finer points of theology. I picked it up in rickety theater chair, sitting in a dimly-lit middle school auditorium. And it has proven to be the most important lesson of my life.

# THE ARMY WE HAVE

After a long time the master of those servants returned and settled accounts with them. The man who had received five bags of gold brought the other five. "Master," he said, "you entrusted me with five bags of gold. See, I have gained five more."

His master replied, "Well done, good and faithful servant! You have been faithful with a few things; I will put you in charge of many things. Come and share your master's happiness!"

—*Matthew 25:19–21 (NIV)*

In late 1863, President Lincoln had a major problem with one of his generals. General George B. McClellan had far more troops than his Confederate counterparts but largely refused to march the troops out to war.

Fed up with the inactivity, President Lincoln wrote General McClellan a one-sentence letter: "If you don't want to use the army, I should like to borrow it for a while. Yours respectfully, A. Lincoln."

Unlike General McClellan, we must make full use of what we've been given.

Although we always want more, God has blessed us with so many resources already. We have every tool at our disposal to blaze new trails, bring greater healing, and have an impact in this world.

---

*Our prayer today, dear Lord, is not for more, but to use what we have well. Help us be good stewards of our present resources and, with them, build your kingdom. Amen.*

# A QUIET RITUAL

Three times a year Solomon sacrificed burnt offerings and fellowship offerings on the altar he had built for the LORD, burning incense before the LORD along with them, and so fulfilled the temple obligations.

—*1 Kings 9:25 (NIV)*

King Solomon had already accomplished it all. He had built an awesome temple for the Lord. He was known throughout the world for his wisdom. He had tens of thousands of people under his command.

And still, three times a year, Solomon kept a quiet ritual. He went by himself to bring offerings to the Lord on the altar he had built. Solomon did this for his entire life.

Even after we've reached points of success, we must keep our rituals. The quiet prayers, the humble gestures, our solitary approaches to God are even more important after we have "arrived" than before we came. Like King Solomon, let's build these rhythms into our days. And God will honor our diligence.

---

*Dear God, I pattern myself on King Solomon. I will regularly seek your face, outside of public view. I will always keep your commands. Amen.*

# THE JUDGMENT SEAT

> But why do you judge your brother? Or why do you show contempt
> for your brother? For we shall all stand before the judgment seat of
> Christ.
>
> —*Romans 14:10 (NKJV)*

We shall all stand before the judgment seat of Christ. Every robber, every
king, every slave, every freeman, every pauper, every billionaire, and everyone in between.

There will be a great leveling, a time when all our sins are laid bare
before our Father. So today, let's be careful not to judge: "For we shall all
stand before the judgment seat of Christ."

---

*God, place within me a humble and contrite heart. Remind me that I am
a sinner, saved only by grace. And that like other sinners, I will stand before
your face. Amen.*

# NEVER WEARY

Let us not become weary in doing good, for at the proper time we will reap a harvest if we do not give up.

—*Galatians 6:9 (NIV)*

I met Reverend Joseph Lowery (one of Dr. Martin Luther King Jr.'s closest confidants and founder of the Southern Christian Leadership Conference) in early 2007 and traveled with him frequently over the next two years. At least once a month, Dr. Lowery would call me and say that he would like to go to another campaign stop and speak on our behalf. I always stopped whatever I was doing and flew or drove with him to these events.

One day we were in Iowa, and Dr. Lowery was addressing a group of young people at local college. Someone thanked Dr. Lowery for fighting for "the younger generation," the kids who were coming behind him. Dr. Lowery, who was eighty-nine years old at the time, laughed and replied, "Son, I'm not just fighting for you. I've got a lot of life left, and I'm fighting for me, too!"

Every day we are presented with a new and beautiful struggle. Every hour is a fresh opportunity to make our mark on the world. Like Dr. Lowery, let's "never become weary in doing good," and press forward with holy tension into the challenges of this day.

———

*Dear God, grant me the energy for a new struggle. Let me never grow weary in doing good. Amen.*

NOTE: This devotional was sent to President Obama on his birthday.

# BOUND TOGETHER

We are so bound together that no man can labor for himself alone.
Each blow he strikes in his own behalf helps to mold the universe.
*—Jerome K. Jerome,* Works of Jerome K. Jerome

Bear one another's burdens, and so fulfill the law of Christ.
*—Galatians 6:2 (ESV)*

Let's be intentional about seeking community.

When we fall, let there be hands behind to catch us. And when others fall, let's help them soften the landing.

There are times for striking out on our own, as Christ did in the wilderness, but we mostly read about him surrounded by twelve followers, twelve friends. Let's find community and do the same.

*Dear God, give me caring friends, friends who reflect your love back to me. And let me be a good friend too. Amen.*

# JUST A BREATH

But He, being full of compassion,
    forgave their iniquity,
    and did not destroy them.
Yes, many a time He turned His anger away,
    and did not stir up all His wrath;
For He remembered that they were but flesh,
    a breath that passes away and does not come again.
                         *—Psalm 78:38–39 (NKJV)*

God lets so many of our iniquities slide, because he knows the frailty of our human condition. Should we not show the same grace to others?

Remember, even our enemies, the ones who mistreat us most, are just "a breath that passes away and does not come again."

That's all. In the grand scheme of things, that's what these lives of ours are. Just a breath.

*Dear God, give me a portion of your grace to extend to those who disappoint me. For like me, they are just a breath. Amen.*

# NEVER DESPAIR

For His anger is but for a moment,
  His favor is for life;
Weeping may endure for a night.
  But joy comes in the morning.

*—Psalm 30:5 (NKJV)*

The day may dawn when fair play, love for one's fellow men, respect for justice and freedom, will enable tormented generations to march forth serene and triumphant from the hideous epoch in which we have to dwell. Meanwhile, never flinch, never weary, never despair.

*—Winston Churchill, last speech to the House of Commons,*
*March 1, 1955*

*Dear God, we ask that you conquer our despair. Any hopelessness in the recesses of our minds must shatter in the face of your promises. The world will not always be just, the sun will not always shine bright, and pain and evil will rear their heads. But you love us—you always have and always will. And so we never despair. Amen.*

# WE LOVE YOU

And yet, I love a certain light, a certain voice
—some scent, some flesh, some morsel—when I love my God.
A light, a sound, a smell, a taste . . .
The embrace of some inner lover.
A splendor that cannot be contained anywhere.
A sound that the passage of time can't ravage.
A fragrance that the wind can't disperse.
A craving that can't be appeased by gorging.
A lust that clings to the senses well after it's fulfilled.
That is what I love, when I love you. My God.
—*St. Augustine,* Confessions, *10.6.8*

*God—we love you. We love that you shaped this form so long ago, in our mother's womb.*

*We love that you ordered our tentative first steps into the world, the early barrage of living that shaped our ascent.*

*We love the valleys—cold and long—that have toughened our skin.*

*And we love the overcoming. The surpassing. The triumph of a life lived fully, in your embrace.*

*We love you, dear God. Amen.*

# LETTING IT PLAY OUT

He also spoke this parable: "A certain man had a fig tree planted in his vineyard, and he came seeking fruit on it and found none. Then he said to the keeper of his vineyard, 'Look, for three years I have come seeking fruit on this fig tree and find none. Cut it down; why does it use up the ground?' But he answered and said to him, 'Sir, let it alone this year also, until I dig around it and fertilize it. And if it bears fruit, well. But if not, after that you can cut it down.'"

—*Luke 13:6–9 (NKJV)*

As the parable of the fig tree teaches us, let's give our strategies time to play out.

Sometimes God's plans take time. The yield is not always immediate, but there may still be a harvest on the horizon.

We serve a God of patience, whose plans can unfold over months and years. When it comes to the things he has planted deep within—let's give it time.

*Dear God, pace me. Slow my anxious mind, and help me remember to give your plans time to play out. Amen.*

# IMMORTAL

So we fix our eyes not on what is seen, but on what is unseen, since what is seen is temporary, but what is unseen is eternal.
—*2 Corinthians 4:18 (NIV)*

Let every man and woman count himself immortal. Let him catch the revelation of Jesus in his resurrection. Let him say not merely, "Christ is risen," but "I shall rise."
—*Phillips Brooks, in* Herald Gospel of Liberty, *vol. 114*

Immortal. Imagine that.

This frame of ours, as delicate as rice paper after a rain, lasts just a few ticks on the stopwatch of the eternal.

But as Christ rose and lives, so shall we. The deeper part of us lives on. It makes one think about which part to cultivate.

*Dear God, fix my eyes on what is unseen, not just what's seen. Remind me of the brevity of this life and the length of my life with you. Amen.*

# HOLY GROUND

Now when Joshua was near Jericho, he looked up and saw a man standing in front of him with a drawn sword in his hand. Joshua went up to him and asked, "Are you for us or for our enemies?"

"Neither," he replied, "but as commander of the army of the LORD I have now come." Then Joshua fell facedown to the ground in reverence, and asked him, "What message does my Lord have for his servant?"

The commander of the LORD's army replied, "Take off your sandals, for the place where you are standing is holy." And Joshua did so.

—*Joshua 5:13–15 (NIV)*

Where we sit and read God's word—that's holy ground.

Where we write or type what he inspires within us—that's holy ground.

Where we work to help his people—that's holy ground.

Where we live out his love in the world—that's holy ground.

Let's treat these places with the sanctity they deserve. "For the place where you are standing is holy." Holy ground. *Amen.*

# EVERY COWARDICE

[Be] not frightened in anything by your opponents. This is a clear sign to them of their destruction, but of your salvation, and that from God.

—*Philippians 1:28 (ESV)*

Here one must leave behind all hesitation;
  here every cowardice must meet its death.

—*Dante Alighieri,* Inferno

Every cowardice must meet its death.

Every hesitation, every fear.

Two paths before us—backward or forward. With God at our side, we choose, today, to press on.

"Here one must leave behind all hesitation;
here every cowardice must meet its death."

~~~

*Lord, help me leave behind hesitation today, and charge forward into the future you've ordained. Amen.*

# DIGGING DEEP

But from there you will seek the LORD your God and you will find him, if you search after him with all your heart and with all your soul.

—*Deuteronomy 4:29 (ESV)*

Life is so generous a giver, but we, judging its gifts by their covering, cast them away as ugly or heavy or hard. Remove the covering, and you will find beneath it a living splendor, woven of love, by wisdom, with power.

—*Fra Giovanni, "A Letter to the Most Illustrious*
*the Contessina Allagia Dela Aldobrandeschi"*

*Oh God, let me dig deep. Beneath the slender veneer and the crusty subtext. Beneath the glazed-over glance, the superficial meaning.*

*Help me tap the lower stratum, the ancient places, your closest soil. Push me beyond the surface. Let me, Lord, dig deep.*

*Amen.*

# GOOD REASONS

> Then the children of Israel did evil in the sight of the LORD, and served the Baals; and they forsook the LORD God of their fathers, who had brought them out of the land of Egypt; and they followed other gods from among the gods of the people who were all around them, and they bowed down to them; and they provoked the LORD to anger.
>
> —*Judges 2:11–12 (NKJV)*

When the Israelites forsook the Lord and served other gods, no one said they didn't have a good reason.

Maybe there was drought in the area and God had thus far sent no rain. Maybe other tribes berated the Israelites and forced them to bow down at the tip of a sword. Maybe they could not hear God's voice clearly and wondered if he had left them.

There are always reasons to pick from, viable excuses to leave the presence of God. And they always lead to destruction.

Let us not be so weak that we're led astray even for good reason. Our compelling justification for staying close to our Savior is always stronger than the reasons to do otherwise.

---

*Dear God, let me look past the opportunities for disobedience and ever toward your light. Amen.*

# FOR RIGHTEOUSNESS

The LORD rewarded me according to my righteousness;
According to the cleanness of my hands He has recompensed me.
—*Psalm 18:20 (NKJV)*

*Dear God, we want to be righteous today.*

*We want to look down at these hands of ours and see that they are clean.*

*We know that there are beautiful things you wish to place in these hands—beautiful, holy, precious things.*

*And so, we will make them ready. We will guard them for your coming reward.*

*Amen.*

# THE WALKING CONQUERED

The Philistine, with his shield bearer in front of him, kept coming closer to David. He looked David over and saw that he was little more than a boy, glowing with health and handsome, and he despised him. He said to David, "Am I a dog, that you come at me with sticks?" And the Philistine cursed David by his gods. "Come here," he said, "and I'll give your flesh to the birds and the wild animals!"

David said to the Philistine, "You come against me with sword and spear and javelin, but I come against you in the name of the LORD Almighty, the God of the armies of Israel, whom you have defied. . . ."

David ran quickly toward the battle line to meet him. Reaching into his bag and taking out a stone, he slung it and struck the Philistine on the forehead. The stone sank into his forehead, and he fell facedown on the ground. . . .

David ran and stood over him. He took hold of the Philistine's sword and drew it from the sheath. After he killed him, he cut off his head with the sword.

—*1 Samuel 17:41–45, 48–49, 51 (NIV)*

I love the man that can smile in trouble, that can gather strength from distress, and grow brave by reflection. 'Tis the business of little minds to shrink; but he whose heart is firm, and whose conscience approves his conduct, will pursue his principles unto death.

—*Thomas Paine,* The American Crisis

Let's relish the uncertainty, the trouble, even the danger of this day. Like David staring down Goliath, let's see our giants as the Walking Conquered, ready to fall at our feet. Weaker men avoid problems, but we, the strong, run toward them, with God at our side. Let's grab our sling and fling our stone.

*Dear God, let me charge into battle this day. Let trouble fall before me like Goliath and, like David, I will give you the praise. Amen.*

# STRAIGHT UP

> But a certain man named Ananias, with Sapphira his wife, sold a possession. And he kept back part of the proceeds, his wife also being aware of it, and brought a certain part and laid it at the apostles' feet. But Peter said, "Ananias, why has Satan filled your heart to lie to the Holy Spirit and keep back part of the price of the land for yourself? While it remained, was it not your own? And after it was sold, was it not in your own control? Why have you conceived this thing in your heart? You have not lied to men but to God."
>
> —*Acts 5:1–4 (NKJV)*

We have to be straight up with God.

Ananias and Sapphira, two Christians in the early church, brought an offering to the church that they claimed was the full proceeds from a sale of one of their possessions. However, they knew in their hearts that they only brought a portion of the profit. And Peter called them out. "While it remained, was it not your own? And after it was sold, was it not in your own control? . . . You have not lied to men, but to God."

Ananias and Sapphira had no reason to lie—they could have been straight up and said that they were only bringing a portion. Or they could have brought nothing at all and been honest about that. Falling short would have been a sin but at least an honest one. Instead, they lied, not "to men but to God." And they paid a horrible price.

Wherever we are, whatever we're going through, however we have fallen short, it behooves us to be transparent with ourselves and with God. God cannot use us until we have come to terms with our own shortcomings. When we do, he will always be there.

*Lord, let me never be like Ananias and Sapphira, bringing only part of myself to you. I come to you straight up, flaws and all. In honesty, I stand before you and give you what I have. Amen.*

# THE GOD OF MORNING

To him whose elastic and vigorous thought keeps pace with the sun, the day is a perpetual morning.

*—Henry David Thoreau,* Walden

The Sovereign LORD has given me a well-instructed tongue,
    to know the word that sustains the weary.
He wakens me morning by morning,
    wakens my ear to listen like one being instructed.

*—Isaiah 50:4 (NIV)*

It is now morning. The curtains have opened, and light is pouring in.

And it will remain so as long as we stand with God.

His light is greater than the darkness. His radiance eliminates the afternoon shadows and the approaching night.

When we need illumination, when the world closes in, let's return to his side. Because there it is always, always morning.

<hr />

*Lord, thank you for being a God of the morning. There is none like you, and in you there is always light. Amen.*

# THE "ACCURSED THINGS"

> And you, by all means abstain from the accursed things, lest you become accursed when you take of the accursed things, and make the camp of Israel a curse, and trouble it. . . .
>
> But the children of Israel committed a trespass regarding the accursed things, for Achan . . . took of the accursed things; so the anger of the LORD burned against the children of Israel.
>
> —*Joshua 6:18; 7:1 (NKJV)*

We have to leave "accursed things" behind.

Led by Joshua, God delivered the city of Jericho into the Israelites' hands. God just had one requirement: after the city is conquered, the Israelites should leave the "accursed things"—the idols, the spoils, the wicked items that corrupted Jericho—behind. After the victory, most of the Israelites obeyed God's command. But one man, Achan, "took of the accursed things; so the anger of the LORD burned against the children of Israel."

We have to scan our lives to see if there are items within them not of God. Are we watching, consuming, or participating in things that the enemy can use for our destruction? If so, we have to leave them behind—not only for our sake, but for our children, and our children's children.

---

*Dear God, help me leave behind the "accursed things." Break me of any dependencies, and bring me into your light. Amen.*

# EXPRESSING OUR HEARTS

God is the friend of silence. We need to find God, but we cannot find Him in noise, in excitement. See how nature—the trees, the flowers, the grass—grows in deep silence. See the stars, the moon and the sun move in silence. . . . We need this silence in order to touch souls.

—*Mother Teresa, in* Mother Teresa's Lessons of Love & Secrets of Sanctity

A fool has no delight in understanding,
    But in expressing his own heart.

—*Proverbs 18:2 (NKJV)*

We need not always express our own heart.

Some meditations are best kept there, as thoughts between us and God. Today, we seek circumspection, the ability to discern when to speak and when to be silent.

*Dear God, give me wisdom in my expressions. Help me know when to speak up and when to be silent. Amen.*

# GAMALIEL

Gamaliel was a Pharisee, a teacher of the law held in high regard. So he was the type of guy predisposed to hating the new Apostles, Peter and John, followers of the risen radical Savior, Jesus.

But when the teachers of law plotted to kill Peter and the other Apostles, Gamaliel gave a stirring speech that led to their release:

> Therefore, in the present case I advise you: Leave these men alone! Let them go! For if their purpose or activity is of human origin, it will fail. But if it is from God, you will not be able to stop these men; you will only find yourselves fighting against God.
>
> —*Acts 5:38–39 (NIV)*

When we are attacked, God will raise up advocates on our behalf. And if we're walking in his way, no weapon formed against us will prosper. In unseen rooms and behind closed doors, God has empowered our Gamaliels.

*Lord, thank you for my Gamaliels, known and unknown. Continue to raise up advocates on my behalf, and show me how to advocate for others. Amen.*

# WE, HIS CREATION

For by him all things were created, in heaven and on earth, visible and invisible, whether thrones or dominions or rulers or authorities—all things were created through him and for him.

*—Colossians 1:16 (ESV)*

I see the marks of God in the heavens and the earth, but how much more in a liberal intellect, in magnanimity, in unconquerable rectitude, in a philanthropy which forgives every wrong, and which never despairs of the cause of Christ and human virtue.

*—William Ellery Channing, "Likeness to God"*

All things are God's creation—will we live up to that label?

Will our integrity shine like a silvery pearl? Will our honesty hold firm like the oak? Will our joy ripple like the ocean's waves? Will we be as forgiving as the replenishing earth?

God expects his creation to be beautiful, and that includes us.

*Dear God, like this land that you created, let me reflect your beauty and character. Amen.*

# SHREWD SERVANTS

So the master commended the unjust steward because he had dealt shrewdly. For the sons of this world are more shrewd in their generation than the sons of light.

*—Luke 16:8 (NKJV)*

God needs shrewd soldiers in his army. Believers are not supposed to navigate the world blindly, without regard for sound business dealings and efficient process.

No, our Father wants us to be even more shrewd than the people of this world so that we can be responsible stewards of his blessings. In fair but shrewd dealings, we will see a Godly increase.

～～～

*Dear God, help me be a wise and shrewd steward of what you have blessed me with. Give me a compassionate heart and a sharp mind. Amen.*

# DON'T DWELL

The Holy Spirit would lead us to think much upon our own sins. It is a dangerous thing for us to dwell upon the imperfections of others.
—*Ichabod Spencer, in* Dictionary of Burning Words of Brilliant Writers

Therefore you are inexcusable, O man, whoever you are who judge, for in whatever you judge another you condemn yourself; for you who judge practice the same things.
—*Romans 2:1 (NKJV)*

Let's avoid judgment today.

If the same gaze we cast on others was directed at ourselves, we'd likely shiver in response. There's one who holds eternal scales and who measures righteousness and sin—and he is not us. Let's meet our brothers and sisters with the same grace with which God meets us.

~~~

*Dear God, rid me of a judging spirit. Help me remember to love others as you love me. Amen.*

# UNFORCED ERRORS

Then Satan entered Judas, surnamed Iscariot, who was numbered among the twelve. So he went his way and conferred with the chief priests and captains, how he might betray Him to them. And they were glad, and agreed to give him money. So he promised and sought opportunity to betray Him to them in the absence of the multitude.

*—Luke 22:3–6 (NKJV)*

Oftentimes, Judas Iscariot—the disciple who betrayed Jesus and led him to his death—is portrayed as a hapless character, a pawn in the hands of the powerful chief priests. But we find here in the Gospel of Luke that Judas knew exactly what he was doing. In fact, he approached the chief priests and offered them his services. They were more than glad to accept.

We all can strive to be like Jesus, but we all have Judas qualities as well. Too often the enemy does not even have to come to us; we offer ourselves to him. We walk directly into situations we know will cause us to stumble. We have enough pitfalls in our lives already; let's be careful not to be like Judas and create more for ourselves.

*Dear God, help me avoid the unforced errors of this day, the bad decisions that I am completely cognizant of. Keep me in your path. Amen.*

# GOING BIG

Whoever can be trusted with very little can also be trusted with much.

—*Luke 16:10 (NIV)*

There is a great and crying evil in modern society. It is want of purpose. It is that narrowness of vision which shuts out the wider vistas of the soul. It is the absence of those sublime emotions which, wherever they arise, do not fail to exalt and consecrate existence.

—*Felix Adler, "Address of May 15, 1876"*

It's time to go big.

Big like building a boat to survive a millennial flood.

Big like swinging a rock at the face of a giant.

Big like refusing to bow down when a fiery furnace is the likeliest fate.

Big like grasping the Savior's hand and stepping out onto raging waters.

Big like sacrificing everything for the good of the world.

We don't serve a little God. We serve a big one. And it's time for us to go big.

*Dear God, plant within me a purpose today. Ground me in it, and move me toward it. Help me go big. Amen.*

# OUR DEDICATION

King Solomon had poured his riches, his heart, his life into building a temple for the Lord. But when it was finished, here's how he dedicated it:

> But will God indeed dwell on the earth? Behold, heaven and the heaven of heavens cannot contain You. How much less this temple which I have built!
>
> —*1 Kings 8:27 (NKJV)*

King Solomon went on to ask a simple request of God: that God's eyes would "be open toward this temple" and that God would "hear the prayer which Your servant makes toward this place."

Our works will never be enough. We can't accumulate enough, build enough, love enough, serve enough to merit our place on this earth.

But here's what we can have: relationship. Relationship with the Almighty God. The creator of this world can open his eyes toward us, and hear our prayers, and commune with us. If that was enough for Solomon after all his labors, that will be more than enough for us.

---

*Dear God, I dedicate my works to you. I know they're not enough, but what I have is yours. All I ask is that you abide with me. And I will abide with you. Amen.*

# MOVE

What good is it, my brothers, if someone says he has faith but does not have works? Can that faith save him? If a brother or sister is poorly clothed and lacking in daily food, and one of you says to them, "Go in peace, be warmed and filled," without giving them the things needed for the body, what good is that? So also faith by itself, if it does not have works, is dead.

—*James 2:14–17 (ESV)*

I find the great thing in this world is not so much where we stand, as in what direction we are moving: To reach the port of heaven, we must sail sometimes with the wind and sometimes against it, but we must sail, and not drift, nor lie at anchor.

—*Oliver Wendell Holmes,* Autocrat of the Breakfast Table

We must move.

Toward God, toward justice, toward progress, toward peace.

Standing still is simply not an option. Either with the wind, or against it—today, toward God's purposes, we have to move.

~~~

*Dear God, place a fire within me. Let me not become comfortable in my current position. Help me move. Amen.*

# REMEMBER ME

Remember me, my God, for good, according to all that I have done for this people.

—*Nehemiah 5:19 (NKJV)*

---

*Remember me, my God.*

*Remember how I labored—the long, sincere hours I spent.*

*Remember how I loved those who did not love me back, how I absorbed barb after barb.*

*Remember the sacrifices—time with my family, resources, rest—that I have made in service of a larger purpose. Today, like Nehemiah, I pray that you would "remember me, my God, for good, according to all that I have done for this people." And I will always remember you. Amen.*

# JOHNNY CASH

I do not understand what I do. For what I want to do I do not do, but what I hate I do. . . . What a wretched man I am! Who will rescue me from this body that is subject to death? Thanks be to God, who delivers me through Jesus Christ our Lord!

—*Romans 7:15, 24–25 (NIV)*

Well, if they freed me from this prison,
If that railroad train was mine,
I bet I'd move it on
A little farther down the line,
Far from Folsom Prison,
That's where I want to stay,
And I'd let that lonesome whistle,
Blow my blues away.

—*Johnny Cash, "Folsom Prison Blues"*

Johnny Cash was a glutton for redemption. The country, blues, and gospel music great, the "Man in Black" and bard of working-class folks everywhere, constantly reminds us that we're all just a step away from the edge.

Perhaps that's why he spent so much time performing to inmates in prisons—*Johnny Cash at Folsom Prison* and *Johnny Cash at San Quentin* were among his most celebrated albums. Perhaps that's why he wrote lyrics that help us identify with the down and out, people who, in fits of rage or despair, unleashed harm on the world.

Whether it's by Johnny Cash or the Apostle Paul, we must be constantly reminded that we are prone to darker things. This fact should prompt forgiveness to well up within us, even when we have been wronged, because on so many occasions, it was us who did the wronging.

*Dear God, when faced with a decision to forgive or begrudge, let me choose the former. For I know that so often I am in need of forgiveness. Amen.*

# GIVE US YOUR PRESENCE

If I say, "Surely the darkness will hide me
    and the light become night around me,"
even the darkness will not be dark to you;
    the night will shine like the day,
    for darkness is as light to you.

                                 *—Psalm 139:11–12 (NIV)*

O Christ Jesus,
when all is darkness
and we feel our weakness and helplessness,
give us the sense of Your presence,
Your love, and Your strength.
Help us to have perfect trust
in Your protecting love
and strengthening power,
so that nothing may frighten or worry us,
for, living close to You,
we shall see Your hand,
Your purpose, Your will through all things.

                                    *—St. Ignatius of Loyola*

*When all is darkness, give us your presence, your purpose, and your will. Amen.*

# SEPTEMBER

## MARRIAGE

It started on the campaign trail in 2008. We were in the back of a black SUV, heading to the Saddleback Civil Forum in Orange County, California. After quizzing me on the Ten Commandments (and poking fun at my friend and his body man, Reggie Love, for not knowing all of Moses's instructions by heart), then-Senator Obama looked at me with a wry smile and said: "You know, you really should get married."

"I'm working on in, Senator, I really am. Things are going pretty well with my girlfriend . . ."

"Well, you should get married. Time for you to settle down."

It was the first of several inquisitions. There was the time we gathered in the Oval Office with a dozen faith leaders to launch the Faith-Based Advisory Council, when President Obama interrupted the proceedings to ask, "You engaged yet?"

There was Father's Day 2010, when we visited a local nonprofit, and backstage before his remarks, the president introduced me to a group of fathers and kids by saying, "And this is Joshua, my faith-based director. He's a great guy, but he's not a dad yet himself—he'll get there, if we could only get him married."

And there was the afternoon before a picnic on the White House lawn. We had invited teenage boys from local high schools to the White House, along with some famous adult mentors. I was sitting in a foyer called the Diplomatic Reception Room when President Obama walked in. Before I could begin briefing him on the event, he interrupted me. "Really, what's the holdup? Why haven't you popped the question?"

Surprised but grateful for the opportunity to have a longer conversation on the subject, I started in with a range of excuses. "Sir, I'm saving more money for a ring, and a wedding. . . . I'm waiting for the job to slow down a bit so that we have more time to spend together. . . . I'm—"

And the president interrupted me again. "Listen, Joshua. Do you love her? Do you think she'll be a great wife?"

"Well, yes. Yes sir, I do."

"Then you can't let that other stuff stop you. Marriage is the best decision you can make; it sounds trite, but it really does complete a person, rounds you out. If you've made up your mind that you want her to be your wife and the mother of your children, then that's all you need to know. You really should think about popping the question—you need to get married."

Marriage ran deep for President Obama. In fact, I came to know it as the mooring force for his life. Growing up with his grandparents and seeing their relationship firsthand, the future president embraced their marriage as an island of stability in an often-tumultuous childhood.

And when this globe-trotting, big-thinking, ambitious young man met Michelle Robinson in Chicago in the summer of 1989, his itinerant legs grew roots, and grew strong. At the end of full days then and now, navigating the world and its challenges, Michelle had a way of reminding Barack of what was most important. In photos and joint interviews that shed light on their private moments, we see the president leaning on his wife, both physically and in spirit. She is his place for replenishment, for grounding, for rest, and for joy.

I remember being on the first lady's airplane—sometimes (incorrectly) referred to as Air Force Two—heading to Nashville, Tennessee, where she was giving a speech to a large church gathering. It was the day that the United States Supreme Court was to rule on the constitutionality of the Affordable Care Act, the landmark health care bill better known as Obamacare. We were mid-flight when the telephone rang with a call for the first lady (somehow the U.S. Air Force is able to keep consistent phone service, even at 20,000 feet). The caller said that the Court had ruled in favor of the government; Obamacare was upheld. And who was ringing the first lady to share the news and celebrate? It was the president on the line, calling to rejoice with his wife.

I realized after our conversation in the foyer and after witnessing moments like the one on the first lady's plane that when it came to marriage, President Obama wasn't just chiding me for sport. Instead, he wanted me to have what he had, something so hard to find in the world of politics—a love that doesn't fade based on circumstance, an anchor for my days.

And I wanted that too. So I got to work. I heard clearly from God that Michelle (my then-girlfriend) was the one; I loved her, she was my best friend, she was brilliant, she helped me worship, and critically, she made me laugh. So I put a plan together to make the weekend of May 5, 2012, her thirtieth birthday weekend, a memorable one.

Michelle loved Yorkshire Terriers, those little, energetic (some would say maniacal) dogs. She had owned two Yorkies over the course of her life, but they had both passed away, God bless their souls. I had convinced Michelle that at that point in her life as a busy working woman living in a small D.C. apartment, it didn't make sense to get another puppy.

On May 5, we went for a stroll through Lafayette Square, a lovely oasis of statues, trees, and winding paths right across the street from the White House. A young couple was walking toward us, and as they came into view we could see that they were leading an adorable Yorkshire puppy, tripping over himself on a short leash.

Michelle knelt down to pet the dog—as I knew she would—and gushed over him. "It's beautiful!" she said to the couple, whom she did not recognize. "Where'd you get him? How old is he?"

The man walking the puppy replied, "Well actually, it's yours."

She looked up at him and then me, absolutely confused. "What? My dog?"

I chimed in, "Hun, I got you a dog for your birthday—it's your dog."

Shrieks ensued. After the young couple walked away and she had a few moments to pet him, I asked, "What's that around the dog's collar?"

Michelle ignored me at first, so I asked again. "Babe, is there something around his collar?"

She turned the dog's collar around . . . and there was the engagement ring.

Michelle's eyes watered, and I bent down on one knee, and told her what she meant to me, and how honored I would be if she would agree to be my wife. And she said, "Yes."

It was an amazing weekend; we celebrated that evening and on Sunday with family and friends. On Monday, I had to travel to New York for a previously scheduled speech, and on the way there, I received a call from a blocked number on my cell phone.

"Mr. DuBois, the president is on the line for you. Do you have time to speak?"

There's only one answer to that question—"Yes, of course."

President Obama joined the line and got right to it.

"So you did it! I'm proud of you. That's the best decision you will ever make. And I have to say—it's about time."

I agreed with him on both points. It has proven to be the best decision I ever made. And yes, it was about time.

# HERE TO WORK

Whatever you do, work heartily, as for the Lord and not for men.
—*Colossians 3:23 (ESV)*

There's a story told about the American Revolution and a group of soldiers who were found on a road working to repair a small fortification that had fallen apart. The group's commander was lording over them, shouting instructions but making no attempt to help. A stranger went past and asked the commander why he wasn't helping. The commander replied, "Sir, I am a corporal!" The stranger then stooped down with the men, and lent a hand.

After the job was completed, the stranger turned to the corporal and said, "Mr. Corporal, next time you have a job like this and not enough men to do it, go to your commander in chief, and I will come and help you again." The corporal then recognized that the stranger was General George Washington.

As General Washington shows us, in the face of work to do, we must never think so highly of ourselves that we're afraid to get our hands dirty. The fact remains that God's purposes must be accomplished and we must work "as for the Lord and not for men."

———

*Dear God, give me a spirit of diligence in all tasks, large or small. In doing so, let me set an example for others. Amen.*

# MORAL LEADERSHIP

Now Nadab the son of Jeroboam became king over Israel in the second year of Asa king of Judah, and he reigned over Israel two years. And he did evil in the sight of the LORD, and walked in the way of his father, and in his sin by which he had made Israel sin.

—*1 Kings 15:25–26 (NKJV)*

Just as King Solomon's peace filtered out through all the land, bringing Israel into a season of progress, so King Nadab's sin led all of Israel astray. "And in his sin by which he had made Israel sin."

God reminds us that our moral leadership matters. As we walk uprightly, so will our family, our friends, and those who follow us. When we stray, others are more likely to do so. Let us be more like Solomon than Nadab and avoid leading others into sin.

*Dear God, keep me reminded of the example I set. Let my character and integrity make me a model for those looking on. Amen.*

# WHY WE WORK

The worker must work for the glory of his handiwork, not simply for pay; the thinker must think for truth, not for fame.

—*W. E. B. DuBois,* The Souls of Black Folk

Whatever you do, work at it with all your heart, as working for the Lord, not for human masters, since you know that you will receive an inheritance from the Lord as a reward. It is the Lord Christ you are serving.

—*Colossians 3:23–24 (NIV)*

The same God who knit us together in our mother's womb, who formed our emotions and character and innate worth, who orchestrated our lives up until this point—that God placed us where we are today. In our jobs, in our families, in this place.

There are some moments when the light of that purpose burns clear and bright but others when we can barely discern it through the fog. Regardless, we must work "as working for the Lord." Serving a heavenly Christ, even through our earthly tasks.

*Dear God, help me work for the right reasons—not for man's purposes, but for yours. Amen.*

# A MOMENT FOR WORSHIP

The floods have lifted up, O LORD,
   The floods have lifted up their voice;
   The floods lift up their waves.
The LORD on high is mightier
   Than the noise of many waters,
   Than the mighty waves of the sea.

*—Psalm 93:3–4 (NKJV)*

There are moments just right for worship.

When we recall how far God has brought us, over the winding roads behind.

When we open our eyes wide and see the fullness of his blessings, the gifts he's bestowed that are so often hidden in the shadows of our busy days.

We should sit in that gratitude. Reside in his goodness. And after it settles in, let's imitate the organs of his creation—the floods, the waters, the mighty waves—and praise his name.

*Thank you, God. Thank you for blessing me. Amen.*

# WAITING LIKE DAVID

The Yiddish mentality is not haughty. It does not take victory for granted. It does not demand and command but it muddles through, sneaks by, smuggles itself amidst the powers of destruction, knowing somewhere that God's plan for Creation is still at the very beginning.
—*Isaac Bashevis Singer, Nobel lecture*

So David and Abishai went to the army by night, and there was Saul, lying asleep inside the camp with his spear stuck in the ground near his head. Abner and the soldiers were lying around him.

Abishai said to David, "Today God has delivered your enemy into your hands. Now let me pin him to the ground with one thrust of the spear; I won't strike him twice."

But David said to Abishai, "Don't destroy him! Who can lay a hand on the LORD's anointed and be guiltless? As surely as the LORD lives," he said, "the LORD himself will strike him, or his time will come and he will die, or he will go into battle and perish. But the LORD forbid that I should lay a hand on the LORD's anointed."
—*1 Samuel 26:7–11 (NIV)*

Saul, David's former mentor and present tormentor, was within David's grasp. Saul was sleeping within mere feet of David, ready to be slain, and David's aggressive servant, Abishai, declared: Let me at him!

But David said: Wait. Whatever happens to Saul will happen. Who am I, David declared, to get ahead of God's plan? God has a purpose for every single person on this earth—even our enemies. It is not our job to stand in the way. We may be tempted in the coming days to drive the knife in, and then deeper, perhaps deservedly so. But the great ones—like David, like Christ—show grace. And let God work out the rest.

*Dear Lord, help me not only forgive my enemies but also show to them life-giving grace. I trust you, fully, to work out the rest. Amen.*

# A COLOSSIANS PRAYER

A prayer for today:

> Let the peace of Christ rule in your hearts, to which indeed you were
> called in one body; and be thankful. Let the word of Christ richly
> dwell within you, with all wisdom teaching and admonishing one
> another with psalms and hymns and spiritual songs, singing with
> thankfulness in your hearts to God. Whatever you do in word or
> deed, do all in the name of the Lord Jesus, giving thanks through
> Him to God the Father.
>
> —*Colossians 3:15–17 (NAS)*

*Amen.*

# THE GREAT EQUALIZERS

Then Peter opened his mouth and said: "In truth I perceive that God shows no partiality. But in every nation whoever fears Him and works righteousness is accepted by Him."

*—Acts 10:34–35 (NKJV)*

The book of Acts tells us that the fear of God and work of righteousness are the great equalizers.

All of us who labor together in his vineyard, seeking to create greater justice and love in the world, are equal to one another and accepted by God.

We live in a world of brothers and sisters. Everywhere we go, there are allies in the fight. That fact should encourage us, as we thank God for those in each nation who are serving him, and serving each other.

---

*Dear God, thank you for the fact that the works of righteousness know no boundaries. Connect me with brothers and sisters around the world who share the same goals. Amen.*

# RULES OF THE ROAD

On one occasion an expert in the law stood up to test Jesus. "Teacher," he asked, "what must I do to inherit eternal life?"

"What is written in the Law?" he replied. "How do you read it?"

He answered, " 'Love the Lord your God with all your heart and with all your soul and with all your strength and with all your mind'; and, 'Love your neighbor as yourself.' "

"You have answered correctly," Jesus replied. "Do this and you will live."

*—Luke 10:25–28 (NIV)*

There's a story about the greatest (and most self-assured) boxer of all time, Muhammad Ali, aboard an airplane that was about to take off. Ignoring the intercom, Ali did not fasten his seatbelt. A flight attendant came by and asked him to buckle up, to which Ali replied, "Superman don't need no seatbelt!" The attendant shot back, "Mr. Ali, Superman don't need no airplane, either." Ali laughed and buckled up.

As Ali learned, there are certain inviolable rules of the road.

For believers, Jesus makes these rules simple, and every one of us, to a person, needs them in order to fly: love God with all your heart, soul, and mind. And then, love your neighbor—but not with just any love. Love your neighbor *as much as you love yourself.*

We must buckle ourselves up in each of these simple rules, every day.

※

*Dear God, plant within me your decrees, particularly the ones you called most important: loving you and loving my neighbor. Amen.*

# BRING OUR SINS TO HIM

Suppose one of you has a hundred sheep and loses one of them. Doesn't he leave the ninety-nine in the open country and go after the lost sheep until he finds it? And when he finds it, he joyfully puts it on his shoulders and goes home. Then he calls his friends and neighbors together and says, "Rejoice with me; I have found my lost sheep." I tell you that in the same way there will be more rejoicing in heaven over one sinner who repents than over ninety-nine righteous persons who do not need to repent.

*—Luke 15:4–7 (NIV)*

Not only does God refuse to condemn us for our sins—he rejoices when we bring them to him!

He's not a God who loves the righteous—because none are righteous, none.

He's not a God who values those who have it all together, because who among us really does?

No, Jesus tells us in the book of Luke that when a sinner comes before him and repents, a party is thrown in heaven, and the heavenly hosts rejoice!

Won't we give him a moment of levity, and bring our sins to him? He's waiting, and ready to shout for joy.

*Dear God, I confess my sins to you today, the ways that I have fallen short of your purpose. I rejoice with you that I am forgiven, even now. Amen.*

# GLORIFY YOUR NAME

Now My soul is troubled, and what shall I say? "Father, save Me from this hour"? But for this purpose I came to this hour. Father, glorify Your name.

*—John 12:27–28 (NKJV)*

The chief purpose of life, for any of us, is to increase according to our capacity our knowledge of God by all means we have, and to be moved by it to praise and thanks.

*—J. R. R. Tolkien,* Myth, Morality, and Religion

"Father, glorify Your name." At the end of the day—that's it, isn't it?

Will the sum of our actions, our collective strivings, our hopes and dreams and daily machinations—will they bring glory to God? Do they reflect the light of his glory into this darkened world?

Jesus could press through his greatest moments of agony because he knew that the answer to that question was "yes." He did not ask God to save him from the cross. He did not ask for safety, or riches, or comfort. His only requested was "Father, glorify Your name."

Let that be our prayer today as well. *Amen.*

# GOD BURIED MOSES

> So Moses the servant of the LORD died there in the land of Moab, according to the word of the LORD. And He buried him in a valley in the land of Moab, opposite Beth Peor; but no one knows his grave to this day.
>
> —*Deuteronomy 34:5–6 (NKJV)*

The God of the universe came down and buried Moses. I had never noticed this verse before—it stopped me in my tracks.

Moses, who rose from a son of a slave to the most important leader in all of ancient Israel; who spoke with God and carried his commandments; who knew failure, anger, and disappointment. When he died, Moses had such an intimacy with God that God himself came down. God held Moses's lifeless body and dug his grave. Perhaps he even said words of remembrance. And then, when it was time for his mortal frame to be put to rest, God buried Moses.

Let us have a sliver of that legacy. When we pass from this world into the next, let the loss of our presence on this earth be such that in our final moments, even God comes down. *Amen.*

# ON WASHING FEET

Jesus, knowing that the Father had given all things into His hands, and that He had come from God and was going to God, rose from supper and laid aside His garments, took a towel and girded Himself. After that, He poured water into a basin and began to wash the disciples' feet, and to wipe them with the towel with which He was girded. Then He came to Simon Peter. And Peter said to Him, "Lord, are You washing my feet?"

Jesus answered and said to him, "What I am doing you do not understand now, but you will know after this."

Peter said to Him, "You shall never wash my feet!"

Jesus answered him, "If I do not wash you, you have no part with Me."

—*John 13:3–8 (NKJV)*

They serve God well,
Who serve his creatures.
—*Caroline Elizabeth S. Norton, "The Lady of La Garaye"*

Service rounds out relationship.

Leaders speak, leaders command, leaders cast visions, and leaders implement plans. But it is not until a leader has humbled him- or herself to the point of service—even bending down and washing a follower's feet—that the leader and follower become one.

How will we serve today? How can we stoop down before the people who always support us? How can we let them know that we care—that we're not too big to serve?

—◦◦◦◦◦—

*Dear God, give me a servant's heart. Show me whose feet I must wash—and give me the courage to do it. Amen.*

# LEADING LIKE SOLOMON

And Judah and Israel dwelt safely, each man under his vine and his fig tree, from Dan as far as Beersheba, all the days of Solomon.

*—1 Kings 4:25 (NKJV)*

*Lord, help me to lead like Solomon, son of David—bringing peace to my domain. Use me to ease tensions and increase provisions for those who have least.*

*Bring safety all around me, particularly to those who are most insecure. And let my legacy be like the land of Israel under wise Solomon:*

And Judah and Israel dwelt safely, each man under his vine and his fig tree, from Dan as far as Beersheba, all the days of Solomon.

*Amen.*

# NO LABELS

Once there was this man who had two sons. One day the younger son came to his father and said, "Father, eventually I'm going to inherit my share of your estate. Rather than waiting until you die, I want you to give me my share now." And so the father liquidated assets and divided them. A few days passed and this younger son gathered all his wealth and set off on a journey to a distant land. Once there he wasted everything he owned on wild living. He was broke, a terrible famine struck that land, and he felt desperately hungry and in need. He got a job with one of the locals, who sent him into the fields to feed the pigs. The young man felt so miserably hungry that he wished he could eat the slop the pigs were eating. Nobody gave him anything.

So he had this moment of self-reflection: "What am I doing here? Back home, my father's hired servants have plenty of food. Why am I here starving to death? I'll get up and return to my father, and I'll say, 'Father, I have done wrong—wrong against God and against you. I have forfeited any right to be treated like your son, but I'm wondering if you'd treat me as one of your hired servants?'" So he got up and returned to his father. The father looked off in the distance and saw the young man returning. He felt compassion for his son and ran out to him, enfolded him in an embrace, and kissed him.

The son said, "Father, I have done a terrible wrong in God's sight and in your sight too. I have forfeited any right to be treated as your son."

But the father turned to his servants and said, "Quick! Bring the best robe we have and put it on him. Put a ring on his finger and shoes on his feet. Go get the fattest calf and butcher it. Let's have a feast and celebrate because my son was dead and is alive again. He was lost and has been found."

*—Luke 15:11–24 (The Voice translation)*

This story is often known as the tale of the prodigal son—but interestingly, that particular phrase is found nowhere in the Bible. Instead, scripture describes the son's "prodigal *living.*" His actions were sinful—but the son himself—*he* was not prodigal. He was just . . . a son.

We have to be careful not to label those who are sinful—and we should refrain from putting labels on ourselves as well. We are children of God, simple as that. We may stray, even severely, but we are still his daughters and sons.  And to him we can always return.

*Dear God, help me avoid placing labels on others and on myself. Remind me that we are all sinners who encounter your grace. And to you we can always return. Amen.*

# RESURRECTION

Martha said to Him, "I know that he will rise again in the resurrection at the last day."

Jesus said to her, "I am the resurrection and the life. He who believes in Me, though he may die, he shall live."

—*John 11:24–25 (NKJV)*

Up out of this sea, expectancy rises reborn again and sees heaven open—reborn.

—*Søren Kierkegaard,* Eighteen Upbuilding Discourses

Martha's brother Lazarus had died four days earlier. Before his death, Martha called to Jesus to save him, but Jesus came too late. Still, Martha believed. She declared that God's will would be done, if not now, then in the future, on that great Resurrection Day. And Jesus said in response: Martha, today is your resurrection. In me, there is life, each day. And then Jesus called Lazarus forth into life.

Our Lord is telling us: today is our resurrection.

In Christ, we are renewed, every day. The old things, the broken things, the depressed and dead things, are behind us. Through the blessing of an intimate relationship with our eternal God, this flesh of ours perishes each morning and our spirit is renewed. A personal springtime. A fresh awakening. Our resurrection.

---

*Dear God, I humbly accept my renewal. Let me believe in your ability to restore. Put the old things behind me, and move me forward into my resurrection day. Amen.*

# EARNEST PRAYER

And He was withdrawn from them about a stone's throw, and He
knelt down and prayed, saying, "Father, if it is Your will, take this
cup away from Me; nevertheless not My will, but Yours, be done."
Then an angel appeared to Him from heaven, strengthening Him.
And being in agony, He prayed more earnestly. Then His sweat
became like great drops of blood falling down to the ground.
—*Luke 22:41–44 (NKJV)*

Like Jesus, let's increase the earnestness of our prayers.

Let's throw away all conceits, all traditional words and lofty praises.

Bring God our hopes, our worship, our pain.

Let's pour it out to him, like Christ in the garden.

God will strengthen us when we seek him earnestly; he will honor our
prayers.

—∽∾∽—

*Dear God, I remove all pretense and bring these thoughts to you: _____.*
*Amen.*

# GREATER WORKS

We are but as the instrument of heaven.
Our work is not design, but destiny.
>           —*Owen Meredith, "Clytemnestra"*

Most assuredly, I say to you, he who believes in Me, the works that I do he will do also; and greater works than these he will do, because I go to My Father.
>           —*John 14:12 (NKJV)*

Jesus left a lot to do, here on earth. And he intends for us to do it.

Today is not meant for trivial tasks. It is not to be consumed with consumption or used up with self-glorification. No, it's time to take things up a notch. To serve more. To love more of the unloved. To build more temples to God's glory here on earth. "He who believes in Me, the works that I do he will do also; and greater works than these."

It's not a day for the mundane, for the usual, for less. It's a day for greater, and greater, and greater works.

—∞∞∞—

*God, let me be a striver. Help me reach not toward my own high calling but toward yours. And in your name, let me accomplish great things. Amen.*

# SOMEONE ELSE'S PROPERTY

So if you have not been trustworthy in handling worldly wealth, who will trust you with true riches? And if you have not been trustworthy with someone else's property, who will give you property of your own?

—*Luke 16:11–12 (NIV)*

We must be faithful, even with things that are not our own.

Places where we live, items we borrow, temporary situations in which we find ourselves.

Acknowledging that all good things come from God, let's take great care to honor the possessions in our hands, even if they don't belong to us.

---

*Dear God, let me treat each temporary possession as if it were my own. Because I know that all good and perfect things come from you. Amen.*

# IN ALL THINGS, LOVE

Give us courage and gaiety and the quiet mind. Spare to us our friends, soften to us our enemies. Bless us, if it may be, in all our innocent endeavors. If it may not, give us the strength to encounter that which is to come, that we be brave in peril, constant in tribulation, temperate in wrath, and in all changes of fortune and down to the gates of death, loyal and loving one to another.

—*Robert Louis Stevenson, "For Success"*

If I speak in the tongues of men or of angels, but do not have love, I am only a resounding gong or a clanging cymbal. If I have the gift of prophecy and can fathom all mysteries and all knowledge, and if I have a faith that can move mountains, but do not have love, I am nothing. If I give all I possess to the poor and give over my body to hardship that I may boast, but do not have love, I gain nothing.

Love is patient, love is kind. It does not envy, it does not boast, it is not proud. It does not dishonor others, it is not self-seeking, it is not easily angered, it keeps no record of wrongs. Love does not delight in evil but rejoices with the truth. It always protects, always trusts, always hopes, always perseveres.

Love never fails. But where there are prophecies, they will cease; where there are tongues, they will be stilled; where there is knowledge, it will pass away. For we know in part and we prophesy in part, but when completeness comes, what is in part disappears. When I was a child, I talked like a child, I thought like a child, I reasoned like a child. When I became a man, I put the ways of childhood behind me. For now we see only a reflection as in a mirror; then we shall see face to face. Now I know in part; then I shall know fully, even as I am fully known.

And now these three remain: faith, hope and love. But the greatest of these is love.

—*1 Corinthians 13 (NIV)*

❧

*Amen.*

# WE POINT BACK

Jesus had ascended into heaven, but his disciples were still on the move. Peter and John had just healed a disabled man outside the gate called "Beautiful," and the crowd marveled, wondering how they'd done it. Peter's reply was powerful, and telling:

> He responded to the people: "Men of Israel, why do you marvel at this? Or why look so intently at us, as though by our own power or godliness we had made this man walk? The God of Abraham, Isaac, and Jacob, the God of our fathers, glorified His Servant Jesus, whom you delivered up and denied in the presence of Pilate, when he was determined to let Him go. But you denied the Holy One and the Just, and asked for a murderer to be granted to you, and killed the Prince of life, whom God raised from the dead, of which we are witnesses. And His name, through faith in His name, has made this man strong, whom you see and know. Yes, the faith which comes through Him has given him this perfect soundness in the presence of you all."
>
> —*Acts 3:12–16 (NKJV)*

"His name . . . has made this man strong."

In this stirring speech, Peter and John gave glory to God, to the "Prince of life." When we reach our moments of acclaim, let's remember to do the same.

*Dear God, after all my strivings, all my work, all my victories, I will point back to the source. I will point back to you. Amen.*

# TAKE TO THE OARS

If the wind will not serve, take to the oars.

*—Latin proverb*

Then Samson said,
    "With a donkey's jawbone
       I have made donkeys of them.
    With a donkey's jawbone
       I have killed a thousand men."

*—Judges 15:16 (NIV)*

We seek an improvising spirit. We may not have it all; circumstances may not have aligned exactly as we would have chosen. But what God has given us, that's what we'll use. To serve his people. To build. To grow. To love.

Like Samson, we seek an improving spirit. And, "If the wind will not serve, take to the oars."

———∞∞∞———

*God, grant me ingenuity and flexibility. Let me use whatever is around me to accomplish your purposes. This I pray in Jesus's name. Amen.*

# WORTH IT

Love anything and your heart will certainly be wrung and possibly broken. If you want to make sure of keeping it intact you must give it to no one, not even an animal. Wrap it carefully round with hobbies and little luxuries, avoid all entanglements, lock it up safe in the casket or coffin of your selfishness. But in that casket—safe, dark, motionless, airless—it will change. It will not be broken; it will become unbreakable, impenetrable, irredeemable.

—*C. S. Lewis, "To Love Is to Be Vulnerable"*

Then Jesus went with his disciples to a place called Gethsemane, and he said to them, "Sit here while I go over there and pray." He took Peter and the two sons of Zebedee along with him, and he began to be sorrowful and troubled. Then he said to them, "My soul is overwhelmed with sorrow to the point of death. Stay here and keep watch with me."

—*Matthew 26:36–38 (NIV)*

The flip side of a child's laughter is the hollow ache we feel when they're gone. The sweet comfort we derive from a spouse's closeness is in direct proportion to the cold, stinging distance that hits us when things aren't right.

When we pay full price for love, we do receive that love in full, but we also receive pain as change. It's built into the equation; no less than our Savior has shown us that, as he agonized in these verses over his coming death. But he also shows us love is worth the pain.

⁓∘∾∘⁓

*Lord, keep watch with me when love seems distant; stay near when it returns. Amen.*

# A FUTURE NOT OUR OWN

It helps, now and then, to step back and take a long view.
The kingdom is not only beyond our efforts, it is beyond our vision.
We accomplish in our lifetime only a tiny fraction of the magnificent enterprise that is God's work.
Nothing we do is complete, which is another way of saying that the kingdom always lies beyond us.
No statement says all that could be said.
No prayer fully expresses our faith.
No confession brings perfection.
No pastoral visit brings wholeness.
No program accomplishes the Church's mission.
No set of goals and objectives includes everything.
This is what we are about:
We plant the seeds that one day will grow.
We water the seeds already planted, knowing that they hold future promise.
We lay foundations that will need further development.
We provide yeast that produces effects beyond our capabilities.
We cannot do everything, and there is a sense of liberation in realizing that.
This enables us to do something, and to do it very well.
It may be incomplete, but it is a beginning, a step along the way,
an opportunity for God's grace to enter and do the rest.
We may never see the end results,
but that is the difference between the master builder and the worker.
We are workers, not master builders, ministers, not messiahs.
We are prophets of a future not our own.

—*Bishop Kenneth Untener,*
*"Prophets of a Future Not Our Own"*

*Dear God, remind me of my own limits. Help me not seek to do everything, but to do something for your people and your kingdom. In this limiting, liberating reality, let me be set free. Amen.*

# SITUATIONAL OBEDIENCE

He answered, "Then I beg you, father, send Lazarus to my family, for I have five brothers. Let him warn them, so that they will not also come to this place of torment."

Abraham replied, "They have Moses and the Prophets; let them listen to them."

"No, father Abraham," he said, "but if someone from the dead goes to them, they will repent."

He said to him, "If they do not listen to Moses and the Prophets, they will not be convinced even if someone rises from the dead."

—*Luke 16:27–31 (NIV)*

So often we think that if God does one more miracle—answers one more request—then, we'll trust him and obey. "Just prove yourself one more time, Lord," we say. "Show me evidence of your power on this occasion, and I'll never forget it."

But it doesn't work that way. Jesus told a story of a man burning in hell, who begged Father Abraham to allow him to return to earth and warn his brothers so that they would avoid the same fate. Abraham declined the man's request because Abraham knew that even if these brothers saw their own resurrected sibling, they still would not change their ways.

We must avoid making our obedience situational, dependent on some miraculous action of God. Either we belong to him and follow his instructions, or we don't. Let's not make God prove his worth.

*Dear God, my love and obedience for you is not dependent on any particular blessing. You are more than my provider—you are my Father. And I will love you as such. Amen.*

# OUR BEST STRENGTH

*Success is . . . knowing that you did your best to become the best that you are capable of becoming.*
—*Coach John Wooden,* Coach Wooden One-on-One

*When Joab saw that the battle line was against him before and behind, he chose some of Israel's best and put them in battle array against the Syrians. . . . Then he said, "If the Syrians are too strong for me, then you shall help me; but if the people of Ammon are too strong for you, then I will come and help you. Be of good courage, and let us be strong for our people and for the cities of our God. And may the LORD do what is good in His sight."*
—*2 Samuel 10:9–12 (NKJV)*

Let's put our best effort on the field today, and let God take care of the rest.

Joab did as much. The Syrians, his mortal enemies, were on one side, and the Ammonites were on another. Joab was in a tough spot, but he controlled what was in his power to control: his courage, his team, his strength. "Be of good courage, and let us be strong for our people and for the cities of our God. And may the LORD do what is good in His sight."

*Let that be our prayer today. And like Joab, we will overcome. Amen.*

# WELLNESS

As he was going into a village, ten men who had leprosy met him. They stood at a distance and called out in a loud voice, "Jesus, Master, have pity on us!"

When he saw them, he said, "Go, show yourselves to the priests." And as they went, they were cleansed.

One of them, when he saw he was healed, came back, praising God in a loud voice. He threw himself at Jesus' feet and thanked him—and he was a Samaritan.

Jesus asked, "Were not all ten cleansed? Where are the other nine? Has no one returned to give praise to God except this foreigner?" Then he said to him, "Rise and go; your faith has made you well."

*—Luke 17:12–19 (NIV)*

Ten lepers met Jesus on the road to Jerusalem. They cried out for healing, and Jesus responded, making them clean: "And as they went, they were *cleansed.*"

After they were healed, only one of the former lepers came back to Christ to give him thanks. Jesus said, "Were not all ten cleansed? Where are the other nine? Has no one returned to give praise to God except this foreigner? . . . Rise and go; your faith has made you *well.*"

Jesus shows that there's a difference between temporary cleansing and permanent wellness. We can keep going back to God to "fix" us, to remedy our immediate circumstances, and then go on our way. Or we can return to him, lay our lives at his feet, and give him glory.

The former practice will make us temporarily clean. But the latter makes us *well.*

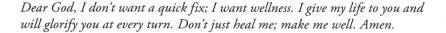

*Dear God, I don't want a quick fix; I want wellness. I give my life to you and will glorify you at every turn. Don't just heal me; make me well. Amen.*

# MORE TO COME

However, as it is written:
"What no eye has seen,
   what no ear has heard,
and what no human mind has conceived"—
   the things God has prepared for those who love him.
                                    —*1 Corinthians 2:9 (NIV)*

It is astounding how much of our story is yet unwritten.

In the Bible, the great forefather Abraham was seventy years old when God commanded him to leave his home and begin his journey to the Promised Land. His wife Sarah was ninety years old when she gave birth to Isaac, cementing her own legacy and place among the giants. Fannie Lou Hamer was born in 1917, but she remained a poor sharecropper, working the fields of Mississippi until 1962. It took forty-five years for her legend to come about, for something to stir within that began her civil rights activism.

The narrative of our lives has been fascinating up until now; there has been no shortage of twists and turns. But we serve a God who still surprises—and it may be that the greatest of our stories is yet to come. We must be ever watchful, living in a spirit of holiness that enables God to use us, and with expectant minds, looking for a change in plot, a brand-new theme, or an unforgettable conclusion.

———

*Dear God, give me the joy of hopefulness. Use me to paint your narrative in the world. I am patient and grateful for the story you have given me, but I am open to a new chapter as well. Amen.*

# LOYALTY

> Then Saul said to his servants who stood about him, "Hear now, you Benjamites! Will the son of Jesse give every one of you fields and vineyards, and make you all captains of thousands and captains of hundreds? All of you have conspired against me."
>
> —*1 Samuel 22:7–8 (NKJV)*

King Saul was in hot pursuit of David, God's chosen leader of Israel. Saul burned with jealous rage because of David's triumphs and would do anything to take David down.

In these verses we find Saul angry because those loyal to David would not give him up, even if they obtained "fields and vineyards" and became "captains of thousands." Saul foolishly thought that he could bribe the Israelites into loyalty to him rather than to their beloved David.

We learn from these verses that the loyalty of those around us—our loved ones, our family, our friends—is not gained through what we can give to them or do for them. It is established through the way we love them. David knew this and loved his people deeply, thereby engendering great devotion. King Saul never figured this out, and he brooded in isolation, jealousy, and fear.

―∞∞∞―

*Dear God, let me never "purchase" love; rather, let me earn it through the love that I show. Amen.*

# NINA SIMONE

Birds flying high, you know how I feel
Sun in the sky, you know how I feel
Breeze drifting on by, you know how I feel
It's a new dawn!
It's a new day!
It's a new life for me
And I'm feeling good.

*—Nina Simone, "Feeling Good"*

The great America jazz singer Nina Simone has a funny song called "Feeling Good." It has a driving, ominous beat—think: the feverishly dark rhythm of "Hit the Road, Jack." One could imagine the bass line playing in a movie—a mafia flick right before the hit job or when the main character, in a moment of despair, is contemplating a leap from the Golden Gate Bridge. And that rhythmic context is exactly why the upbeat lyrics are so jarring. With dark music surrounding her words . . . why is Nina feeling good?

The contrast reminds me of David in Psalm 59. David first writes fearfully, of stalkers and invaders camped around him.

See how they lie in wait for me!
    Fierce men conspire against me
    for no offense or sin of mine, LORD. . . .
They return at evening,
    snarling like dogs,
    and prowl about the city.
They wander about for food
    and howl if not satisfied.

But, counterintuitively, he concludes,

I will sing of your strength,
    in the morning I will sing of your love;

for you are my fortress,
  my refuge in times of trouble.
You are my strength, I sing praise to you;
  you, God, are my fortress.

—*Psalm 59:3, 14–15, 16–17, (NIV)*

Nina Simone and David remind us of one unimpeachable fact: whatever situations we face, the lyrics we sing today are completely up to us. We can choose to shout above the din outside our window and sing louder than the ominous noise approaching our lives. We can worship God today. We can love today, even when it's tough. We can take control of our song, our Psalm.

—◦◦◦—

*Dear God, let me be a composer. Even though dark rhythms may emerge around me, help me write my own song. Amen.*

# ESTABLISH THE WORK OF OUR HANDS

Let Your work appear to Your servants,
    And Your glory to their children.
    And let the beauty of the LORD our God be upon us,
And establish the work of our hands for us;
    Yes, establish the work of our hands.

—*Psalm 90:16–17 (NKJV)*

The Psalm says, "Let the beauty of the LORD our God be upon us, and establish the work of our hands." A plea for beauty, and a call for work.

Let it be so today. Let the Spirit of God within us come out of us, not just to accomplish tasks but to manifest beauty in the world. Let the work of our hands be both useful and inspirational, fulfilling a purpose and beckoning the world to him.

~∞~

*"Let the beauty of the LORD our God be upon us, and establish the work of our hands." Amen.*

# OCTOBER

## NO SPIN

Sitting around a large conference table, I was genuinely convinced that the Obama campaign would fail, the world would end, and it would be my fault.

Dramatic, I know. But in that moment in downtown Chicago, I really thought life as I knew it was over.

A few days earlier, the *Wall Street Journal* had broken one heck of a story. Senator Obama's pastor, Reverend Jeremiah Wright, was caught on video hurling a series of statements that flew in the face of most notions of patriotism and decorum. Other news outlets picked up the statements, and in a matter of a day, the controversy snowballed nearly out of control.

As the "faith guy," the president's spiritual advisor and the person in charge of faith-based outreach, I thought that managing this disaster was supposed to be my problem. In my head, if the president lost the election because of this, as many were suggesting, it would be my fault.

I had a short but intense history with Reverend Wright. Starting from the beginning of the campaign, I spent time in his private study and his church, getting to know him and his family. I knew he was very progressive, fiery even, with a heart for mentoring black pastors around the country. But I had no idea that he had spoken the specific statements from that famous video, and I knew that Senator Obama was not aware of those remarks, either.

By the end of a difficult week, Obama thought it was time to issue a statement to the American people, explaining the issue directly. My job that evening was to sit around a table with two of the sentator's most senior advisers—much more senior than I—and write a first draft of his statement to the nation. The three of us were supposed to encapsulate thoughts about race, religious divides, patriotism, and politics in a few paragraphs that would ultimately explain how a man's pastor could say such things. To say I felt the pressure was an understatement.

With a pen and paper and a couple of laptops, we tried, and tried again. After a few rounds of edits, we had a passable statement that sought to put the best possible light on Reverend Wright, Senator Obama, and the issue at hand. It didn't tell the whole truth, but it didn't lie. It left a healthy political gloss on the facts, just enough to try to put this whole ordeal behind us. The statement wasn't perfect, but we thought it would work.

And then, Senator Obama walked in. He read our draft quickly, then read it again. And he then said something I will never forget: "Guys, I appreciate what you tried to do here. I know you gave it your best shot. But here's the thing: in times like this, you just can't—I mean, you really cannot—'spin.' You have to tell the truth."

He continued: "The bottom line is, my pastor said some things I disagree with. I was a very busy man over the last few years, and I was not in church nearly as much as I should have been. I didn't hear him say these things, but that doesn't take away from what he said.

"At the end of the day, we have to be honest with the American people. If they know what Reverend Wright said and decide that it disqualifies me from the presidency, then so be it. But if they think that my character and my vision are more important than my pastor's sermons, then they will elect me.

"But it's up to them. And it's up to us to tell the truth so that they can make their decision. In times like this—you just can't spin."

Senator Obama then took out his pen and rewrote the statement. He was honest about his feelings for his pastor, and about the things Reverend Wright had said. We issued the statement later that evening, and it helped a bit. The senator later expounded on his initial statement in a speech in Philadelphia on race in America, a courageous address, one that I will never forget. In that speech, he addressed not only Reverend Wright but also deep issues of race and class in our country, divides that had existed for generations.

When his Philadelphia speech was over, Senator Obama e-mailed me a note that simply said when it came to handling this tough issue of race, religion, and Reverend Wright, "I'm proud of you." He had no idea how proud *I* was of *him*. And by Election Day, the American people had affirmed his approach and elected him to the highest office in the land.

Whenever I was faced with difficult issues and controversy in the months and years that followed, I always tried to remember the core lesson from that conference room. In the toughest times, when our backs are absolutely against the wall, when our own fates, or our families', or even—as in this case—the country's hang in the balance, we have to approach issues with full honesty and integrity. Half-measures of truth are not enough; our character and our God demand much more. When it's all on the line—"you just can't spin."

# MARIAN ANDERSON

Nobody knows the trouble I've seen
Nobody knows my sorrow
Nobody knows the trouble I've seen
Glory, hallelujah!
*—Traditional Negro spiritual, made famous by Marian Anderson*

Jesus answered them, "Do you now believe? Indeed the hour is coming, yes, has now come, that you will be scattered, each to his own, and will leave Me alone. And yet I am not alone, because the Father is with Me. These things I have spoken to you, that in Me you may have peace. In the world you will have tribulation; but be of good cheer, I have overcome the world."

*—John 16:31–33 (NKJV)*

Trouble comes first, but triumph has the last laugh. Jesus knew this, and Marian Anderson knew it as well.

The great African American contralto—one of the most celebrated singers of the twentieth century of any race—was used to trouble. In 1939, she hoped to perform for an integrated audience at the Daughters of the American Revolution (DAR) Constitution Hall in Washington, D.C., but was quickly rebuffed by the DAR. Undeterred, Ms. Anderson scheduled her own open-air concert on the steps of the Lincoln Memorial with some help from Eleanor Roosevelt. The concert—to seventy-five thousand enraptured listeners and over a million tuning in on the radio—was a sensation. Like the Negro spiritual she made famous, for Ms. Anderson, what started with "trouble" ended with, "Glory, hallelujah."

Jesus said as much in John 16. Our days will be winding and some nights will be long. In those moments, it is incumbent upon us to "be of good cheer." For Christ, our Savior, has "overcome the world."

*Dear God, bring forth within me the courage of the spirit of Christ. Let me remember that at the end of my trouble is a "glory, hallelujah." Amen.*

# HELD HOSTAGE

The ransom of a man's life is his riches,
But the poor does not hear rebuke.

*—Proverbs 13:8 (NKJV)*

If we are not careful, wealth can literally hold us hostage. We become hostages to growing it, protecting it, shielding it from loss. The fact of having wealth alone does not harm us, but when held too closely, our riches become our ransom. Let's pray and ask God to help us avoid this bondage or, if now held captive, to set us free.

*Dear God, let me not be held hostage by money or material things. Let me know the freeness of a life lived for you. Amen.*

# THE TREASURES AHEAD

And as every present state of a simple substance is naturally a consequence of its preceding state, so its present is pregnant with its future.
—*Gottfried Leibniz,* Discourse
on Metaphysics and Other Writings

However, as it is written:
"What no eye has seen,
   what no ear has heard,
and what no human mind has conceived"—
   the things God has prepared for those who love him.
—*1 Corinthians 2:9 (NIV)*

It's hard for us to grasp the brightness of our future, the treasures that lie ahead in the bends of those coming winding roads.

The flavors we'll taste, the melodies we'll hear, the lands we'll explore, the love we'll feel, poignantly and deep. An all-seeing God knows all about it. But our feeble eyes have not seen, nor our ears heard, nor our minds conceived, what he has in store.

---

*Eagerly, we wait! Come now, Jesus. Bring the bounty you foretold. Amen.*

# PAUL'S PRAYER FOR THE COLOSSIANS

For this reason, since the day we heard about you, we have not stopped praying for you. We continually ask God to fill you with the knowledge of his will through all the wisdom and understanding that the Spirit gives, so that you may live a life worthy of the Lord and please him in every way: bearing fruit in every good work, growing in the knowledge of God, being strengthened with all power according to his glorious might so that you may have great endurance and patience, and giving joyful thanks to the Father, who has qualified you to share in the inheritance of his holy people in the kingdom of light.

—*Colossians 1:9–12 (NIV)*

———〜∞∞〜———

*Help us live a life worthy of you, God, pleasing in every way. Let us bear fruit in every good work, grow in your knowledge, become strong with your power. Give us great endurance and patient, joyful, and thankful hearts. And we humbly ask for our share of "the inheritance of the saints, in the kingdom of light." Amen.*

# UNEARNED SUFFERING

Blessed are you when people insult you and persecute you, and falsely say all kinds of evil against you because of Me. Rejoice and be glad, for your reward in heaven is great; for in the same way they persecuted the prophets who were before you.

—*Matthew 5:11–12 (NASB)*

I am not unmindful that some of you have come here out of great trials and tribulations. And some of you have come fresh from narrow jail cells. Some of you have come from areas where your quest—quest for freedom left you battered by the storms of persecution and staggered by the winds of police brutality. You have been the veterans of creative suffering. Continue to work with the faith that unearned suffering is redemptive.

—*Dr. Martin Luther King Jr., "I Have a Dream"*

*Dear God, we rejoice in unearned suffering, because we know that it is redemptive. Our trials are creating for us rewards that we can hardly perceive. Thank you for the models you've given us, like our Christ and Dr. King. May we follow in their footsteps, as veterans of creative suffering, rejoicing all the way. Amen.*

# HERE AND NOW

Then Peter said, "See, we have left all and followed You."

So He said to them, "Assuredly, I say to you, there is no one who has left house or parents or brothers or wife or children, for the sake of the kingdom of God, who shall not receive many times more in this present time, and in the age to come eternal life."

—*Luke 18:28–30 (NKJV)*

God does not want us to live a life of drudgery, in fact, he wants to bless us, here and now, "in this present time."

But here's the thing—we have to leave our old lives behind. Our old way of thinking. Our prior priorities.

Doing so is not just an investment in the afterlife, in heaven above. According to Jesus, as spoken to Peter, it also changes our situation here and now.

*Dear God, help me leave everything that does not matter and follow you. Amen.*

# TOGETHER

And let us consider how to stir up one another to love and good works, not neglecting to meet together, as is the habit of some, but encouraging one another, and all the more as you see the Day drawing near.

—*Hebrews 10:24–25 (ESV)*

The value and dignity of the individual . . . is threatened whenever it is assumed that individual desires, hopes and ideals can be fitted with frictionless harmony into the collective purposes of man. The individual is not discrete. He cannot find his fulfillment outside of the community; but he also cannot find fulfillment completely within society. In so far as he finds fulfillment within society he must abate his individual ambitions. He must "die to self" if he would truly live. In so far as he finds fulfillment beyond every historical community he lives his life in painful tension with even the best community, sometimes achieving standards of conduct which defy the standards of the community with a resolute "we must obey God rather than man."

—*Reinhold Niebuhr,* The Irony of American History

---

*Lord, wrap me not only in your love but also in connections with other people. Show me the way toward brothers and sisters who will edify me, and I them. Place me within your community. Amen.*

# STANDING FOR TRUTH

Pilate, therefore, wishing to release Jesus, again called out to them. But they shouted, saying, "Crucify Him, crucify Him!"

Then he said to them the third time, "Why, what evil has He done? I have found no reason for death in Him. I will therefore chastise Him and let Him go."

But they were insistent, demanding with loud voices that He be crucified. And the voices of these men and of the chief priests prevailed. So Pilate gave sentence that it should be as they requested.
—*Luke 23:20–24 (NKJV)*

It will not always be easy to defend Christ and his truths.

Like the crowd surrounding Pilate demanding Jesus's crucifixion, the voices beckoning us toward sin and death will be loud, and their imperatives strong.

We have to be ready for this, be ready to stand our ground for the Gospel message of Christ's love. The reward for standing up to the shouting demands of sin are great; conversely, as we see with Pilate, the price to pay for acquiescence to these demands is terrible indeed.

※

*Dear God, help me build the resilience to stand up for your truths, even in tough times. Let me grow stronger under pressure, and let me never break. Amen.*

# THE DESERT BEAUTIFUL

If there were no darkness, this morning light would not seem so sweet.

If we never endured pain, the ease of wellness could hardly be enjoyed.

How would we know God's goodness if the enemy did not battle us each day?

The delight of excitement fills our veins only because we've known the mundane.

Let's greet our lower moments with patience today, because:

> "What makes the desert beautiful . . . is that somewhere it hides a well."
>
> —*Antoine de Saint-Exupéry,* The Little Prince

*"What makes the desert beautiful . . . is that somewhere it hides a well."*
*Amen.*

# REST ON EVERY SIDE

In 1 Kings 5:3–5 (NKJV), Solomon said that his father David "could not build a house for the name of the LORD his God because of the wars which were fought against him on every side." But Solomon continued, "now the LORD my God has given me rest on every side; there is neither adversary nor evil occurrence. And behold, I propose to build a house for the name of the LORD."

———∞∞∞———

*There is a season for needful warring and a season for productive rest. Dear Lord, we pray that the former season would swiftly conclude and the latter swiftly come, so that we would have "rest on every side." Amen.*

# SLOW RECOGNITION

> The teachers of the law and the Pharisees brought in a woman caught in adultery. They made her stand before the group and said to Jesus, "Teacher, this woman was caught in the act of adultery. In the Law Moses commanded us to stone such women. Now what do you say?" They were using this question as a trap, in order to have a basis for accusing him. But Jesus bent down and started to write on the ground with his finger. When they kept on questioning him, he straightened up and said to them, "Let any one of you who is without sin be the first to throw a stone at her." . . . At this, those who heard began to go away one at a time, the older ones first, until only Jesus was left, with the woman still standing there. Jesus straightened up and asked her, "Woman, where are they? Has no one condemned you?"
>
> "No one, sir," she said.
>
> "Then neither do I condemn you," Jesus declared. "Go now and leave your life of sin."
>
> *—John 8:3–11 (NIV)*

The accusers of this adulterous woman were challenged by Jesus to stone her, but only if they were themselves without sin. As Jesus waited, the people in the crowd slowly came to terms with their own fallibility and dispersed—from the oldest to the youngest. I imagine that the oldest had lived long enough to recognize quickly that they were sinners. The younger ones, however, stood around for a while longer, holding on to some sense of infallibility—until that myth fell apart.

Let's not hold on to our judgmental spirit as long as these young ones. When we encounter someone who has fallen short, we should immediately recognize our own fallen nature and extend to them the grace that God has given us. Who are we to throw stones?

*Dear God, help me meet evidence of sin and failure in others with the recognition that I, too, am a sinner. Fill my heart with your grace. Amen.*

# REST FOR THE WEARY

Come to me, all you who are weary and burdened, and I will give you rest.

—*Matthew 11:28 (NIV)*

Drop, drop—in our sleep, upon the heart
sorrow falls, memory's pain,
and to us, though against our very will,
even in our own despite,
comes wisdom
by the awful grace of God.

—*Aeschylus,* Agamemnon

His love never ceases.

Even when we beg for it to stop. Even when we bar the door, screaming from the inside to the out, refusing to let him in.   When we sit in the corner, collapsed and overwhelmed. He beckons. He pleads. He whispers and yells.

Unending. Unyielding. Ever present.

"Come to me, all you who are weary and burdened, and I will give you rest." And rest, we shall.

*Dear God, thank you for pursuing me. I'll let your grace overtake me. I accept your rest in my life. Amen.*

# IN OUR WEAKNESS

In the same way, the Spirit helps us in our weakness. We do not know what we ought to pray for, but the Spirit himself intercedes for us through wordless groans. And he who searches our hearts knows the mind of the Spirit, because the Spirit intercedes for God's people in accordance with the will of God.

—*Romans 8:26–27 (NIV)*

Remembering speechlessly we seek the great forgotten language, the lost lane-end into heaven, a stone, a leaf, an unfound door.

—*Thomas Wolfe,* Look Homeward, Angel

Our language is full of infinite capacity and equally boundless limitation. Infinite, because when we are at our best, the words come quickly to us, words that fit our human condition like a glove. We describe the skyscraper towering, the wind roaring, the love lost, all with the highest fidelity and starkest relief.

But when we are at our worst, when the mass of the morning weighs heavy upon us, when time stacks upon time and our thoughts become jumbled, when weariness or sorrow or just plain mundanity fills our souls, the words are lost. We grope in the darkness. And nothing, it seems, can find them.

And that is when "the Spirit helps us in our weakness." That is when we lay bare our jumbled thoughts in prayer to a God of supreme order. And when "we do not know what we ought to pray for . . . the Spirit himself intercedes for us."

God is not looking for the perfect words. He is looking for perfect submission.

—∞∞∞—

*Dear God, I don't need my prayer to be perfect. I just need to bring it to you. I submit to you my wants, needs, desires and ask you to make sense of it, for your glory. Amen.*

# TOUCHING THE HEM

And a woman was there who had been subject to bleeding for twelve years, but no one could heal her. She came up behind him and touched the edge of his cloak, and immediately her bleeding stopped.

"Who touched me?" Jesus asked.

When they all denied it, Peter said, "Master, the people are crowding and pressing against you."

But Jesus said, "Someone touched me; I know that power has gone out from me."

Then the woman, seeing that she could not go unnoticed, came trembling and fell at his feet. In the presence of all the people, she told why she had touched him and how she had been instantly healed. Then he said to her, "Daughter, your faith has healed you. Go in peace."

—*Luke 8:43–48 (NIV)*

Today, we seek "touch the hem" faith. So many times in the Bible, men from Abraham to Jairus needed God's physical presence to assure them of his power. They needed Christ to come to their house, to perform some grand act, to establish his authority before their eyes.

But this woman, a hemophiliac, who had been bleeding for twelve years, didn't need all of that. She *knew* if she could just get close enough to touch the hem of Jesus's robe, she would be healed.

Imagine the potency of that faith—faith that required no grand occurrence, no predetermined standard. Faith that says, "God, just draw close enough, let me graze the outer reaches of your presence, and I will be healed."

God rewards such audacity with miracles beyond our comprehension. Like the woman with the issue of blood, let's seek such "touch the hem" faith today.

*Dear God, you don't have to do anything grand for me to be assured of your power. I stretch my faith toward you. I know you can heal what ails me and make me whole. Amen.*

# HIS DICTATION

We are therefore Christ's ambassadors, as though God were making his appeal through us.

*—2 Corinthians 5:20 (NIV)*

Harriet Beecher Stowe's landmark novel, *Uncle Tom's Cabin,* took the country by surprise and shook it to its core. It was a sensation, and everyone wanted a piece of Stowe.

One day a woman accosted Stowe, saying, "I just want to hold the hand of the woman who has written such a great work." Stowe replied, "I did not write it. God wrote it. I merely did his dictation."

---

"I merely did his dictation."

*Give us that spirit today, oh Lord. Let us write down the words you have placed on our hearts and live out your intended deeds. Every action we take is for a higher purpose; every word we speak brings either life or death. We choose to represent you faithfully. Amen.*

# A THIEF'S PRAYER

Then one of the criminals who were hanged blasphemed Him, saying, "If You are the Christ, save Yourself and us."

But the other, answering, rebuked him, saying, "Do you not even fear God, seeing you are under the same condemnation? And we indeed justly, for we receive the due reward of our deeds; but this Man has done nothing wrong." Then he said to Jesus, "Lord, remember me when You come into Your kingdom."

And Jesus said to him, "Assuredly, I say to you, today you will be with Me in Paradise."

—*Luke 23:39–43 (NKJV)*

A criminal hanging on a cross next to Jesus received the most exalted send-off imaginable: "Today you will be with Me in Paradise."

This criminal was rewarded for confessing God's perfection and power, in his desperate final breath.

How much more is in store for us, if we confess Christ now—even borrowing the words of this common thief?

Confess that we must "fear God" for we are "under . . . condemnation," as sinners.

Confess that our sin brings death, "the due reward of our deeds." Confess that Christ is perfect sacrifice for our sin: "This Man has done nothing wrong."

And finally, confess that he alone can save us and bring eternal life—"Lord, remember me when You come into Your kingdom."

*Dear God, I pray the prayer of the dying thief. I remind myself of his life-giving confession and renew my commitment to you. Amen.*

# WATERING SEED

In all labor there is profit.

*—Proverbs 14:23 (NKJV)*

Have no mean hours, but be grateful for every hour, and accept what it brings. The reality will make any sincere record respectable. No day will have been wholly misspent, if one sincere, thoughtful page has been written. Let the daily tide leave some deposit on these pages, as it leaves sand and shells on the shore.

*—from the journals of Henry David Thoreau*

Some days are not for planting or for harvest. Some days are just for watering seed.

We should pray and ask God to prime our impulses for action. But if that impulse does not come, if the day seems somewhat wasted, that's okay. It's never too late to water a seed.

To write one page. To say one kind word. To make one good decision about our bodies, our families, our minds.

"Let the daily tide leave some deposit on these pages, as it leaves sand and shells on the shore." Place even a drop of water on a seed.

--~∞∞~--

*Dear God, let me do my best, whatever that best is. Show me both my ceiling and my floor, and help me to not go beyond them. Amen.*

# FLOWING THROUGH

> On the last day, that great day of the feast, Jesus stood and cried out, saying, "If anyone thirsts, let him come to Me and drink. He who believes in Me, as the Scripture has said, out of his heart will flow rivers of living water."
>
> —*John 7:37–38 (NKJV)*

Our spiritual journey is not just about our personal nourishment; we are also here to nourish others.

Jesus is food for our souls, and living water as well. But once filled with him, John 7 tells us that the rivers of our newfound joy are supposed to flow out into the world.

This Christian walk is not about us; it's about God and his broader kingdom. Today, let's not keep our peace to ourselves; let's allow our words, actions, and love to irrigate dry soil.

---

*Dear God, let your living waters flow through me to those who are parched and in need of encouragement. Let me be a vessel. Amen.*

OCTOBER 19

# FAIR DEALING

The first step toward greatness is to be honest, says the proverb; but the proverb fails to state the case strong enough. Honesty is not only "the first step toward greatness," it is greatness itself.
—*Christian Nestell Bovee, in* Many Thoughts of Many Minds

Honest weights and scales are the LORD's;
All the weights in the bag are His work.
—*Proverbs 16:11 (NKJV)*

God is a God of fair dealing. The answer to the question of whether we should cut corners, deprive our brothers and sisters of their full and honest share, or cheat or steal in any way is always consistent and always clear: no.

When we place our portion on the Lord's scale with confidence that the measure is correct, imagine the smile that creeps across our Savior's face. Well done, honest servant. Well done.

⁓∞∞⁓

*Dear God, in my business dealings and finances, help me be honest in all my ways. Not for man's pleasure, but that you might be glorified. Amen.*

# DIRTY WORK

> Now behold, there was a man named Joseph, a council member, a good and just man. He had not consented to their decision and deed. He was from Arimathea, a city of the Jews, who himself was also waiting for the kingdom of God. This man went to Pilate and asked for the body of Jesus. Then he took it down, wrapped it in linen, and laid it in a tomb that was hewn out of the rock, where no one had ever lain before. That day was the Preparation, and the Sabbath drew near.
>
> *—Luke 23:50–54 (NKJV)*

God needs servants to do the quiet, difficult, dirty work of the Kingdom. Joseph of Arimathea was "a good and just man." He had social standing in the time of Jesus, described in Luke's gospel as "a council member."

But after Jesus's death on the cross, Joseph of Arimathea felt a solemn call. He carefully took Jesus's beaten, bloody, deceased body down from the cross—literally lifting him off of the nails. Joseph cleansed the body, and wrapped it in new linen. And then he laid it in the tomb. Handling the dead was far beneath Joseph's station as an observant Jew and member of the council. But called by God, he did what he had to do.

Let us similarly be willing to do the dirty work of the kingdom, serving in ways that are difficult, even with people who are spiritually dead and dying. We never know how God will use this service, in the course of bringing dead things back to life.

---

*Dear God, make me like Joseph of Arimathea. Let me never hesitate to do the hard work you require when I hear the prompting of your spirit. Amen.*

# WITHIN

God lends us a little of His reasoning powers and that is how we think: He puts a little of His love into us and that is how we love one another. When you teach a child writing, you hold its hand while it forms the letters: that is, it forms the letters because you are forming them. We love and reason because God loves and reasons and holds our hand while we do it.

*—C. S. Lewis,* Mere Christianity

Examine yourselves to see whether you are in the faith; test yourselves. Do you not realize that Christ Jesus is in you—unless, of course, you fail the test?

*—2 Corinthians 13:5 (NIV)*

We are not God. But every day when we wake up, a bit of God dwells within us. The atom of real love that we feel for our fellow man—unalloyed and pure—is a bit of God's love. The shimmer of clarity that we catch in our furthest glimpse, a moment of perspective in a cloudy world—that's a bit of God's understanding. Flashes of knowledge amidst confusion, the times when uncertainty finally gives way to conviction—that's God's wisdom. Imagine that, we mortals, endowed with shreds of God!

He has placed within us just enough to whet the taste. And he beckons: If you want more, just ask. Ask that I dwell within you. Ask for my wisdom. Ask for ever greater, more righteous, things. You mortal, if you desire immortality, then come to my throne—and ask.

---

*Dear God, I want to experience more of you. I am awed that the God of the universe would dwell within me, and I give more and more room within this mortal frame to your presence. Take charge. Amen.*

# CORRECTION

Harsh discipline is for him who forsakes the way,
And he who hates correction will die.

—*Proverbs 15:10 (NKJV)*

Correction is essential.

We will never walk a perfectly straight path. And the only way to right our steps—and avoid going straight off a cliff—is to be corrected. Either by ourselves, God, or our brothers and sisters.

Failure to recognize this can lead to our destruction; as the book of Proverbs says, "He who hates correction will die."

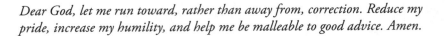

*Dear God, let me run toward, rather than away from, correction. Reduce my pride, increase my humility, and help me be malleable to good advice. Amen.*

# WISDOM AND UNDERSTANDING

Now King Solomon sent and brought Huram from Tyre. He was the son of a widow from the tribe of Naphtali, and his father was a man of Tyre, a bronze worker; he was filled with wisdom and understanding and skill in working with all kinds of bronze work. So he came to King Solomon and did all his work.

—*1 Kings 7:13–14 (NKJV)*

*Dear Lord, like Huram from Tyre, who was called upon by King Solomon to build your temple, give us not just the practical skill to do our work but also "wisdom and understanding." We don't want to just be productive practitioners; we want to be wise in all that we do. And let the efforts of our minds, mouths, and hands bring you glory. Amen.*

# EVERLASTING VISION

Incline my heart to Your testimonies,
　　And not to covetousness.
Turn away my eyes from looking at worthless things,
　　And revive me in Your way.
　　　　　　　　　　*—Psalm 119:36–37 (NKJV)*

Vision is the art of seeing things invisible.
　　　　*—Jonathan Swift,* The Works of Dr. Jonathan Swift

If only we could place on our faces filtering glasses, which would let only goodness through.

Our vision would be filled with the light of this day, and the smiles of our loved ones, and the shining goals toward which we strive.

Blocked out would be the material things that so quickly pass away—the momentary offenses and slights, the hurt that only lasts a measure in God's eternal song.

We do not have those glasses, but we do have a direct line into the One who controls our sight. And we can pray for clearer vision, free from worthless distractions and filled with everlasting things.

———◦◦◦◦◦———

*Dear God, be my vision. Help me see past and beyond. Help me see into the eternal. Amen.*

# THE STORY OF OUR PAIN

Now as Jesus passed by, He saw a man who was blind from birth. And His disciples asked Him, saying, "Rabbi, who sinned, this man or his parents, that he was born blind?"

Jesus answered, "Neither this man nor his parents sinned, but that the works of God should be revealed in him. I must work the works of Him who sent Me while it is day; the night is coming when no one can work. As long as I am in the world, I am the light of the world."

—*John 9:1–5 (NKJV)*

Our pain has an important story to tell.

The blind man that Jesus passed did not sin; neither did his parents. Christ said that the man was blind so that God's glory could be demonstrated through him.

Perhaps that glory was demonstrated in the way the blind man lived his life, the story it told—one of quiet strength or fierce determination. We know God's glory was demonstrated in what happened next in the story—Jesus anointed the eyes of the man and brought him sight. Either way, his pain, like ours, served a purpose.

Let's not discount the value of our trials. Someone needs to hear what we have overcome, and in doing so, they will grow closer to God.

⸻⚬⚬⚬⸻

*Dear God, tell a story through my pain. Let my struggles be a lesson and a blessing to others. Amen.*

# PREEMPTIVE LOVE

I call this a Divine humility because it is a poor thing to strike our colours to God when the ship is going down under us; a poor thing to come to Him as a last resort, to offer up "our own" when it is no longer worth keeping. If God were proud He would hardly have us on such terms: but He is not proud, He stoops to conquer, He will have us even though we have shown that we prefer everything else to Him, and come to Him because there is "nothing better" now to be had.

—*C. S. Lewis,* The Problem of Pain

God is our Savior, even when we've made him our last resort. When we cry out in desperation, at the end of our rope, he answers. But why wait until then?

At this particular moment, we are not at our breaking point. Life, while not perfect, is far from over. How beautiful a thing would it be to grasp God's hand now, when disaster is not imminent, when it's a choice of ours rather than an imperative? Might God honor this preemptive love?

*Dear Lord, you exist not just at the end of my rope—you're at the beginning of it. Help me walk with you in good times as well as bad. Amen.*

# HOW WE CLIMB

Very truly I tell you Pharisees, anyone who does not enter the sheep pen by the gate, but climbs in some other way, is a thief and a robber.
—*John 10:1 (NIV)*

How we ascend the ranks of leadership matters.

If we climb with integrity, honesty, and right dealing, the foundation beneath us will be lasting and strong. But if we cut corners—climbing "in some other way"—we will have shaky ground beneath us, just like one whose wealth is acquired by being "a thief and a robber."

Today, what door will we enter? How will we climb?

*Dear God, never let the light of future glory blind me from the path I should take to get there. Help me ascend the right way. Amen.*

# HE KNOWS OUR FAULTS

But he said to me, "My grace is sufficient for you, for my power is made perfect in weakness." Therefore I will boast all the more gladly of my weaknesses, so that the power of Christ may rest upon me.
—*2 Corinthians 12:9 (ESV)*

The mercies of the Lord are greater than our iniquities. He can pardon you more sins than you can commit, as your malice is finite and his mercy is infinite.
—*Saint Theodore Guérin,* Journals and Letters of Mother Theodore Guérin

God would rather have us kneeling before the throne of forgiveness every day than hiding away from him in shame.

It is never too late, we are never too sullied, and he is never too far away. Let's approach him now, with intimate humility. He is a God who knows our faults and loves us nonetheless.

—◆◆◆—

*Dear God, I never want my sin to keep me away from you. Draw me near. Amen.*

# THE LONG FEAR

The LORD is my light and my salvation—
  whom shall I fear?
The LORD is the stronghold of my life—
  of whom shall I be afraid?

*—Psalm 27:1 (NIV)*

I am no prophet—and here's no great matter;
  I have seen the moment of my greatness flicker,
  And I have seen the eternal Footman hold my coat, and snicker,
  And in short, I was afraid.
    *—T. S. Eliot, "The Love Song of J. Alfred Prufrock"*

The world is a fearsome thing.

Not just fear of dark alleys and bankruptcy and muggers and the meanness of love. Rather, that long fear. That fear that when we are old and gray, and go to unlock the padlock on the storehouses of our lives, and step gingerly on its creaky floor, and stoop over to gather the accomplishments we've been tucking away all these years . . . instead of the clang of gold and platinum, we will feel flowing through our fingers the fleeting silk of sand.

That's where Christ comes in. See, for those who know him, who love him, we have burned our individual storehouses to the ground. Instead, every day that we spend worshipping him and loving our neighbor, we add a newly baked brick to his storehouse, his Kingdom. It's a building not our own, indeed. But it's one that holds no sand.

---

*Dear God, help me confront the fear of the eternal. Allow me to give that fear over to you and rest in the comfort of your love and your purpose for me. I'm not building my own house, God, but yours. And I thank you for that eternal freedom. Amen.*

OCTOBER 30

# WHAT WE'RE HERE FOR

Finally, brothers and sisters, whatever is true, whatever is noble, whatever is right, whatever is pure, whatever is lovely, whatever is admirable—if anything is excellent or praiseworthy—think about such things. Whatever you have learned or received or heard from me, or seen in me—put it into practice. And the God of peace will be with you.

—*Philippians 4:8–9 (NIV)*

There's a story about Hank Aaron in the 1957 World Series. Yogi Berra was his catcher at the time, and when Aaron approached the plate, Yogi noticed that his bat was facing the wrong way.

Yogi stopped Aaron and said, "Turn the bat around, Hank, so you can see the trademark." Aaron replied, "Didn't come up here to read. Came up here to hit."

Hank Aaron had his priorities straight—something the Bible advises for all believers.

There are a million ways we could spend our time today, a thousand worthy tasks. But we find ourselves at home plate in the biggest game possible, this life of ours. We have to make a decision about how we're going to use our time. Will we dwell on the past, on regrets, on jealousies and envies and trifling accumulations? Or will we focus on the most important things: pouring our lives into our neighbors and loving God with all our hearts, investing our time in him?

The choice is clear—we came here for greater things. "Whatever is true, whatever is noble, whatever is right, whatever is pure, whatever is lovely, whatever is admirable—if anything is excellent or praiseworthy—think about such things."

We didn't come up here to read. We came up here to hit.

*Dear God, orient me around your purpose; guide my choices throughout the day. Amen.*

# A STEADFAST HEART

Give us, O Lord, a steadfast heart, which no unworthy affection may drag downwards; give us an unconquered heart, which no tribulation can wear out; give us an upright heart, which no unworthy purpose may tempt aside. Bestow upon us also, O Lord our God, understanding to know thee, diligence to seek thee, wisdom to find thee, and a faithfulness that may finally embrace thee; through Jesus Christ our Lord.

—*Thomas Aquinas, in* The Westminster
Collection of Christian Prayers

*A steadfast heart. An unconquered heart. Understanding to know you, diligence to seek you, wisdom to find you, and faithfulness to embrace you. Through Jesus Christ our Lord, we pray. Amen.*

# NOVEMBER

## CRITICS

I thought I had tough skin.

When you're generally the youngest person in the room and you spend your day working on faith and politics—two subjects that really get people riled up—it is a fact of life that you'll have a few detractors.

There was the liberal religion reporter who didn't believe that government should ever partner with faith-based organizations, and wrote variations on the same headline about my office—"Faith-Based Failure"—so many times that we joked it must be a physical reflex for her. There was the political operative who gave blind quotes to reporters and sent surreptitious memos to my bosses in the White House, claiming that I did everything wrong and he could do things better. And then there were religious leaders, often dear friends of mine, who—whenever they were upset about a particular policy—brought their anxiety to me in countless e-mails, phone calls, and in-person meetings. Criticism came with the territory, and I tried to take it in stride.

But I guess it eventually stacked up because on February 21, 2012, I had had enough. It was a long day anyway—the religious liberty conversation with the Catholic Church was boiling over, and we were in the middle of tough fights on Capitol Hill—then, to top it off, the former director of my office under the previous president, a guy named Jim Towey, went to the newspapers with a doozy of an attack.

Now, I had never met Mr. Towey. He had never called to ask about my work or the programs we ran with faith-based groups around the country.

But that did not stop him from going to the pages of a popular D.C. publication with an opinion piece titled, "Faith-Based Farce," filled with claims that anyone who knew our work would never recognize.

Reading the article, I was angry and hurt. How could this person—a fellow believer—publicly attack someone he doesn't know, or care to know? Doesn't he understand the long hours I put in, the staff who depend on me, the people we're trying to help every day? To be honest, I felt a little victimized, and I called my fiancée to complain.

I ran through the litany of abuses in the article, expecting sympathy. Michelle paused. After a few seconds I had to ask her, "Hello? You still there?"

"I'm here," she replied. "I just don't know how to say this, so I'm just going to say it. Babe, you're working in a job you love. You're helping change people's lives every day. You're not starving, you have your health, and you have a great woman by your side." (She chuckled there, and I had to laugh.) "You are definitely not on Robben Island. In the grand scheme of things, a little criticism from a guy you hardly know really shouldn't rattle your cage."

Robben Island was the prison in which Nelson Mandela was imprisoned for twenty-seven years during the apartheid era in South Africa; Michelle had just returned from South Africa, and Mandela was on her mind. Her point could not have been clearer.

I thought about my great-grandmother growing up in the American South where people questioned her very humanity. I thought about ancestors who labored their lives away as slaves or struggled to reach an Underground Railroad. And I thought about Jesus. My struggles with folks like Jim Towey had nothing to do with the denial of my basic humanity, my dignity, or my right to live. Instead, they were daily challenges that came with the territory of my blessings.

If the people who came before me, who were despised and faced such great evil, could love in the midst of the struggles they faced, couldn't I respond to Jim Towey's relatively mundane attack as a Christian should? So after a bit of thinking, I prayed. And I didn't just pray by myself—I organized a conference call of at least fifty believers around the country, and we all prayed for Jim Towey. We prayed long and hard. We prayed not for Towey's "defeat," but for his family, for his happiness—for his good success.

In the days since, I have tried to develop a fast "prayer reflex"—the urge to lift any critics to my Father as quickly as I can, before I respond to them myself. I have not been perfect, but I have learned that God, rather than I, always knows best what to do. As Exodus 14:14 (NIV) says, "The LORD will fight for you; you need only to be still."

# WE BOUNCE BACK

We are hard pressed on every side, but not crushed; perplexed, but not in despair.

*—2 Corinthians 4:8 (NIV)*

The great boxer Joe Louis was fighting Tony Galento when Galento knocked him down with a surprise left hook. Louis bounced back from the mat before the referee could even start his ten count.

Louis's trainer was furious, saying to Joe, "I keep teaching you to take a count when you're knocked down. Now why didn't you stay down for nine like I've always taught you?" Louis angrily responded, "What . . . and let him get all that rest?"

Like Joe Louis, we bounce back.

We will not give the enemy the pleasure of even one more second on the mat.

*Dear God, give us a resilient spirit, a spirit that returns to face this day even in the shadow of yesterday's challenges. Help us, today, to bounce back. Amen.*

# On Judgment

There is only one test of someone's belief in Christ:

> If you confess with your mouth the Lord Jesus and believe in your
> heart that God has raised Him from the dead, you will be saved.
> —*Romans 10:9 (NKJV)*

Until we have the ability to perceive the pulses of a human heart, we
will never know the results of that test.

So let's avoid the ways of the Pharisees, who created various other mea-
suring sticks for godliness:

> Therefore some of the Pharisees said, "This Man is not from God,
> because He does not keep the Sabbath."
> —*John 9:16 (NKJV)*

Let's leave the judgments to God and walk a loving path in our own
lives.

*Dear Lord, help me never be a judger, but instead love my neighbor as myself.
Amen.*

# FROM THE MARGINS

> Then they came to Jericho. As Jesus and his disciples, together with a large crowd, were leaving the city, a blind man, Bartimaeus (which means "son of Timaeus"), was sitting by the roadside begging. When he heard that it was Jesus of Nazareth, he began to shout, "Jesus, Son of David, have mercy on me!"
>
> Many rebuked him and told him to be quiet, but he shouted all the more, "Son of David, have mercy on me!"
>
> Jesus stopped and said, "Call him." . . .
>
> "What do you want me to do for you?" Jesus asked him.
>
> The blind man said, "Rabbi, I want to see."
>
> "Go," said Jesus, "your faith has healed you." Immediately he received his sight and followed Jesus along the road.
>
> —*Mark 10:46–52 (NIV)*

In these verses in the Gospel of Mark, Jesus had just finished a powerful prophecy and was walking out of Jericho with a purpose. He had places to go, a great crowd around them, and disciples moving the whole operation forward.

But suddenly, he stopped. A voice cried out from nowhere: "Son of David, have mercy on me!" It was old blind Bartimaeus, a beggar who folks generally just passed by.

The crowd tried to get Bartimaeus to be quiet; surely Jesus, this great prophet, had no time for trifling requests. But Bartimaeus cried out again. Jesus answered, and he healed him.

Like Jesus, we must listen for those crying out from the margins of our lives—the voices that we generally dismiss, the cries that are not readily heard. Perhaps someone in our lives is in need of our touch. If so, like Christ, we should make the time.

---

*Dear God, prick my ears to hear those crying out from the margins: those I encounter who may need my help and support. And when I hear them, give me the courage and capacity to act. Amen.*

# OLD WISDOM

> Then they took [Paul] and brought him to a meeting of the Areopagus, where they said to him, "May we know what this new teaching is that you are presenting? You are bringing some strange ideas to our ears, and we would like to know what they mean." (All the Athenians and the foreigners who lived there spent their time doing nothing but talking about and listening to the latest ideas.)
>
> —*Acts 17:19–21 (NIV)*

Paul was in Athens, in the Areopagus, and the Athenians were fascinated by this strange apostle. They were always looking for the latest fad to gossip about, the latest issue to discuss. In many ways, it was the Twitter-sphere of the ancient world.

But in response to their fascination, Paul did not give the Athenians something new. Instead, he went on to proclaim a lasting truth—that God is sovereign, and that we should seek him through his son, Jesus Christ.

Like Paul, but unlike the Athenians, let's not become obsessed with discovering the latest theme, idea, or truth. Instead, let's dwell on the old wisdom that so often sustains.

*Dear God, give me an appreciation of ancient wisdom and long-held truths today. Amen.*

# KEEPING WATCH

Be on your guard; stand firm in the faith; be courageous; be strong.
—*1 Corinthians 16:13 (NIV)*

As nightfall does not come all at once, neither does oppression. In both instances, there is a twilight when everything remains seemingly unchanged. And it is in such twilight that we all must be most aware of change in the air—however slight—lest we become unwitting victims of the darkness.
—*Supreme Court Justice William O. Douglas, letter to the Young Lawyers Section of the Washington State Bar Association*

Let's keep watch. Let's perceive the slow creep of oppression, wherever it might move. Let's be aware of the darkness in our world—or even in our own soul—that seeks, like a fungus, to grow.

When we see it, or feel it, we pray that Christ would come into it and strike it out, making us new.

We will not be victims. Nor will we be oppressors. No—today, we will keep watch.

---

*Dear God, open my eyes not just to blessings but also to the potential of evil in the world. And when I perceive it, help me move against it. Amen.*

# TRADITION

Yet if the only form of tradition, of handing down, consisted in following the ways of the immediate generation before us in a blind
or timid adherence to its successes, "tradition" should positively be
discouraged. We have seen many such simple currents soon lost in
the sand; and novelty is better than repetition. Tradition is a matter
of much wider significance. It cannot be inherited, and if you want
it you must obtain it by great labour.
> —*T. S. Eliot, "Tradition and the Individual Talent"*

See to it that no one takes you captive by philosophy and empty
deceit, according to human tradition, according to the elemental
spirits of the world, and not according to Christ.
> —*Colossians 2:8 (ESV)*

We must all learn the difference between sacred tradition and simple
repetition.

There is value in tradition, in time-tested practices that remind us
of our principles. But perhaps there are other things passed down from
previous generations that we should leave behind: behaviors, attitudes,
misplaced beliefs. We must not be captive to those things, if they do not
meet the test of Christ.

*Dear God, free me from unnecessary tradition, from the sins of my forefathers
that threaten to bind me this day. Wed me only to those habits that are edifying and true. Amen.*

# BROUGHT LOW

Every man alive in the world is a beggar of one sort or another, every last one of them, great and small. The priest begs God for grace, and the king begs something for something. Sometimes he begs the people for loyalty, sometimes he begs God to forgive him. No man in the world can have endured ten years without having begged God to forgive him.

—*William Saroyan, "The Beggars"*

So people will be brought low
    and everyone humbled,
      the eyes of the arrogant humbled.

—*Isaiah 5:15 (NIV)*

Every man alive will be brought low.

As a mighty earthquake rattles a mountaintop, sending rocks tumbling down, so the position of our own skyward precipice is never safe. We're all just a strong wind away from a steep fall.

For nonbelievers, this is a sobering reality, because being at the top matters most. But for those of us who trust in God, it is liberating, because if we take seriously his commandments to maintain a spirit of humility, we are indeed already low. Sin has floored us, and it is only in Christ that we're exalted. Nothing can change that—no disaster, no death, no disease, no displacement. "Blessed are the meek"—for these humble souls are never shaken, and they will indeed "inherit the earth" (Matt. 5:5).

---

*Dear God, help me maintain a spirit of humility in my highest highs and my lowest lows. Let me only be exalted in you. Amen.*

# TO BE KNOWN

And if anyone thinks that he knows anything, he knows nothing yet as he ought to know. But if anyone loves God, this one is known by Him.

—*1 Corinthians 8:2–3 (NKJV)*

Let's seek to be known by God—not simply to know.

Sure, we will accumulate knowledge over time. Our understanding will expand with each passing day.

But at the end of life, our store of wisdom will still be but a molehill to a mountain—a teardrop in the broader sea.

More than knowing, we seek to be known. We want the God of the universe to say that we sought him and loved him, and he loved and knew us in return. That's our prayer today. *Amen.*

# SCIENCE AND LOVE

The antagonism between science and religion, about which we hear so much, appears to me to be purely factitious—fabricated, on the one hand, by short-sighted religious people who confound a certain branch of science, theology, with religion; and, on the other, by equally short-sighted scientific people who forget that science takes for its province only that which is susceptible of clear intellectual comprehension, and that outside the boundaries of that province, they must be content with imagination, with hope, and with ignorance.

—*Thomas Henry Huxley, "The Interpreters of*
*Genesis and the Interpreters of Nature"*

Oh, the depth of the riches of the wisdom and knowledge of God!
    How unsearchable his judgments,
        and his paths beyond tracing out!

—*Romans 11:33 (NIV)*

~∞∞∞~

*Dear God, today, help me hold equally to the wonders of your creation, and the glory of your presence. Remove the tension between what I can explain and what I cannot; allow them to coexist easily within me. Thank you for being the God of both science and love. Amen.*

NOVEMBER 10

# The Places You Dwell

However, the Most High does not dwell in temples made with hands,
as the prophet says:

> "Heaven is My throne,
>     And earth is My footstool.
> What house will you build for Me?" says the LORD,
>     "Or what is the place of My rest?
> Has My hand not made all these things?"

—*Acts 7:48–50 (NKJV)*

———✦———

*Dear God, bring me to the places where you dwell.*
*If it is not in temples made by hand, then take me where you are.*
*Outside, with your creation. In the valleys, where your light breaks through*
*darkness. With the poor and outcasts, those whom you love. In the quiet spaces,*
*where it's just me and you. "The Most High does not dwell in temples made*
*with hands." Then, Lord, bring me to the places where you dwell. And there,*
*let me encounter you.*
*    Amen.*

# TEMPTATION

> Jesus, full of the Holy Spirit, left the Jordan and was led by the Spirit into the wilderness, where for forty days he was tempted by the devil. He ate nothing during those days, and at the end of them he was hungry.
>
> *—Luke 4:1–2 (NIV)*

Scripture tells us that Jesus was tempted by the devil at his weakest moment in three major ways: with bread when he was hungry, with the praise of men and all the power in the world, and with a request to prove his authority by throwing himself down from the temple. Some scholars call this the "Three Temptations of Christ," temptations of "miracle, mystery, and authority."

But Luke 4:2 reveals something curious, often skipped by readers of this passage. Before these three major tests, Jesus was tempted, for many days, in other, smaller ways: "for forty days he was tempted by the devil." We will never know what exactly Christ went through in this period, but we know that at the end of these trials, Jesus was spent.

The Lord reminds us that our chief battle every day will be with temptation. We may not always be tempted with major things, existential crises or dramatic moral decisions. But the smaller pulls on our character, actions, and conscience are still critically important. Let us be on our guard against these temptations and ask God to prevent the enemy from gaining a foothold in our lives.

~~~~~

*Dear God, lead me not into temptation, but deliver me from evil. Prepare my mind to spot signs of temptation and condition my response. Amen.*

# WE SHALL GET IN

> At present we are on the outside of the world, the wrong side of the door. We discern the freshness and purity of the morning, but they do not make us fresh and pure. We cannot mingle with the splendours we see. But all the leaves of the New Testament are rustling with the rumour that it will not always be so. Some day, God willing, we shall get *in*.
>
> —*C. S. Lewis,* The Weight of Glory

"Some day, God willing, we shall get *in*."

Through the gates of eternal glory.

To fields that know no pain.

Dwelling among a perfect knowledge and consummate peace. So far from temptation, sin, and sorrow that our mouths can't form the words. God willing, we shall get in some day. Until then, let's live in hopeful anticipation of this great reward.

*Dear God, help me work hard while it is still day, so that I can join you later, in paradise. Amen.*

# INTEGRITY

But they cried out, "Away with Him, away with Him! Crucify Him!"
Pilate said to them, "Shall I crucify your King?"
The chief priests answered, "We have no king but Caesar!"
*—John 19:15 (NKJV)*

The chief priests—men who had devoted their entire lives to God's service—rejected their own God in an instant in service of crucifying Christ.

When challenged by Pilate, the chief priests lifted Caesar as their king instead of God. "We have no king but Caesar!" they exclaimed. This appears to be in direct contravention of the priests' own penultimate principle: Exodus 20:3 (NKJV), "You shall have no other gods before Me."

We see here that our opponents will not always adhere to their own principles, especially if abandoning them means taking us down. But even in the face of their shattered integrity, we are still commanded to keep ours. If Christ can do this in the face of death, so can we.

---

*Dear God, let my integrity not be dependent on someone else's. Let it come from within and be unshakable. Amen.*

# LIFE TOGETHER

They devoted themselves to the apostles' teaching and to fellowship, to the breaking of bread and to prayer. Everyone was filled with awe at the many wonders and signs performed by the apostles. All the believers were together and had everything in common. They sold property and possessions to give to anyone who had need. Every day they continued to meet together in the temple courts. They broke bread in their homes and ate together with glad and sincere hearts, praising God and enjoying the favor of all the people. And the Lord added to their number daily those who were being saved.

*—Acts 2:42–47 (NIV)*

All men live not by the thought they spend on their own welfare, but because love exists in man.

I knew before that God gave life to men and desires that they should live; now I understood more than that.

I understood that God does not wish men to live apart, and therefore he does not reveal to them what each one needs for himself; but he wishes them to live united, and therefore reveals to each of them what is necessary for all.

I have now understood that though it seems to men that they live by care for themselves, in truth it is love alone by which they live. He who has love, is in God, and God is in him, for God is love.

*—Leo Tolstoy, "What Men Live By"*

⸺᪣⸺

*Today God, bind me with my community in love. No matter who I encounter, let that tie be established, and let it never be broken. Amen.*

# JUST ME AND YOU

> But when you pray, go into your room and shut the door and pray
> to your Father who is in secret. And your Father who sees in secret
> will reward you.
>
> —*Matthew 6:6 (ESV)*

When Bill Moyers served as President Lyndon Baines Johnson's press secretary, he was famous for being a calming presence in the face of larger-than-life LBJ.

One day at lunch, Moyers was in the middle of saying grace when Johnson exclaimed, "Speak up, Bill! I can't hear a d__n thing!" Moyers quietly replied, "I wasn't addressing you, Mr. President."

Moyers knew that prayer is a conversation between us and God—nothing more, and nothing less. The God of this universe wants to talk with us, hear our trouble, and guide our steps. Let's take advantage of that wonderful opportunity and spend time communing with him.

———∞∞∞———

*Dear God, I appreciate the opportunity to be in conversation with you. I bring to you my praise, confessions, requests, and thoughts. It's just me and you. Amen.*

# A GENTLE BATTLE

Rejoice in the Lord always. I will say it again: Rejoice! Let your gentleness be evident to all. The Lord is near. Do not be anxious about anything, but in every situation, by prayer and petition, with thanksgiving, present your requests to God. And the peace of God, which transcends all understanding, will guard your hearts and your minds in Christ Jesus.

Finally, brothers and sisters, whatever is true, whatever is noble, whatever is right, whatever is pure, whatever is lovely, whatever is admirable—if anything is excellent or praiseworthy—think about such things. Whatever you have learned or received or heard from me, or seen in me—put it into practice. And the God of peace will be with you.

*—Philippians 4:4–9 (NIV)*

Every morning we awaken to a gentle battle. The first few thoughts will either march out in the direction of busyness, worry, weariness, lust, depravity, or indifference. Or they will stand their ground for peace, for holiness, for love, for joy.

We must not underestimate the difficulty of this fight, nor its import. Of all the negotiations and decisions of our day—this one is the most important. How will our minds be focused? As soldiers, in what direction will we march?

"Whatever is true, whatever is noble, whatever is right, whatever is pure, whatever is lovely, whatever is admirable—if anything is excellent or praiseworthy—think about such things."

---

*Dear God, ground me, not in my own wisdom, but in yours. Return my thoughts to the things that matter most. Amen.*

# RELIGION

Do not merely listen to the word, and so deceive yourselves. Do what it says.

*—James 1:22 (NIV)*

I would not so dishonour God as to lend my voice to perpetuate all the mad and foolish things which men have dared to say of Him. I believe that we may find in the Bible the highest and purest religion . . . most of all in the history of Him in whose name we all are called. His religion—not *the Christian religion,* but *the religion of Christ*—the poor man's gospel; the message of forgiveness, of reconciliation, of love; and, oh, how gladly would I spend my life, in season and out of season, in preaching this!

*—James Anthony Froude,* The Nemesis of Faith

We have to peel back the layers of religion to find Christ. When our churches, our pastors, our leaders point us toward Jesus, toward his word and his love, they deserve our full embrace.

But when we encounter religion and leave feeling less connected with Christ than when we began, we know something's amiss. That's when we must return to the basics: reading the Bible for ourselves, experiencing a prayerful communion with God, and engaging in gentle fellowship with other believers.

Religion is either an up-escalator to our Savior or a down-escalator to something else. When it goes up, let's ride. When it goes down, let's be sure to get off.

---

*Jesus, be my religion. Help me find the support necessary to grow closer to you. Amen.*

# PLUNGING IN

There are two approaches to a risen Savior, a King who has triumphed over death and brought us to life.

After Jesus was raised from the dead, he presented himself to the disciples, who were fishing in the Sea of Tiberias. Jesus stood on the shore and called out to them, and after he performed a miracle, they knew it was him.

Most of the disciples rowed their boat back in to greet Jesus. But Peter, "that disciple whom Jesus loved," took a different approach:

> Now when Simon Peter heard that it was the Lord, he put on his outer garment . . . and plunged into the sea.
>
> —*John 21:7 (NKJV)*

Peter couldn't hold himself back—in his excitement, he just plunged in!

God is still moving in the world, raising dead and broken things to life—an exciting fact indeed. The knowledge of what he continues to do in this world should never be mundane to us, should never feel ordinary. Rather, it should build within us such excitement that when we see evidence of God, like Peter, we plunge in.

---

*Dear God, light a fire within me when I see your healing manifested in the world. Help me greet evidence of you with excitement and great joy. Amen.*

# PATIENCE

There are two main human sins from which all the others derive: impatience and indolence. It was because of impatience that they were expelled from Paradise; it is because of indolence that they do not return. Yet perhaps there is only one major sin: impatience. Because of impatience they were expelled, because of impatience they do not return.

—*Franz Kafka,* The Blue Octavo Notebooks

Be still before the LORD
    and wait patiently for him;
do not fret when people succeed in their ways,
    when they carry out their wicked schemes.

—*Psalm 37:7 (NIV)*

Kafka is wrong to place impatience above all other sins, but he's right to shine a light on its potential harm.

If Abraham had not been patient, he and Sarah would have never borne Isaac in their old age.

If Joseph had not been patient, he would have never endured the scorn of false accusation and imprisonment to become ruler over so many.

If Job had not been patient, his lessons in perseverance would not have blessed the world.

Our time is coming, and then will come again; it always does. Until then, we ask God for patience.

─── ∞ ───

*Dear Lord, place within me a spirit of Abraham, Joseph, and Job; let me await with ease your coming blessing. Amen.*

# POWER MADE PERFECT

Blessed are you when people insult you and persecute you, and falsely say all kinds of evil against you because of Me. Rejoice and be glad, for your reward in heaven is great; for in the same way they persecuted the prophets who were before you.

*—Matthew 5:11–12 (NASB)*

Three times I pleaded with the Lord to take it away from me. But he said to me, "My grace is sufficient for you, for my power is made perfect in weakness." Therefore I will boast all the more gladly about my weaknesses, so that Christ's power may rest on me. That is why, for Christ's sake, I delight in weaknesses, in insults, in hardships, in persecutions, in difficulties. For when I am weak, then I am strong.

*—2 Corinthians 12:8–10 (NIV)*

What burden—what pain and sorrow—could have broken the Apostle Paul to the point that he pleaded with God three times to take it away?

This is Paul: mighty defender of the Gospel. Second to Jesus, the most important figure in all of Christianity. Imprisoned frequently, flogged severely, shipwrecked thrice, and still—always—standing.

But something got to him. Something drove Paul to his knees to cry out, "God, take it away." Rejected, he pleaded again. Spurned, he begged for reprieve a third time.

And God said: No. I will not remove this thorn from your side. But here's what I will do: I will show myself strong through your weakness. My grace will wash over your pain. My name will be glorified in your time of trouble, and others will see my saving power.

Our suffering is a legacy of prophets and apostles. Let us embrace it, for the glory of one whose triumph outlasts our pain.

*Dear God, remind me that my momentary struggles are just that—momentary. Fix my eyes on what is eternal. Amen.*

# QUIETED MY SOUL

LORD, my heart is not haughty,
  Nor my eyes lofty.
Neither do I concern myself with great matters,
  Nor with things too profound for me.

Surely I have calmed and quieted my soul,
  Like a weaned child with his mother;
  Like a weaned child is my soul within me.

O Israel, hope in the LORD
  From this time forth and forever.

—*Psalm 131:1–3 (NKJV)*

*This is our prayer today, dear Lord. Surely I have calmed and quieted my soul. Amen.*

# PLEASING HIM

I love those who love me,
> and those who seek me diligently find me.

> —*Proverbs 8:17 (ESV)*

I have said that God is pleased with nothing but love; but before I explain this, it will be as well to set forth the grounds on which the assertion rests.

All our works, and all our labours, how grand 'soever they may be, are nothing in the sight of God, for we can give Him nothing, neither can we by them fulfil His desire, which is the growth of our soul; as to Himself He desires nothing of this, for he has need of nothing, and so, if He is pleased with anything it is with the growth of the soul; and as there is no way in which the soul grows more than in becoming in a manner equal to Him, for this reason only is He pleased with our love.

> —*John of the Cross,* The Complete Works of Saint John
> of the Cross of the Order of Our Lady of Mount Carmel

Money and power impress man, and dominance impresses animals. Neither do much for God.

God loves our souls. He wants to see them grow strong. He hopes that our every action will be motivated by an abundance of love.

We should ask ourselves whom it is we desire to impress. If the answer is God, we know the steps we should take.

~~~

*Dear God, it is you that I want to impress. I don't want to boast of wealth or power, but of pleasing you with my life. Amen.*

# A BETTER VIEW

> Jesus entered Jericho and was passing through. A man was there by the name of Zacchaeus; he was a chief tax collector and was wealthy. He wanted to see who Jesus was, but because he was short he could not see over the crowd. So he ran ahead and climbed a sycamore-fig tree to see him, since Jesus was coming that way.
>
> When Jesus reached the spot, he looked up and said to him, "Zacchaeus, come down immediately. I must stay at your house today." So he came down at once and welcomed him gladly.
>
> —*Luke 19:1–6 (NIV)*

Let's never hesitate to move to get a better view of God.

There are times when, like Zacchaeus, things are standing in the way of our vision of the Lord. Maybe it's a person in our life who distracts from God's purpose. Maybe it's a place we frequent that leads us down the wrong path. Maybe it's a habit or ritual that never ends well.

Whatever the obstruction is, once identified, we would do well to flee from it, to get a better view of Christ. Zacchaeus, the rich tax collector, did so, climbing up a tree even at the risk of appearing foolish. He was rewarded with a passing glimpse of Jesus, and then an audience with him.

What's in store for us if, like Zacchaeus, we are willing to forsake obstructions and move?

*Dear God, let me be anchored only in your will and word. Let my ties to other foundations always be loose enough to allow me to move. Amen.*

# LET IT SHINE

You are the light of the world. A town built on a hill cannot be hidden. Neither do people light a lamp and put it under a bowl. Instead they put it on its stand, and it gives light to everyone in the house. In the same way, let your light shine before others, that they may see your good deeds and glorify your Father in heaven.

*—Matthew 5:14–16 (NIV)*

All those treasures that lie in the little bolted box whose tiny space is
Mightier than the room of the stars, being secret and filled with
    dreams:
All those treasures—I hold them in my hand—are straining
    continually
Against the sides and the lid and the two ends of the little box in
    which I guard them;
Crying that there is no sun come among them this great while and
    that they weary of shining;
Calling me to fold back the lid of the little box and to give them
    sleep finally.
But the night I am hiding from them, dear friend, is far more des-
    perate than their night!
And so I take pity on them and pretend to have lost the key to the
    little house of my treasures;
For they would die of weariness were I to open it, and not be
    merely faint and sleepy
As they are now.

*—William Carlos Williams, "Slow Movement"*

We must let our light shine. Many have come before who did not, and we don't even know enough about them to regret it. If we have a message in our bones, a song in the back of our throats, an idea in our brains, it's time to let it out. Like fox fire, it will glow brightly when it hits the air.

*Dear God, give me the courage today to let my many lights shine. Let them burn brightly for your glory and lead others to you. Amen.*

# GLORIOUS INADEQUACY

> Then the LORD turned to [Gideon] and said, "Go in this might of yours, and you shall save Israel from the hand of the Midianites. Have I not sent you?"
>
> So he said to Him, "O my Lord, how can I save Israel? Indeed my clan is the weakest in Manasseh, and I am the least in my father's house."
>
> And the LORD said to him, "Surely I will be with you, and you shall defeat the Midianites as one man."
>
> —*Judges 6:14–16 (NKJV)*

God is glorified in our inadequacy.

Gideon was a bold warrior for God, but the chips were stacked against him. When God told Gideon that he would use him to defeat the Midianites, Gideon replied that he was ill-suited for the task: "My clan is the weakest in Manasseh," Gideon said, "and I am the least in my father's house." We can almost see God smile as Gideon utters these words. Our Lord loves our inadequacy, because when our capabilities are lacking and victory still comes, he gets the glory.

Gideon marched out with an army of three hundred men (fewer than he started with, after God told him to cut the numbers down). He defeated thousands of Midianites in a historic rout. This story has been told throughout the ages, not in praise of Gideon—but in honor of God. To make his name and his power known in all the earth.

Let's ask God to show up in our inadequacy. Far from fearing our weaknesses, let's embrace them and ask God to come into them. And use them for his glory.

*Dear God, when I am weak, you are strong. Work through my weakness to bring your victory to this world and glory to your name. Amen.*

# THINKING ABOUT YOU

What can you ever really know of other people's souls—of their temptations, their opportunities, their struggles? One soul in the whole of creation you do know: and it is the only one whose fate is placed in your hands. If there is a God, you are, in a sense, alone with Him. You cannot put Him off with speculation about your neighbours or memories of what you have read in books.

—*C. S. Lewis,* Mere Christianity

Like many adolescent boys, I was a self-conscious child, especially when it came to girls. For a few years there, I was constantly adjusting my clothing and gait and speech, hoping to calibrate the perfect approach to those seemingly untouchable doyennes of fifth grade. And when I took the act too far, obsessing too much over a furtive glance or perceived slight, my mother always said the same thing: "Boy, nobody's thinking about you! They've got enough to worry about themselves!"

Isn't that the truth! We spend so much time guessing at the intentions of others, the unseen corners of our neighbors' hearts, topics we can never—will never—comprehend. All the while, God beckons to us: "Explore your relationship with me. Delve into your own motives, desires, eternal fate. Don't waste another minute attempting to discern the thoughts of others, thoughts you'll never know."

---

*Dear God, let me never obsess over the motives, desires, and beliefs of others. Point me inward, into my own soul, and then to you. Amen.*

# OUR SECOND WIND

So we do not lose heart. Though our outer self is wasting away, our inner self is being renewed day by day.

*—2 Corinthians 4:16 (ESV)*

My great-grandmother Ola Mae Webb is well north of eighty years old. Yet every Sunday, she remains active in community service at church. If you ask her, "Granny, what are you doing after church today?" she will reply without a hint of irony, "Well, I have to go feed these little old seniors."

When our days grow long and weary, we might be tempted to recede into the background and let life push on without us. But no matter where we are, people still need us, God still has a plan for us, and his calling still rings in our ears. Let's rest up for the journey ahead and get our second wind.

---

*Thank you, dear God, that this life is never over and your work never complete. I will rejuvenate and get ready for the road ahead. Amen.*

# NO MAN IS AN ISLAND

Let us therefore make every effort to do what leads to peace and to mutual edification.

*—Romans 14:19 (NIV)*

Only when we see ourselves in our true human context, as members of a race which is intended to be one organism and "one body," will we begin to understand the positive importance not only of the successes but of the failures and accidents in our lives. My successes are not my own. The way to them was prepared by others. The fruit of my labors is not my own: for I am preparing the way for the achievements of another. Nor are my failures my own. They may spring from failure of another, but they are also compensated for by another's achievement. Therefore the meaning of my life is not to be looked for merely in the sum total of my own achievements. It is seen only in the complete integration of my achievements and failures with the achievements and failures of my own generation, and society, and time.

*—Thomas Merton,* No Man Is an Island

Today, we must not listen to one another just to receive information. We must also listen so that others might be heard. We should not smile as we look in another's eyes simply because we are happy to see them. We must also smile so others will feel the warmth of our greeting. Our communication is not intended simply to get our point across, to elicit action or laughter or applause. Instead, we must choose words that will build our brothers and sisters up, words that nourish and edify.

This life is not about us. In fact, we are just one small part of God's larger plan. He intends for our lives to be lived in service to others.

~~~~~

*Dear God, reduce my self and increase my desire for others. Let me get outside of my own head a bit and see the world through another's eyes. Amen.*

# PRESS TOWARD THE MARK

I press toward the mark for the prize of the high calling of God in Christ Jesus.

*—Philippians 3:14 (KJV)*

Green Bay Packers coach Vince Lombardi was famous for his drive and his hatred of losing. After one important victory, he was asked how important winning was to him. Lombardi responded, "Winning isn't everything, but wanting to win is."

~~~~~~

*Dear Lord, like Vince Lombardi, we have the desire to win. We "press toward the mark" of your calling on our lives. We may not make it today. We may not make it tomorrow. But we press, and press more, until our victory has come. Amen.*

# RESISTING

You stubborn people! You are heathen at heart and deaf to the truth. Must you forever resist the Holy Spirit? That's what your ancestors did, and so do you!

—*Acts 7:51 (NLT)*

—◦◦◦—

*Lord, let me resist not your Spirit. When I hear your voice, let me move. Even when it's tough. Open my ears today. Increase my flexibility. Remove distractions that would drown you out. Let me resist not your Spirit. And when you speak, let me move. Amen.*

# DECEMBER

## As Wonders Unfold

In early 2012, I decided it would be my last year in the White House. I decided to leave.

In the months and years before, such a move would have been unthinkable for me. At the ripe old age of twenty-six, I had literally been given the job of a lifetime: executive director of President Obama's faith-based initiative. In the president, I had a boss I cared for and trusted deeply; I had a wonderful support system of mentors, staff, colleagues, and friends all around me.

And still—God was separating me. He was telling me, "It's time to go."

The process actually started a year before, in January 2011. At that time, I felt driven back to my Bible in a way I hadn't in years. Having been uneven with my daily scripture reading, I heard God say that it was time to reengage. So, encouraged by my prayer partner, Eugene Schneeberg, I downloaded a one-year Bible reading plan on my iPad and started to work my way from Genesis to Revelation. And the subsequent twelve months turned out to be the most rewarding and revealing of my life.

In that time, I learned through God's word about his vision for love, which led me to propose to my fiancée—now my wife. I learned about courage, which buttressed me in the tough times to come, particularly in the debates we had within the White House about the Catholic Church and religious liberty. And most importantly, I learned where my foundation was. For so long, I had defined my very worth by the institutions in which I sat. For a poor kid from the South, I took great pride in the fact that I made it to Boston University and then to Princeton. For someone who was in awe of politics and policy and always wanted to break into an "inner circle," I held my roles in the United States Senate and the 2008 Obama campaign closely.

And then, there was the White House. That ultimate institution of American life. Those broad and gleaming columns, the storied West Wing, the hallways that just decades before would have been inaccessible to someone who looked like me. The fact that I could call the president of the United States a mentor and friend, go to church with him, spend time with his family, support him spiritually. I, Joshua DuBois, from Nashville, Tennessee, worked in the White House! And beyond just working there, I contributed to its daily pulse. In my eyes, for a long time, that building held my worth.

But my renewed journey through the Bible that year told me otherwise. First I learned in Psalm 146:3 that no institution of man, even those great institutions in Washington, is worth endowing with all my trust. Then Romans 8 reminded me that God loves me completely, no matter where I work, and he has big plans for my future, plans he was just beginning to reveal. Finally, Proverbs 17 assured me that true relationships—from the president to my colleagues to our outside partners—will last, because they depend not on the title on my business card, but on a shared bond between brothers and sisters whom I love. I discovered these and more truths in Deuteronomy and Numbers, Ezra and 2 Corinthians, Luke and John. I pondered them and wrote them down in devotionals for the president. I did my best to write them on my own heart.

And in January 2012, God told me that it was time to go. I didn't speak a word to anyone other than my fiancée; I just prayed and asked God to reveal the right moment. I knew that the president would be reelected—I had the utmost confidence in his campaign team and in God's purpose for him—so job security wasn't a factor. And after the November election, God gave the signal.

For a while, I tried to micromanage my exit, hoping to leave at the end of November, and then early December. But tasks kept popping up—from helping with the inauguration to staffing the president at church—and my final day was pushed back.

Because my departure was delayed, President Obama asked me to stay around to help him with the 2013 National Prayer Breakfast, an annual event for Christians around the country, held the first week in February at the Washington Hilton hotel. I assisted with the logistical preparations for the Prayer Breakfast as I had done for many years prior, and then staffed the president when he arrived at the Hilton early in the morning of February 7. We exchanged a few jokes—laughing that due to the early rise, we would prefer that they change it to the "National Prayer *Brunch*"—and then President Obama took the stage. But before his formal remarks, the president had a surprise for me.

Standing behind a podium and speaking to a crowd of thousands, he began with the normal pleasantries, which I was following in the prepared text:

> To Mark and Jeff, thank you for your wonderful work on behalf of this breakfast. To all of those who worked so hard to put this together; to the heads of state, members of Congress, and my Cabinet, religious leaders and distinguished guests. To our outstanding speaker. To all the faithful who've journeyed to our capital, Michelle and I are truly honored to be with you this morning.

But then, the president went off script. He continued:

> Before I begin, I hope people don't mind me taking a moment of personal privilege. I want to say a quick word about a close friend of mine and yours, Joshua DuBois. Now, some of you may not know Joshua, but Joshua has been at my side—in work and in prayer—for years now. He is a young reverend, but wise in years. He's worked on my staff. He's done an outstanding job as the head of our Faith-Based office.
>
> Every morning he sends me via e-mail a daily meditation—a snippet of scripture for me to reflect on. And it has meant the world to me. And despite my pleas, tomorrow will be his last day in the White House. So this morning I want to publicly thank Joshua for all that he's done, and I know that everybody joins me in wishing him all the best in his future endeavors—including getting married.

I was stunned. I had helped him with the speech and had no idea he would say anything about me in it, especially not a dedication in front of thousands of people. It was a beautiful waypoint on this long journey, and I could not have designed a better way to wrap up my tenure of service to this good president, and this good country. Instead of micromanaging my exit, when I gave up control and increased my faith, God showed me that he knew what he was doing.

Looking at my life after I left the White House—beginning a career reporting, writing, and running a company, and, most important, getting married to the love of my life—I realized that my purpose in life only became clear when I learned to trust God and daily seek his word.

I am certain it will be the same for you as life's wonders continue to unfold with joyful revelations every single day.

# THE SABBATH

So then, there remains a Sabbath rest for the people of God, for whoever has entered God's rest has also rested from his works as God did from his. Let us therefore strive to enter that rest.

*—Hebrews 4:9–11 (ESV)*

The great Supreme Court Justice Louis Brandeis was once criticized for taking a vacation before an important trial. When asked for an explanation, Brandeis is reported to have said: "I need the rest. I find that I can do a year's work in eleven months—but I can't do it in twelve."

Every good leader must invest in rest. Our families, our country, our souls need to drink deeply from the fountain of ease and solitude with as much of a sense of purpose as that with which we pursue productivity. It's why God created the Sabbath, for his rest, and our worship. We must remember to keep that Sabbath and guard our times of rest as often as we can.

*Dear God, pull me toward rest, and give me occasions to rest deeply. Amen.*

# OUR GOD'S HISTORY

One day Jesus said to his disciples, "Let us go over to the other side of the lake." So they got into a boat and set out. As they sailed, he fell asleep. A squall came down on the lake, so that the boat was being swamped, and they were in great danger.

The disciples went and woke him, saying, "Master, Master, we're going to drown!"

He got up and rebuked the wind and the raging waters; the storm subsided, and all was calm. "Where is your faith?" he asked his disciples.

In fear and amazement they asked one another, "Who is this? He commands even the winds and the water, and they obey him."

—*Luke 8:22–25 (NIV)*

We must not quickly forget.

The same disciples who saw Jesus awaken from sleep on a boat, speak to a storm, and rebuke the wind and waves—these same disciples just moments later would doubt their Savior's power.

Our God has a history; he and we have been through some things. We must spend time recalling his prior triumphs, the wind and waves that he has rebuked in our lives, the fact that today, we still stand. Unlike the disciples on the boat, let's not so quickly forget. Let's remember his faithfulness and carry it with us always.

*Dear God, help me recall the moments of your prior triumph. Let me remember the times you've rebuked the winds and rains that buffeted me. You will do it again, because you've done it before. Amen.*

# SILENCE

It is better to remain silent at the risk of being thought a fool, than to talk and remove all doubt of it.

*—Maurice Switzer,* Mrs. Goose, Her Book

Even a fool is counted wise when he holds his peace;
When he shuts his lips, he is considered perceptive.

*—Proverbs 17:28 (NKJV)*

As Proverbs maintain, and Maurice Switzer made famous, let's seek to hold our tongues today as much as we can. Listening ears say more about us than active mouths.

*Dear God, help me use my words judiciously and learn to covet silence. Amen.*

# THE THINGS THAT EDIFY

> Let us pursue the things which make for peace and the things by which one may edify another.
>
> —*Romans 14:19 (NKJV)*

Pursue the things that make for peace. And the things that edify. In the end, isn't that the filter?

The filter through which we see our relationships and our disagreements. By which we choose our battles and keep our powder dry.

Will our actions make for peace? Will they build up our brothers and our sisters? If not, then perhaps they're not as important as they seem. This is the message of the Apostle Paul in Romans 14. And a worthy message for our days.

---

*Dear Lord, help me pursue the things that make for peace and the things that edify. Help me pump the brakes when I'm heading in a direction of unnecessary conflict. Amen.*

# AUTHORITY

Because power corrupts, society's demands for moral authority and character increase as the importance of the position increases.

—*John Adams, in* The Quotable John Adams

What is my reward then? That when I preach the gospel, I may present the gospel of Christ without charge, that I may not abuse my authority in the gospel.

—*1 Corinthians 9:18 (NKJV)*

We seek to use authority wisely.

God has given us great jurisdiction, expansive control. People in our lives respect what we say, and many will follow where we lead.

Like Paul, let's seek to never lead those under us toward our own reward, but to something greater than ourselves. We seek to lead them to healing, to understanding, to God.

*Lord, help me use my authority wisely—not for my benefit, but in service to others. Amen.*

# FOR ALLIES

Then the churches throughout all Judea, Galilee, and Samaria had peace and were edified. And walking in the fear of the Lord and in the comfort of the Holy Spirit, they were multiplied.

—*Acts 9:31 (NKJV)*

~∞∞∞~

*Dear Lord,*

*As I fear you and seek your spirit, send others around me who are doing the same. And let our numbers multiply. Send me like-minded allies, friends who build me up. Send me co-laborers for this journey, brothers and sisters who don't mind the hard work as we press toward our reward.*

*Like the early church in Acts, give us peace and edification. And as we walk in the fear of the Lord and the comfort of the Holy Spirit, multiply us.*

*Amen.*

# IMPERFECT PEOPLE

For a multitude of the people, many from Ephraim, Manasseh, Issachar, and Zebulun, had not cleansed themselves, yet they ate the Passover contrary to what was written. But Hezekiah prayed for them, saying, "May the good LORD provide atonement for everyone who prepares his heart to seek God, the LORD God of his fathers, though he is not cleansed according to the purification of the sanctuary." And the LORD listened to Hezekiah and healed the people.
—*2 Chronicles 30:18–20 (NKJV)*

For the first time in a very long time, King Hezekiah wanted the people of Israel to practice their most important custom: he wanted them to participate in the Passover.

But at the time of the feast, some of the Israelites had not completed their ritual cleansing, a practice necessary to join in the Passover. Instead of turning them away, Hezekiah prayed to God on their behalf: "May the good LORD provide atonement for everyone who prepares his heart to seek God." So these "unclean" people participated in the Passover and brought honor to God.

Like Hezekiah, let's remember that those we love and lead are not always going to be perfect. We should intercede with God for their imperfections and help them move in the right direction. In the meantime, let's accept them for who they are.

*Dear Lord, help me accept the imperfections of those around me with grace. And help me lead them in your direction. Amen.*

# ON GOD'S SIDE

Then Jesus came to them and said, "All authority in heaven and on earth has been given to me. Therefore go and make disciples of all nations . . . teaching them to obey everything I have commanded you."

—*Matthew 28:18–20 (NIV)*

Before the Civil War, a group of Southerners came to visit President Abraham Lincoln at the White House to warn him that when it came to the coming conflict, the South would prevail, because God was on their side. Lincoln famously said in response, "It is more important to know that we are on God's side."

Like these Southerners, we spend so much time asking God to come into our situations, our requests, our hopes, and our dreams. But have we asked God what it is he wants us to do? Do we know his side?

———

*Lord, we want to know your side. We're willing to put down our own desires and pick up your cause, for the building of your kingdom. We will shift toward righteousness as you command. Amen.*

# BEYOND OUR SENSES

"What no eye has seen,
   what no ear has heard,
and what no human mind has conceived"—
   the things God has prepared for those who love him.
                                        —*1 Corinthians 2:9 (NIV)*

We differ, blind and seeing, one from another, not in our senses, but
in the use we make of them, in the imagination and courage with
which we seek wisdom beyond the senses.
                              —*Helen Keller,* The World I Live In

---

*Dear Lord, grant us wisdom beyond our senses.*

*We are fearfully and wonderfully made, but our flesh is nonetheless limited.*

*Give us perspective beyond what our eyes behold, perception clearer than
our ears, sensitivity beyond our touch.*

*Help us go beyond the limits of these senses today and experience true
wisdom.*

*Amen.*

# A LEVITE SPIRIT

The Levitical priests—indeed the whole tribe of Levi—are to have no allotment or inheritance with Israel. They shall live on the food offerings made to the LORD, for that is their inheritance.
—*Deuteronomy 18:1–2 (NIV)*

In Jewish tradition, the Levites—members of the Hebrew tribe of Levi—play a unique and important role. When Joshua led the Israelites into the land of Canaan, the Levites were the only tribe that was not allowed to be landowners, "because the Lord the God of Israel himself is their inheritance" (Joshua 13:33, DRA).

In return for the Levites' service, the landed tribes were expected to pay them a tithe, known as the Maaser Rishon, or the Levite Tithe. The greatest figures in the Bible were Levites: Moses and his brother, Aaron, Miriam, Samuel, Ezekiel, Ezra, Malachi, John the Baptist, Mark the Evangelist, Matthew the Evangelist, and Barnabas . . . and Jesus himself.

It's counterintuitive really—that the most powerful in Israel would be those who didn't have an inheritance, people who couldn't accumulate wealth themselves or pass anything down to their children. Instead, the Israelite notion of power was wrapped up in how one served God and served the community—not material acquisitions, but closeness to God, and closeness to man.

Let's meditate on how we might seek this kind of power . . . so that the Lord the God of Israel himself might also be our inheritance.

⚬⚬⚬⚬

*Dear God, help me have the spirit of a Levite. Help me store treasures that are incorruptible, in service to others and to you. Amen.*

# A TIME TO REJOICE

It's toughest to forgive ourselves. So it's best probably to start with other people. It's almost like peeling an onion. Layer by layer, forgiving others, you really do get to the point where you can forgive yourself.

—*Patty Duke, in* Conquer the Fear of Death

Ezra the priest brought the Law before the assembly of men and women and all who could hear. . . . Then he read from it in the open square that was in front . . . before the men and women and those who could understand; and the ears of all the people were attentive to the Book of the Law. . . .

And Nehemiah, who was the governor, Ezra the priest and scribe, and the Levites who taught the people said to all the people, "This day is holy to the LORD your God; do not mourn nor weep." For all the people wept, when they heard the words of the Law.

—*Nehemiah 8:2–3, 9 (NKJV)*

For the first time in a very long time, Nehemiah and Ezra had just reintroduced the Israelites to the word of God. And the people became overwhelmed. When the word was read, the Israelites realized how far they had strayed from God's presence, from his commands. They realized the error of their ways, their sinful nature. And they began to weep.

But Nehemiah and Ezra stopped them. The prophet and priest said: Don't cry! This is a time to worship God, to thank him for your new understanding. It's a holy day.

Like the Israelites, when we come to terms with our own error, our own brokenness, we should not be crushed. God desires to take our sins upon him, no matter how bad they are, and give us a new start. That's a cause for rejoicing; it's a holy day.

*Lord, thank you for a new start today. I will not bemoan my prior state; instead, I'll worship you. Amen.*

# DO NOT ENTER

> Coming out, He went to the Mount of Olives, as He was accustomed, and His disciples also followed Him. When He came to the place [that he would be betrayed], He said to them, "Pray that you may not enter into temptation."
>
> —*Luke 22:39–40 (NKJV)*

To set the scene, this was one of the worst days of Jesus's life—except for the day of his crucifixion. He was fully aware that in just a few moments, one of his own disciples, Judas Iscariot, would betray him and hand him over to Pontius Pilot. The dominoes would fall from that moment until the agony of his crucifixion. Scripture tells us Jesus's agony was so great that he prayed three times for God to "take this cup away," praying so hard that "his sweat became like great drops of blood falling to the ground" (Luke 22:42, 44).

So one wonders: What were Jesus's final words to his disciples before he was led away to death? What did he say to his best friends, his confidants, those who had been with him in the most important part of his ministry? Did he bid a warm farewell? Did he offer a poignant departing speech?

No. Christ chose to offer one final thought at this moment: "Pray that you may not enter into temptation." He wanted his disciples to be diligent about avoiding those sins that were foreseeable to them. Maybe for some it was pride. Maybe for others it was lust, sexual temptation. For others it might have been passivity. Christ knew that it was not the big things, the major world forces, that would derail his followers from implementing his will. Instead, it was the benign "temptations" of life that we can all see coming.

We pray today that we "may not enter into temptation." We identify those faults which are all known to us already and pray for the Holy Spirit's help in tackling them. We can't do it through our own strength, but through the grace of God. *Amen.*

# COVERING TRANSGRESSION

He who covers a transgression seeks love,
But he who repeats a matter separates friends.

—*Proverbs 17:9 (NKJV)*

*Lord, when a wrong has been committed against me, teach me how to forgive and let go. Place my love for you first, my human relationships second, and my own ego far behind. Let me be slow to offense and quick to grace. May I be like you were, and like you are with me. Amen.*

# DARKNESS'S HOUR

> Then Jesus said to the chief priests, captains of the temple, and the elders who had come to Him, "Have you come out, as against a robber, with swords and clubs? When I was with you daily in the temple, you did not try to seize Me. But this is your hour, and the power of darkness."
>
> —*Luke 22:52–53 (NKJV)*

"But this is your hour, and the power of darkness."

Darkness will, in fact, have its hour. We saw hours of darkness in Auschwitz and Treblinka, Newtown and antebellum Mississippi. No one less than Christ affirmed that there are moments when evil moves mightily in the world. The questions become: Do we have confidence in the coming light? Will the darkness overwhelm us, which is always its goal, or will we hold on to the promise of the morning?

Jesus held on to that promise, and in his resurrection and ascension was crowned victorious, in a mantle of light. His confidence is an indicator of how we should meet our own times of darkness, those moments when evil temporarily seems to reign.

*Dear God, in the nighttime, remind me of the day. In the darkness, remind me of your light. I have confidence in the coming morning, and until then I will stand strong. Amen.*

# EDISON'S INTERESTS

Many, Lord my God,
  are the wonders you have done,
  the things you planned for us.
None can compare with you;
  were I to speak and tell of your deeds,
  they would be too many to declare.

*—Psalm 40:5 (NIV)*

There's a story told about Thomas Edison, inventor of the lightbulb, the gramophone, and so many other brilliant things.

Edison was asked to sign a guest book, and in addition to his name and address, the guest book asked him to list what he was "interested in." In that field, Edison wrote: "Everything."

Like Edison, let's cultivate our sense of God-given wonder. There are so many things left to be discovered, so many questions unanswered, both in our own minds and the wider world. Often it just takes us lifting our heads—above the humdrum of the day—to see uncharted territories to explore. Today, we ask God for wonder, and we follow it to startling places.

*Dear God, you've made a big earth here, and I want to see more of it. Help me get beyond the busyness of this day and better realize the wonder of this world. Amen.*

# LIGHT MY PATH

For the cloud of the LORD was upon the tabernacle by day, and fire was on it by night, in the sight of all the house of Israel, throughout all their journeys.

—*Exodus 40:38 (KJV)*

Behold, I say unto thee, *This is the way, walk ye in it,*
neither turn to the right hand nor to the left.
For I shall make the path for thy feet a plain path,
and light shall be there,
and there shall be the shining of My glory.
It shall not be the glory of man. It shall be the glory of God.

—*Frances Roberts,* Dialogues with God

*Dear God, light my path today. Place me within your holy presence, and surround me with your cloud and fire. I won't turn to the left, or to the right. I will move with you. Amen.*

# RISE UP

A certain man lame from his mother's womb was carried, whom they laid daily at the gate of the temple which is called Beautiful, to ask alms from those who entered the temple; who, seeing Peter and John about to go into the temple, asked for alms. And fixing his eyes on him, with John, Peter said, "Look at us." So he gave them his attention, expecting to receive something from them. Then Peter said, "Silver and gold I do not have, but what I do have I give you: In the name of Jesus Christ of Nazareth, rise up and walk." And he took him by the right hand and lifted him up, and immediately his feet and ankle bones received strength.

—*Acts 3:2–7 (NKJV)*

"In the name of Jesus Christ of Nazareth, rise up and walk." What confidence went into that command! What history fell from Peter's lips.

Peter knew this Christ. He knew what Jesus had done. He knew who Jesus had healed. He saw the resurrection and ascension for himself.

And it was in the fullness of that knowledge that Peter grew confident. He was confident in his own ability to heal, to speak wholeness into a broken world. "In the name of Jesus Christ of Nazareth, rise up and walk."

May we have that same confidence. May we look back and remember what God has done and then, in full knowledge of his power, move mightily in this world. May we declare to the most difficult problems, the most broken communities, those who are hurting the most—"In the name of Jesus Christ of Nazareth, rise up and walk."

And then, like Peter, may we take them by the hand, and lift them up. *Amen.*

# ENJOYING THE FRUIT

When the LORD your God enlarges your border as He has promised you, and you say, "Let me eat meat," because you long to eat meat, you may eat as much meat as your heart desires.
—*Deuteronomy 12:20 (NKJV)*

Pick a day. Enjoy it—to the hilt. The day as it comes. People as they come. . . . The past, I think, has helped me appreciate the present—and I don't want to spoil any of it by fretting about the future.
—*Audrey Hepburn, in* What Would Audrey Do?

The book of Deuteronomy is filled with all sorts of rules and regulations for the people of Israel: when to worship, what to sacrifice, with whom to associate. But an often-overlooked commandment is this one: when God has blessed you . . . enjoy it!

Are we truly enjoying the fruits of our blessing today? Yes, there's always something else to acquire, something else to do, one more hill to climb. But we are on top of some hill right now; and it took some doing to get here. So, in the midst of our striving, be sure to look around and savor the God-given view.

---

*Dear God, thank you for who you have made me. There is a lot yet to do, but today, let me not forget that there is a lot you have already done. Bless me with joy, the happiness that comes with the knowledge of you. Amen.*

# WITHDRAW AND PRAY

> Yet the news about him spread all the more, so that crowds of people came to hear him and to be healed of their sicknesses. But Jesus often withdrew to lonely places and prayed.
>
> —*Luke 5:15–16 (NIV)*

We can't give everyone all of us, all the time. Sometimes, like Jesus, we have to withdraw, and pray.

Leadership is not just physically straining; it taps our spirit too. When the water in the well has drawn low, we must be intentional about pressing pause in our public roles and finding quiet spaces in which we can be replenished. Jesus, after pouring himself out for the crowds, "often withdrew to lonely places and prayed." If we're going to continue at maximum capacity and impact, we should regularly do the same.

⚬⚬⚬⚬

*Dear God, let me know when to engage and when to disconnect. Help me find my own "lonely places," where I can go and pray. Amen.*

# PREEMPTIVE PRAISE

Two men look out through the same bars:
One sees the mud, and one the stars.
> —*Frederick Langbridge, "A Cluster of Quiet Thoughts"*

At evening they return,
    They growl like a dog,
    And go all around the city.
They wander up and down for food,
    And howl if they are not satisfied.
But I will sing of Your power;
    Yes, I will sing aloud of Your mercy in the morning;
For You have been my defense
    And refuge in the day of my trouble.
> —*Psalm 59:14–16 (NKJV)*

There is power in preemptive praise. At the very moment when David's enemies were closing in around him, his response was to "sing of Your power . . . of Your mercy in the morning; For You have been my defense."

My slave ancestors used to call this "praising in the middle of the storm." In the spiritual realm, above our human comprehension, it's as if God is delighted that we trust him enough to speak words of praise even in advance of our breakthrough. And he hastens that breakthrough, in fulfillment of our praise.

---

*Dear God, you know the challenges, the fears, the insecurities of my life. Instead of letting them weigh me down, I will use them as fuel for the fire of my praise. I know that you are a deliverer. And I know that you are with me, and I am with you. Amen.*

# LANGSTON HUGHES

As long as it is day, we must do the works of him who sent me. Night is coming, when no one can work.

*—John 9:4 (NIV)*

Let's say we were to visit Harlem. On a whim, between meetings, we drop by the Schomburg Center, that venerable library that tells the history of people of African descent in America. Let's say we were to walk into the atrium and step on its beautifully inlaid floor, set with blue and red and golden stone. We might find ourselves gravitating toward a medallion in the middle of that floor. And as we stood above this medallion, we would be standing above the ashes of Langston Hughes.

Hughes, of course, is not there. The unrivaled poet, of great critical acclaim and historical significance, does not lie beneath the shining floor of the Schomburg. His memory is kept alive by schoolchildren struggling to memorize his lines. His words are held closely by adults who find comfort in the stanzas. Hughes himself is in an eternal place, the exact destination we are not qualified to judge.

We are not on this earth for long. And, as Hughes's ashes at the Schomburg testify, even the finest resting place in the world will not allow us to remain a minute longer than has been determined. All we will leave behind is remnants, and memories, medallions on the floor. We all have some place else to go. So as John 9:4 instructs, let us work while it is still day—without panic, but with urgent determination.

*Dear God, thank you for the time that I have to serve you on this planet. I know it will not last forever; grant me the wisdom to make the best use of what I have. Amen.*

# ELEANOR'S PRAYER

Our Father, who has set a restlessness in our hearts and made us all seekers after that which we can never fully find, forbid us to be satisfied with what we make of life. Draw us from base content and set our eyes on far-off goals. Keep us at tasks too hard for us that we may be driven to Thee for strength. Deliver us from fretfulness and self-pitying; make us sure of the good we cannot see and of the hidden good in the world. Open our eyes to simple beauty all around us and our hearts to the loveliness men hide from us because we do not try to understand them. Save us from ourselves and show us a vision of the world made new.

—*Eleanor Roosevelt, in* The Treasury of American Prayers

*Forbid us to be satisfied. Draw us from base content.*

*Keep us at tasks too hard for us that we may be driven to Thee. Open our eyes to simple beauty; show us a vision of the world made new. These things we pray in Jesus's name.*

*Amen.*

# In the Temple

Now it came to pass, while He blessed them, that He was parted
from them and carried up into heaven. And they worshiped Him,
and returned to Jerusalem with great joy, and were continually in the
temple praising and blessing God. Amen.

—*Luke 24:51–53 (NKJV)*

After Christ ascended into heaven, the disciples did not marvel alone, but
together. They went to the temple, "praising and blessing God."

In our moments of great joy, as well as our times of sorrow, it's important that we come together in God's house. While we can access God anywhere, there is something sacred about his church that lends itself toward
true adulation and worship.

Like the disciples in this penultimate moment, let's make our way to
the church house. In that close encounter with God, we can focus our
hearts on praise.

*Dear God, like your disciples, let me find my way to the temple. Pull me
toward your house, so that I might better praise your name. Amen.*

# MUCH TO OFFER

> Now when the days of her purification according to the law of Moses were completed, they brought Him to Jerusalem to present Him to the Lord (as it is written in the law of the Lord, "Every male who opens the womb shall be called holy to the LORD"), and to offer a sacrifice according to what is said in the law of the Lord, "A pair of turtledoves or two young pigeons."
>
> —*Luke 2:22–24 (NKJV)*

We often fail to recall just how poor Mary and Joseph were. A brief line in the Gospel of Mark says that after Jesus was born, they offered the traditional ritual sacrifice for his birth of "a pair of turtledoves or two young pigeons." The book of Leviticus requires that offering; if we go back to the original source, Leviticus says that pigeons are offered only when the parents "cannot afford a lamb."

Jesus's parents—the two human individuals responsible for presiding over our Savior's entrance into the world—were so poor that they could not offer the traditional sacrifice. They had to settle for two pigeons, or cheaply purchased doves.

Like Mary and Joseph, people struggling with poverty and want have so much to offer us. So much wisdom, so many gifts for the world. Let's be sure to seek this knowledge out and honor them. We must recall that the earthly parents of our heavenly Savior were rich in spirit, but in station, desolately poor.

*Dear God, let me regard highly the contributions of those struggling in poverty. Let me remember to act not just with charity but also with respect for their dignity and worth. Amen.*

# GO, AND SEE

So it was, when the angels had gone away from them into heaven, that the shepherds said to one another, "Let us now go to Bethlehem and see this thing that has come to pass, which the Lord has made known to us." And they came with haste and found Mary and Joseph, and the Babe lying in a manger.

—*Luke 2:15–16 (NKJV)*

Go. And see.

If you hear of God doing a great work.

If your curiosity has been piqued by a tale of righteousness.

If you've been longing to lay your eyes on something that in the pit of your stomach or corner of your mind you believe will be a healing force in your life.

Then don't hesitate. Don't second-guess. Like the shepherds—get up. Take the next step. Go, and see. You never know; Jesus may be at the end of that journey.

─◦◦◦◦◦─

*Dear God, are there new places you want me to travel? New lands to explore? New people to meet? At your prompting, I am ready to go, and see. Amen.*

NOTE: The next several devotionals were sent to the president around Christmas.

# A THOUGHT TO CHRIST

There have been men before . . . who got so interested in proving
the existence of God that they came to care nothing for God Himself . . . as if the good Lord had nothing to do but to exist. There
have been some who were so occupied with spreading Christianity
that they never gave a thought to Christ.

—*C. S. Lewis,* The Great Divorce

Let's give a thought to Christ.

Who was he? What did he care about? How did he spend his time?
What did he feel while working the earth? How must he have received his
death?

Let's delve into our Bibles and our minds to explore the person of Jesus.
Christianity is nothing, nothing, without him.

~~~~~

*Lord, I'd like to reintroduce myself. I have not known you fully, and I'd like
to know you more. Show me your character. And help me be more like you.
Amen.*

# WITH EYES WIDE OPEN

He fights well who shrewdly flies.
— *"The Owl and the Nightingale," Middle English poem*

The utterance of Balaam the son of Beor,
The utterance of the man whose eyes are opened,
The utterance of him who hears the words of God,
Who sees the vision of the Almighty,
Who falls down, with eyes wide open.

*—Numbers 24:3–4 (NKJV)*

"Who falls down, with eyes wide open." These verses introduce us to Balaam, one of the most significant prophets of ancient Israel. Balaam was a man totally immersed in the Spirit of God. When he prophesied, it was as if he was holding the hand of God, feeling God's heartbeat through the grip of his hand, and interpreting the will of God to the people of Israel. Balaam knew the pulse of God.

But even when Balaam fell down to worship God, he did so "with eyes wide open." He saw the world around him. He perceived, he absorbed, he empathized. He maintained the duality of a full immersion in the Spirit, and a full awareness of the things of the world.

Let our prayer today be to be like Balaam. To constantly seek and receive the things of God, but to be attuned to the life around us as well. And let the first of these condition the second.

———

*Dear God, thank you for your prophet Balaam. Thank you for the example he set to "fall down, with eyes wide open." Let me maintain a similar posture, consistently worshipping and seeking you, while perceiving, knowing, and loving my fellow man. In Jesus's name, amen.*

# AMAZING GRACE

Moreover the law entered that the offense might abound. But where sin abounded, grace abounded much more, so that as sin reigned in death, even so grace might reign through righteousness to eternal life through Jesus Christ our Lord.

—*Romans 5:20–21 (NKJV)*

Through many dangers, toils and snares,
I have already come;
'Tis grace has brought me safe thus far,
And grace will lead me home.

—*John Newton, "Amazing Grace"*

⚬⚬⚬

*Dear God, today, we gratefully accept your grace. We don't deserve it; we weren't even looking for it. In a just world, we'd be condemned for our shortcomings. But you encountered us at the moment of our need, and you loved us. We are sinners. But you are our Savior. And your grace abounds more than our sin. Thank you, Lord. Amen.*

# THE CYCLE OF SIN

In Romans 7, we find that even the Apostle Paul was caught in a cycle of his own sin.

> For what I will to do, that I do not practice; but what I hate, that I do.
> —*Romans 7:15 (NKJV)*

We've all been there. The same thing keeps tripping us up, over and over again. The same old flesh. But in Romans 8, we find our reprieve.

> There is therefore now no condemnation to those who are in Christ Jesus, who do not walk according to the flesh, but according to the Spirit. For the law of the Spirit of life in Christ Jesus has made me free from the law of sin and death.
> —*Romans 8:1–2 (NKJV)*

On our own, we can never be set free from the deathly cycle of sin. But in Christ, with his mercy, we can find liberation.

---

*Our prayer, oh God, is for you to come into this flesh of ours. To free us from our sin. We know there will be a struggle, and we accept it; as you suffered, so will we. But our momentary suffering is worth the lasting reward. Amen.*

# NOT USING IT MYSELF

Do not store up for yourselves treasures on earth, where moths and vermin destroy, and where thieves break in and steal. But store up for yourselves treasures in heaven, where moths and vermin do not destroy, and where thieves do not break in and steal. For where your treasure is, there your heart will be also.

—*Matthew 6:19–21 (NIV)*

As the old saying goes, "You can't take it with you."

Great scientist and son of slaves George Washington Carver once lost his entire life savings, seventy thousand dollars, when the Alabama bank where he kept his deposits crashed. Most people would have been devastated, but Carver took it in stride. "I guess somebody found a use for it," he said. "I was not using it myself."

There's a reason the Bible has so many admonishments about money. The pursuit of treasure, while benign in the abstract, can get in the way of higher pursuits and eat away at our souls. We should remember to store up what really matters, in a place that never threatens to crash: the eternal storehouse of our Savior, where charity is the currency valued most.

———∞∞∞———

*Dear God, help me to not value material things over the things that you value most. Let me hold my material possessions loosely and my integrity tightly. Amen.*

# WAITING

I wait for the LORD, my soul waits,
    And in His word I do hope.
My soul waits for the Lord
      More than those who watch for the morning—
      Yes, more than those who watch for the morning.
                           —*Psalm 130:5–6 (NKJV)*

*We're waiting on you, Lord. We're waiting for you to do a new thing. We're waiting for our healing, for our purification, for our rest. We're waiting in expectation, and the fullness of hope.*

    *"My soul waits for the Lord*
    *More than those who watch for the morning—*
    *Yes, more than those who watch for the morning."*

    *Amen.*

# ACKNOWLEDGMENTS

"First giving honor to God . . ." :-) (My friends in the Black church will know what I mean.)

But seriously, I'm grateful for a Savior who has loved me fully and well for a very long time. He redeemed me at my lowest points, and made any heights possible. I hope everyone has a chance to experience a God who calls them friend. I have, and I'm thankful.

To a wife and best friend that I don't deserve, who has worked as hard as anyone to make this book possible. Thank you, Michelle—I love you. To a wonderful team of friends, especially my long-time buddy and partner Michael Wear; my brother in prayer and life Eugene Schneeberg; my dear friend Scott Buckhout; Safiya Simmons, for whom the sky is the limit; and my "assistant" that broke the mold of that title in every way, Maab Ibrahim. Day by day, they push me higher.

To my parents, Rev. W. Antoni and Mrs. Kristy Sinkfield, and my brother and sister, Anah and Tony Sinkfield, who have always been my biggest supporters.

To my wonderful agent, Gail Ross, and the phenomenal HarperOne team, especially Mickey Maudlin, Katy Renz, Noël Chrisman, Suzanne Wickham, and Jennifer Jensen. Their blend of professionalism and heart was felt throughout this process. And to Clare Anne Darragh and Frank PR for always knocking it out of the park.

To Barack Obama, a good president, and a good man.

To Paul DuBois, in memoriam.

To Mark and Roma, for loving so well in all that they do. To Donald Miller for being awesome, and Joel Hunter for being a great pastor, mentor and friend. And to all my friends near and far who contributed thoughts, ideas, endorsements, and support—you know who you are, and I hope you know that I'm grateful.

And finally, to my dog, Cinco, who spared more pages than he ate. *Good boy.*